Advance Praise for *Mont Pèlerin 1947*

"Imagine eavesdropping on one of the most revered and reviled conferences of the twentieth century, the gathering organized by Friedrich Hayek at Mont Pèlerin in 1947. Ever since, commentators have been celebrating or cursing the people attending and the ideas discussed at the famous meeting. Now thanks to Bruce Caldwell you can understand the context, read the discussion, and decide for yourself."

—Douglas Irwin, professor of economics, Dartmouth College

"In 1947, against the persistent specter of totalitarian regimes in Europe and a loss of faith in free markets among a large share, perhaps a majority, of American intelligentsia, capitalism was in a state of crisis. At the initiative and direction of Friedrich Hayek, in April of that year a group of thirty-nine individuals from Europe and the United States gathered in the village of Mont Pèlerin, Switzerland, with the aim of resuscitating the course of liberalism. That meeting would eventuate in the Mont Pèlerin Society, which provided the intellectual foundations of free-market thinking for the remainder of the twentieth century and the early twenty-first century. To mark the seventy-fifth anniversary of the 1947 meeting, in this book Bruce Caldwell makes public for the first time the transcripts of that first meeting. Caldwell, the world's foremost scholar of Hayek's thinking and writing, complements the carefully edited reproduction of the discussions at that founding meeting with a fascinating account of the events leading up to that gathering."

—George S. Tavlas, alternate to the governor, Bank of Greece, and distinguished visiting fellow, Hoover Institution

"In 1947, during the aftermath of world crisis, leading thinkers in Europe and the United States came together to diagnose and, more importantly, look forward. This record of their debates and deliberations is well worth reading amid the challenges of today."

—Jennifer Burns, associate professor of history, Stanford University, and research fellow, Hoover Institution

Mont Pèlerin 1947

Mont Pèlerin 1947

Transcripts of the Founding Meeting
of the Mont Pèlerin Society

Edited by Bruce Caldwell

Foreword by John B. Taylor

HOOVER INSTITUTION PRESS

STANFORD UNIVERSITY | STANFORD, CALIFORNIA

hoover.org

Hoover Institution Press Publication No. 722

Hoover Institution at Leland Stanford Junior University, Stanford, California 94305-6003
Copyright © 2022 by the Board of Trustees of the Leland Stanford Junior University

First printing 2022
28 27 26 25 24 23 22   7 6 5 4 3 2 1

Manufactured in the United States of America
Printed on acid-free, archival-quality paper

Library of Congress Cataloging-in-Publication Data
Names: Mont Pèlerin Conference (1947 : Le Mont-Pèlerin, Switzerland) | Caldwell, Bruce, 1952– editor.
Title: Mont Pèlerin 1947 : transcripts of the founding meeting of the Mont Pèlerin Society / edited by Bruce Caldwell.
Other titles: Hoover Institution Press publication ; 722.
Description: Stanford, California : Hoover Institution Press, Stanford University, 2022. | Series: Hoover Institution Press publication ; no. 722 | Includes bibliographical references and index. | Summary: "Presents transcripts from the founding meeting of the Mont Pèlerin Society and explains its importance in the development of 20th-century liberal thought"— Provided by publisher.
Identifiers: LCCN 2021038039 (print) | LCCN 2021038040 (ebook) | ISBN 9780817924843 (cloth) | ISBN 9780817924867 (epub) | ISBN 9780817924881 (pdf)
Subjects: LCSH: Mont Pèlerin Society—History—Sources. | Liberalism—Congresses. | Free enterprise—Congresses. | Economics—Congresses. | LCGFT: Conference papers and proceedings.
Classification: LCC HB95 .M65 2022 (print) | LCC HB95 (ebook) | DDC 330.12/2—dc23
LC record available at https://lccn.loc.gov/2021038039
LC ebook record available at https://lccn.loc.gov/2021038040

For A., T., and P.,
with gratitude

Contents

Photo section follows after page 126

Foreword

John B. Taylor

It is such a joy to read this book. Bruce Caldwell has skillfully combined modern commentary with historical documents from the very first meeting held by a group of economists and other scholars at the Hôtel du Parc in the village of Mont-Pèlerin, Switzerland, during the first ten days of April 1947. He not only makes you feel as if you were present at that meeting, he also delivers insights on what we need to do now. Indeed, with all that is happening today, the Mont Pèlerin Society is as important now as it was at that original 1947 meeting.

The year 2022 marks the seventy-fifth anniversary of the meeting. The in-person notes from the meeting as reproduced in this book are drawn from the Hoover Institution Library & Archives, and this book makes them accessible to all. Some say that the first 1947 meeting was a key event, but now the publication of the words actually spoken at that meeting allows anyone—not only those who can visit the Hoover Library & Archives—to see and read what people actually said, discussed, and debated. The people who attended the first Mont Pèlerin Society meeting were worried about the move of many countries toward socialist or collectivist policies. As we read this volume, we worry about the same tendency today.

Caldwell's introduction to the volume fits in perfectly with the notes and essays from that first meeting. I found myself going back and forth, reading Caldwell's explanation, then going to the original presentations and discussions that took place seventy-five years ago, and then back again.

The whole volume makes it crystal clear why that meeting spawned a society that continues to thrive today. It was no accident. We learn about how Friedrich Hayek was crucial in organizing the meeting and in the founding of the society. Dorothy Hahn, Hayek's secretary attended and took shorthand notes. These notes serve as a record, though they were not verbatim; they were "intended mainly to indicate the general trend of the discussion," as Hayek later wrote.

We learn how as Hayek traveled to promote his book *The Road to Serfdom*, he talked up the idea of the meeting and raised funds for it. Hayek wanted to invite friends he knew from Vienna, who then lived in the United States, including Ludwig von Mises and Fritz Machlup. He also wanted to invite Frank Knight, Aaron Director, and Milton Friedman, who were then at the University of Chicago.

After he met Harold Luhnow, then president of the Kansas City foundation the William Volker Charities Fund, he followed up with a cable: "If you could provide travel expenses for the following eleven American members Brandt Director Friedman Gideonse Graham Hazlitt Knight Kohn Machlup Mises Stigler." Luhnow agreed. Hayek met Albert Hunold, a Swiss banker who had raised money for a journal to be edited by Wilhelm Röpke. The plan for the journal failed, because Hunold wanted editorial control and Röpke refused. But the funds Hunold raised were available, and they were offered to Hayek for the meeting.

Hayek left most of the final organizing details of the meeting to Hunold. The conference took place over ten days to allow for much informal discussion beyond the formal sessions. Hunold's choice for the location of the meeting was beautiful—a hotel with a view of Lake Geneva. Hunold also arranged for popular excursions that have become a traditional part of Mont Pèlerin Society meetings ever since.

An important goal of the conference was to introduce European liberals—those who saw the advantages of limited government and a reliance on markets—to other liberals from Europe and from the United States. The first week focused on presentations and group discussion of five topics chosen by Hayek.

After opening introductions, the first formal topic—"free" enterprise or competitive order—aimed at contrasting the laissez-faire free-market system with a system where the government had a role of making markets more competitive. The two terms were meant to describe two different systems, and it was the system described by the term "competitive order" that Hayek himself preferred. He led off by saying (as transcribed): "If during the next few years, i.e. during the period in which practical politicians are alone interested, a continued movement towards more government control is almost certain in the greater part of the world, this is due, more than to anything else, to the lack of a real program, or perhaps I had better say, a consistent philosophy of the opposition groups." This first session helped to define this program. The record described by Caldwell shows that Aaron Director's presentation under that first topic was much like a "mainstream introductory economics text of today on market failures and their possible remedies." This was certainly needed then, and it is again needed now.

There was a session that first week on the "future of Germany." While a topic like that could have gone in many directions, the session ended up, according to Caldwell, being the most memorable of the meeting. Walter Eucken, who was in Germany during the years preceding the meeting, could speak with experience, and his hands-on portrayal was a very useful criticism. Eucken became "the star of the conference," as described by Hayek.

Another topic that first week was "liberalism and Christianity." Hayek thought the topic was essential in order to resolve a potential conflict in which liberalism seemed antagonist toward Christianity. Knight opened asking: "Can liberalism be put in such a way as to satisfy man's craving for a religion?" Many joined in, and it turned out to be another interesting session. Eucken, again speaking from experience, noted how the church was often a bulkhead against the totalitarian regime in Germany. "From the experience of a totalitarian system," he is recorded as saying, ". . . such a system makes it impossible to be a Christian."

The topics for the second week were determined by people at the conference and most were about economics, including contra-cyclical measures, full employment, monetary reform, wage policy, trade unions, taxation, poverty, income distribution, and agricultural policy.

There was agreement that a view in which government is responsible for producing full employment and uses Keynesian demand-management policies is dangerous. Milton Friedman argued for monetary policy rules and for a tax system that responds automatically rather than by discretion.

He spoke about "attempts to time public investment" and said there was a "great chance that they will end up making the system more unstable than before." He said, "I think it a fallacy that a free market is something that rich nations can afford, but that poor nations must do without." He argued for a rules-based monetary system, but that "if we go beyond, we get the problem of rules versus regulations."

This book reminds us of the amazing collection at the Hoover Institution Library & Archives. Scholars writing about Hayek, Friedman, and the Mont Pèlerin Society have benefited from the collection, including Jennifer Burns, Bruce Caldwell, myself, and many others.[1] Caldwell speaks for us all when he writes about an experience three decades ago: "My whole approach to my field changed forever after that first transformative week in 1991 that I spent poring over the folders in the Hayek collection at Hoover." And he speaks from long experience as a scholar when he says, "If this book helps in some small way to promote interest in archival-based historical scholarship, it will have served a fine purpose." Read and enjoy.

Note

1. See Jennifer Burns, "Milton Friedman: The Early Years," and Bruce Caldwell, "Mont Pèlerin 1947" (both presented at From the Past to the Future: Ideas and Actions for a Free Society, Mont Pèlerin Society Meeting, Hoover Institution, Stanford University, January 15–17, 2020), https://www.mpshoover.org; and John B. Taylor, "Why We Still Need to Read Hayek," The Hayek Prize Lecture, Manhattan Institute for Policy Research, 2012, https://www.manhattan-institute.org/html/first-principles-five-keys-restoring-americas-prosperity-6150.html.

Preface

The book you are about to read reproduces transcripts of the minutes from a 1947 meeting in Switzerland that resulted in the creation of the Mont Pèlerin Society. The academic side of the meeting was organized by the economist Friedrich A. Hayek, and his secretary, Dorothy Hahn, attended and took shorthand notes on the proceedings. These were not verbatim reproductions but rather were "intended mainly to indicate the general trend of the discussion," as Hayek put it in on the cover page accompanying the minutes. That is an important caveat that should be borne in mind as one reads the materials to come. In addition, certain parts of the discussion went unrecorded due to the occasional absence or exhaustion of Mrs. Hahn. Even with such qualifications, the transcribed notes are, as the reader will see, exceedingly rich.

To ensure that the participants felt free to speak their minds, the minutes were not intended for distribution and have never been made public.[1] They are, however, available for inspection by scholars who visit the Hoover Institution Library & Archives at Stanford University, where the Mont Pèlerin Society papers are housed.[2] I secured the permission of the society to reproduce them for this volume.

The introduction that follows this preface will provide some background on the meeting. Here I will explain why I thought it timely to make these documents available to a wider public. I offer four reasons.

First, 2022 marks the seventy-fifth anniversary of the original 1947 meeting, its diamond jubilee. The Mont Pèlerin Society continues to this day, and this is a fitting commemorative work to mark its seventy-five years of existence.

Second, the minutes are a remarkable and vital document in the history of modern liberalism and, as such, should be more easily accessible, not just to scholars fortunate enough to visit the Hoover Archives.[3] Then, as now, liberalism was under attack. To read the words of some of the greatest liberal scholars of that earlier day as they deliberated and argued over the proper responses to the challenges they faced is edifying. It can also be good fun. Many of the names of those who gathered in the salon of the Hôtel du Parc that April will be familiar. It was an impressive and at times cantankerous group of individuals. The transcript illuminates not only the ideas associated with those names but also the distinctive personalities lying behind them.

A third reason for publishing the transcript is that the 1947 meeting has itself reached almost mythic proportions for critics of liberalism today who see it as a key event in the development of that set of doctrines that they gather under the label of "neoliberalism."[4] Though this is mostly an academic dispute, it is an important one, so a brief digression on the ever-expanding literature on neoliberalism, a term that almost exclusively is used by critics of liberalism, is in order.

"Neoliberalism" has many connotations. Though the first appearance of the term dates back at least to the nineteenth century and various authors employed it in the first half of the twentieth century, including on rare occasion even people like Hayek and Milton Friedman, its popularity has grown over the past forty years or so.[5] In early treatments it referred to the movement toward "market deregulation, state decentralization, and reduced state intervention into economic affairs in general" that began to emerge in places like the United States and Britain in the late 1970s and was given further impetus by the collapse of the Soviet Union and the Eastern Bloc.[6] Later it became associated with the globalization of trade and the imposition of the so-called Washington consensus by transnational organizations like the International Monetary Fund and the World Bank. At least some people view these as largely positive developments, as they have been associated with the worldwide reduction in poverty that the world has experienced over the past thirty years.[7]

In more recent treatments, especially those by academic social scientists and historians, not to mention journalists and public intellectuals, the term has come to be associated with far more sinister and indeed malevolent forces. One overriding theme is that neoliberalism provides the intellectual underpinnings to justify the efforts of huge transnational corporations to use the coercive police and military power of strong states (especially the United States) to advance their own interests.[8] In their effort to construct "a world made safe for corporations," neoliberals essentially elevate crony capitalism from a defect to a desideratum. Furthermore, their quest to advance the interests of the plutocracy makes them inevitably and implacably contemptuous of democracy, which they seek through their theories to undermine.[9] The Iraq War, the 2008 financial crisis, the undermining of scientific expertise, the increase in inequality and rise of the "1 percent," and the attendant emergence of the carceral state to discipline and contain those caught at the margins of society are among the ills that have been laid at the door of neoliberalism by its most severe critics.[10]

A curious feature of the academic literature that is most critical of neoliberalism is the paucity of citations to the people who are supposed to have developed its core doctrines. Critics of neoliberalism tend to cite one another, not original sources such as Hayek or Friedman. There is good reason for this. As those who have read Hayek or Friedman know, these putative originators of these toxic doctrines never advocated anything resembling them in their published work. There is no attribution because there is nothing to attribute; as Angus Burgin gently put it, for its critics neoliberalism is not an "actor-centric category."[11] The response of the critics of neoliberalism to this embarrassing absence of evidence has been twofold.

The first is to say that neoliberalism keeps changing, so that trying to define it precisely is impossible.[12] Now it is certainly true that liberalism is not monolithic, and that there have been changes in emphasis over time. As the reader will see, at the first meeting many different points of view were expressed (as was also true at another meeting of liberals, the Colloque Lippmann). But surely these supposed progenitors of neoliberalism must somewhere have given some clues as to what they believed. The frequent reference to an amorphous "neoliberal thought collective" rather than to the writings of individual actors is one way that critics of neoliberalism have tried to finesse the problem.

The other is to invoke the notion of a "double truth." While publicly parading such platitudinous phrases as the rule of law, freedom to choose, and securing the blessings of liberty, members of the neoliberal thought collective knew that their doctrines, if widely understood, would never be accepted. This is why neoliberals almost never refer to themselves as neoliberals; it is the movement that dare not speak its own name.[13] This is why they found it necessary to form a secretive society, one that would meet in places far away from the public eye, where they could discuss their plans unmolested and undetected.[14] And indeed, the links between the Mont Pèlerin Society and neoliberalism run so deep that, even though none of its critics seem able to identify what neoliberalism is, membership in the Mont Pèlerin Society has been offered as a criterion by which to decide who is and who is not a neoliberal.[15]

The antiliberal tradition is long-lived, and critics of liberalism have over the years frequently offered caricatures of the views they sought to discredit.[16] The most recent critique that targets "neoliberalism," though, has some striking and indeed insidious characteristics. Precisely because people who propound and defend liberalism today seldom refer to themselves as "neoliberals," virtually all the references made to that doctrine in a now burgeoning literature are to a malignant force. A young scholar or naïve student who might want to learn more about the subject and who responsibly began with a survey of that literature would find a uniformly negative representation.[17] The extant academic literature on neoliberalism comes dangerously close to devolving into the purest form of echo chamber. And, of course, that literature inevitably filters down into public discourse, via what Hayek termed the "professional secondhand dealers in ideas."[18] I will simply note that the problem of one-sidedness in historical scholarship is not a new phenomenon. As we will see, Hayek included it as a topic for discussion at the 1947 meeting. Seven years later he would edit a collection of papers under the title *Capitalism and the Historians*.[19] *Plus ça change . . .*

The third reason, then, to make the minutes of the 1947 Mont Pèlerin gathering publicly available is to provide that young scholar or naïve student, or anyone else for that matter, with a summary of the words *actually spoken* by this supposed cabal of corporate apologists at their first meeting. This will not silence those critics who have already made up their minds, but it should allow the reader who has yet to do so to see what these people who gathered on the shores of Lake Geneva seventy-five years ago really said and thought.

A fourth and final reason to bring this document to light through publication by the Hoover Institution Press is to highlight and indeed celebrate the marvelous archival holdings of the Hoover Institution. Its collections contain some of the most fundamental documents in the history of contemporary liberalism. There are records of organizations like the Mont Pèlerin Society, the Institute of Economic Affairs, the Atlas Network, and the Institute for Humane Studies, along with the papers of such figures (to mention only some of the most prominent) as Friedrich Hayek, Milton Friedman, Fritz Machlup, Gottfried Haberler, and Karl Popper. As a historian of economic thought, I can attest that my whole approach to my field changed forever after that first transformative week in 1991 that I spent poring over the folders in the Hayek collection at Hoover. If this book helps in some small way to promote interest in archivally based historical scholarship, it will have served a fine purpose.

I would like to thank the officers of the Mont Pèlerin Society for granting permission to reproduce Dorothy Hahn's notes; Eric Wakin, the director of the Hoover Institution's Library & Archives, who welcomed the proposal for this project; Sarah Patton and the rest of the Hoover Archives staff for their help and support in its execution; Adrianna DeLorenzo for research assistance in preparation of the manuscript; Alain Alcouffe, G. M. Ambrosi, Karen Horn, Stefan Kolev, Paul Lewis, Eddie Nik-Khah, and Sandy Peart for helping me track down some elusive references and providing other invaluable assistance; John B. Taylor for providing a foreword; and at the Hoover Institution Press, Barbara Arellano, senior publications manager, Danica Michels Hodge, editorial manager, Alison Law, book production manager, and Barbara Egbert, copy editor, for their good work.

Bruce Caldwell
July 2021
Durham, North Carolina

Notes

1. As we will see, Hayek's cover letter included the underlined words "Private" and "Not for Distribution."

2. The transcripts may be found in the Mont Pèlerin Society Papers, box 5, folders 12–13 (MPSP 5.12–13), Hoover Institution.

3. Throughout I will use liberalism in its European rather than American sense. The publication of this transcript continues a trend that began a few years ago with the translation and publication of the minutes of the Colloque Lippmann, a meeting that took place in Paris in August 1938 that often is viewed as a precursor of the 1947 Mont Pèlerin event. See Jurgen Reinhoudt and Serge Audier, *The Walter Lippmann Colloquium: The Birth of Neo-Liberalism* (New York: Palgrave Macmillan, 2017). For papers from a recent conference on the Colloque Lippmann, see Karen Horn, Stefan Kolev, David Levy, and Sandra Peart, eds., "Liberalism in the 21st Century: Lessons from the Colloque Walter Lippmann," special issue, *Journal of Contextual Economics—Schmollers Jahrbuch* 139, nos. 2–4 (2019).

4. The title of a leading entry in this literature that links the meeting to neoliberalism, and one that alludes to Hayek's own *The Road to Serfdom*, is wholly representative: Philip Mirowski and Dieter Plehwe, eds., *The Road from Mont Pèlerin: The Making of the Neoliberal Thought Collective* (Cambridge, MA: Harvard University Press, 2009).

5. Stefan Kolev dates its first usage to the nineteenth century: See Stefan Kolev, "Paleo- and Neoliberals: Ludwig von Mises and the 'Ordo-Interventionists,'" in *Wilhelm Röpke (1899–1966) A Liberal Political Economist and Conservative Social Philosopher*, ed. Patricia Commun and Stefan Kolev (Cham, Switzerland: Springer, 2018), 66–68. Rajesh Venugopal shows the rise in the use of the term in social science discourse since the 1990s: "Neoliberalism as Concept," *Economy and Society* 44, no. 2 (May 2015): 165–87. Angus Burgin traces some of the most prominent themes in recent historical literature. See "The Neoliberal Turn" (paper presented at the Center for the History of Political Economy workshop, 2018). Louis Rougier, who organized the Colloque Lippmann, used the term *neo-liberalism* in his foreword to the transcripts from the sessions; see Reinhoudt and Audier, *Lippmann Colloquium*, 93. Friedman used the term in a 1951 article published in Norwegian to describe views quite similar to those he and Aaron Director expressed at the 1947 meeting. In a concise summary of the doctrine, he wrote: "Neo-liberalism would accept the nineteenth century liberal emphasis on the fundamental importance of the individual, but it would substitute for the nineteenth century goal of laissez faire as a means to this end, the goal of the competitive order. It would seek to use competition among producers to

protect consumers from exploitation, competition among employers to protect workers and owners of property, and competition among consumers to protect the enterprises themselves. The state would police the system, establish conditions favorable to competition and prevent monopoly, provide a stable monetary framework, and relieve acute misery and distress. The citizens would be protected against the state by the existence of a free private market; and against one another by the preservation of competition." See Milton Friedman, "Neo-Liberalism and Its Prospects," Collected Works of Milton Friedman Project records, Hoover Institution, https://miltonfriedman.hoover.org/objects/57816/neoliberalism-and -its-prospects?ctx=b8c0f32e-f5a4-4e53-ba3d-cf017b993579&idx=0. The original appeared in Norwegian as "Nyliberalismen og dens Mulligheter," *Farmand*, February 17, 1951, 89–93. Hayek once used the word in an encyclopedia article to refer to the views of the German ordoliberals: F. A. Hayek, "Liberalism" (1978), in *The Collected Works of F. A. Hayek*, vol. 18, *Essays on Liberalism and the Economy*, ed. Paul Lewis (Chicago: University of Chicago Press, forthcoming).

6. John Campbell and Ove Pedersen, eds., *The Rise of Neoliberalism and Institutional Analysis* (Princeton, NJ: Princeton University Press, 2001).

7. In its "Poverty Overview," the World Bank reports that between 1990 and 2015, the number of people living in extreme poverty fell by more than 1.1 billion, from 36 percent to 10 percent of the global population, a remarkable improvement in so short a time. Much of the progress came in China and India as they liberalized their economies with respect to trade. Unfortunately, the COVID-19 pandemic reversed the worldwide trend in 2020. See World Bank, "Poverty," last updated April 15, 2021, https://www.worldbank.org/en/topic/poverty/overview.

8. A representative characterization: "Neoliberalism is first and foremost a theory of how to reengineer the state in order to guarantee the success of the market and its most important participants, modern corporations." See Rob Van Horn and Philip Mirowski, "The Rise of the Chicago School of Economics and the Birth of Neoliberalism," in Mirowski and Plehwe, *Road from Mont Pèlerin*, 161; see also Jamie Peck, *Constructions of Neoliberal Reason* (Oxford: Oxford University Press, 2010), 55, which cites its fundamental imperative as "first seizing and then retasking the state."

9. The original title of Van Horn and Mirowski's "Rise of the Chicago School" was "The Road to a World Made Safe for Corporations." The accusation that liberalism is hostile toward democracy has a rather long history. For illustrative earlier efforts, see Harold Laski, *The Rise of Liberalism: The Philosophy of a Business Civilization* (New York: Harper and Brothers, 1936) and Herman Finer, *Road to Reaction* (Boston: Little, Brown, 1945).

10. In addition to those already cited, see the following: David Harvey, *A Brief History of Neoliberalism* (Oxford: Oxford University Press, 2005); Loïc Wacquant,

Punishing the Poor: The Neoliberal Government of Social Insecurity (Durham, NC: Duke University Press, 2009); Bernard Harcourt, *The Illusion of Free Markets* (Cambridge, MA: Harvard University Press, 2011); and Wendy Brown, *Undoing the Demos: Neoliberalism's Stealth Revolution* (Princeton, NJ: Zone Books, 2015). Some treatments of neoliberalism, though broadly critical and not without flaws, more accurately represent liberal thought. Two examples are Daniel Stedman Jones, *Masters of the Universe: Hayek, Friedman, and the Birth of Neoliberal Politics* (Princeton, NJ: Princeton University Press, 2012) and Quinn Slobodian, *Globalists: The End of Empire and the Birth of Neoliberalism* (Cambridge, MA: Harvard University Press, 2018). As Burgin shows in "The Neoliberal Turn," for academic historians the history of neoliberalism is now poised to supersede earlier literatures on the history of conservatism and of capitalism.

Among economists, the leading critic of neoliberalism has been Philip Mirowski. See, e.g., Mirowski and Plehwe, *Road from Mont Pèlerin*, which contains both Van Horn and Mirowski, "Rise of the Chicago School" and Philip Mirowski, "Postface: Defining Neoliberalism," 417–55. See also Robert Van Horn, Philip Mirowski, and Thomas Stapleford, eds., *Building Chicago Economics: New Perspectives on the History of America's Most Powerful Economics Program* (Cambridge: Cambridge University Press, 2011); Philip Mirowski, *Never Let a Serious Crisis Go to Waste: How Neoliberalism Survived the Financial Meltdown* (New York: Verso, 2013); and Philip Mirowski and Edward Nik-Khah, *The Knowledge We Have Lost in Information: The History of Information in Modern Economics* (New York: Oxford University Press, 2017). For critical assessments of some of these works, see Bruce Caldwell, "The Chicago School, Hayek, and Neoliberalism," in *Building Chicago Economics*, 301–34; and Bruce Caldwell, review of *The Knowledge We Have Lost in Information*, by Philip Mirowski and Edward Nik-Khah, EH.net, November 2017, https://eh.net/book_reviews/the-knowledge-we-have-lost-in -information-the-history-of-information-in-modern-economics.

11. Burgin, "The Neoliberal Turn," 5.

12. Thus we find neoliberalism characterized as a shape-shifter, a "loose and shifting signifier" (Brown, *Undoing the Demos*, 21) that "is anything but a succinct, clearly defined political philosophy" (Mirowski and Plehwe, *Road from Mont Pèlerin*, 1). "The ten-plus commandments of neo-liberalism were not delivered complete and immaculate down from the Mont in 1947," intoned Mirowski (*Serious Crisis*, 41), but rather kept developing, always adapting to new circumstances. This did not, however, prevent that author from repeatedly trying to list those tenets: see Mirowski, "Postface," 434–40; Mirowski, *Serious Crisis*, 53–67; Mirowski and Nik-Khah, *Knowledge We Have Lost*, 54–59; and Philip Mirowski, "Neoliberalism: The Movement That Dare Not Speak Its Name," *American Affairs* 2, no. 1 (Spring 2018), 118–41.

13. See Mirowski "Postface," 440–46, and Mirowski, *Serious Crisis*, 68–83, for an enunciation of the double-truth doctrine. "The Movement That Dare Not Speak Its Name" is the title of Mirowski's 2018 article in *American Affairs*.

14. Thus neoliberalism, "a transnational, reactionary, and messy hybrid right from the start . . . has been the work of many hands, a lot of them hidden" (Peck, *Constructions of Neoliberal Reason*, 39, xi). Note that the subtitle of Wendy Brown's exposé, *Undoing the Demos*, is "Neoliberalism's Stealth Revolution."

15. Mirowski, "Postface," 428: "If the target person or group bore any links to the Mont Pèlerin Society since 1947, directly or at one remove, then we count them as falling squarely within the purview of the neoliberal thought collective."

16. Stephen Holmes, in *The Anatomy of Antiliberalism* (Cambridge, MA: Harvard University Press, 1993), 187, describes some of the tenets of the anti-liberal tradition as follows: "Classical European liberals ignored the social constitution of the individual, were scornful of the common good, disparaged authority, sacrificed the public to the private, belittled political participation, neglected virtue, idolized economic man, declared values to be subjective, reduced man to a pleasure-pain machine, abolished self-restraint, placed excessive faith in Reason, and generally dissolved all nourishing bonds." He goes on to say, "This is a daunting list of allegations. When confronted one at a time with the claims actually defended in classic liberal texts, however, they either seem exaggerated or wrong."

17. For an articulation and defense of the sort of cosmopolitan liberal ideals that followers of Hayek embrace, see Deirdre McCloskey, *Why Liberalism Works: How True Liberal Values Produce a Freer, More Equal, Prosperous World for All* (New Haven, CT: Yale University Press, 2019); and Peter Boettke, *The Struggle for a Better World* (Arlington, VA: Mercatus Center, 2021).

18. See F. A. Hayek, "The Intellectuals and Socialism" (1949), in *Collected Works*, vol. 10, *Socialism and War: Essays, Documents, Reviews*, ed. Bruce Caldwell (Chicago: University of Chicago Press, 1997), 221. For a single data point, see Mehrsa Baradaran, "The Neoliberal Looting of America," *New York Times*, July 2, 2020, where Hayek is identified as "perhaps the most influential leader of the movement . . . known as neoliberalism" whose "governing logic held that corporations could do just about everything better than the government could."

19. Chicago: University of Chicago Press, 1954.

A Note to the Reader

What follows is Dorothy Hahn's transcript of the April 1947 Mont Pèlerin Conference. A few words explaining the conventions I used in preparing the text are in order.

There were often two typed transcripts in the archives, an initial clean one, and then one that had corrections of various sorts added: words crossed out, words crossed out and replaced by others, insertions. All such changes appear to have been done by Friedrich Hayek himself. The corrected version was used to prepare the text. All cross-outs are indicated, straightforwardly enough, by ~~crossing out the relevant section~~. All additions are set in *italics*. All <u>underlining for emphasis</u> in the present text was also in the original. Finally, additions by me as editor are [contained in brackets], the most typical of which is to indicate a spelling error in the text, noted by [*sic*], and any missing accents (e.g., René, Pèlerin) have been silently added. All numbered footnotes have been added by me or, in the case of the appendix to session 2, by Stefan Kolev and Karen Horn.

The beginning information attached to each session, recording the time, date, and title of the session, has been standardized. Dorothy Hahn was British, and British spellings for all words have been preserved in the text. All numbered footnotes, however, as well as the preface and introduction, use American spellings and stylistic conventions.

Following the conference, Albert Hunold prepared for each of the attendees a commemorative album containing photos taken at the meeting. The ones provided in this volume are from F. A. Hayek's copy of the album.

Introduction

Bruce Caldwell

The founding meeting of what would become the Mont Pèlerin Society took place from April 1 through 10, 1947, at the Hôtel du Parc in the village of Mont-Pèlerin, which lies above Vevey, Switzerland, on Lake Geneva.[1] Over the course of their stay, the thirty-nine participants engaged in thirteen substantive sessions covering ten topics, plus six organizational ones, and took trips to nearby sites of interest. The academic side of the conference was organized by the Austrian-born British economist Friedrich A. Hayek while most of the logistical organizing was done by Albert Hunold, who then served as the chief spokesman for the Swiss watch industry. Hunold raised the funds to pay for the conference venue, including room and board, while Hayek garnered the money to pay the travel expenses of ten scholars located in North America who accepted his invitation.

This introduction will provide some background on the meeting, showing how it came about, placing it in the context of its times, introducing the participants, and offering some brief remarks on the sessions. The transcripts from the meeting follow.

Hayek Floats an Idea

Friedrich Hayek first proposed the idea of a postwar international society of liberals in a lecture in February 1944 before the Political Society at King's College, Cambridge.[2] Hayek was worried about the direction—political, social, economic, intellectual, cultural, and moral—of Central Europe after the war and envisaged an organization that would put the few remaining liberals there in contact with peers in other countries as the rebuilding process began. His proposed name was the Acton Society, after the great Cambridge historian Lord Acton, a scholar "half German by education and more than half German in his training as a historian," whose ideas united "the great English liberal tradition with the best there is in the liberal tradition of the continent."[3] Hayek also discussed the possibility of starting a journal and issuing new editions of the works of great German liberal thinkers of the past.

This was not the first time that he had thought about how to advance the cause of liberalism or, perhaps better, to try to slow its decline. Hayek had left Vienna in the early 1930s to teach at the London School of Economics (LSE). Over the course of the decade, he engaged in numerous debates over economics—with John Maynard Keynes over their respective theories of money and the cycle; with socialists of various stripes over the viability of socialism; with the American economist Frank Knight over capital theory—but, by its end, his attention turned increasingly toward the fate of liberalism. Its prospects seemed grim. The Great Depression had undermined people's faith in markets, and on the continent totalitarian systems of various unpalatable sorts were vying for power. For many in England, socialist planning seemed to provide a promising middle path between a discredited free-enterprise system and its communist and fascist alternatives. Hayek's goal was to articulate a renewed version of liberalism, one more suited to the twentieth century, that in economics went beyond the simple nostrums of laissez-faire, and that could more effectively counter the collectivist alternatives. Aside from having affinities with a handful of like-minded souls, people like Lionel Robbins, Arnold Plant, Frederic Benham, and Frank Paish at LSE, or Knight and Henry Simons in the United States, his was very much a minority viewpoint.

The publication in 1937 of the American journalist Walter Lippmann's book *An Inquiry into the Principles of the Good Society* offered a ray of hope.[4] Though Lippmann had progressive roots, by the mid-1930s he had soured on Roosevelt's New Deal and turned toward liberalism. His widely read and discussed book criticized the economics of both laissez-faire and collectivism. It sought instead a middle ground that built on the insight that "the division of labor, democracy, and the method of the common law are organically related and must stand or fall together, because they are different aspects of the same way of life," a view that much appealed to Hayek.[5] Hayek began a correspondence with Lippmann and helped facilitate a meeting in Paris in August 1938 to celebrate the French translation of the book. The event, the Colloque Lippmann, organized by Louis Rougier, brought together liberals from across Europe. Notable among the attendees were Hayek and Michael Polanyi from Great Britain; Raymond Aron, Jacques Rueff, and Étienne Mantoux from France; Alfred Schütz from Austria; Alexander Rüstow from Turkey; Ludwig von Mises and Wilhelm Röpke, identified not by their birth countries (both were by then in Geneva) but by "École Autrichienne" ("Austrian School"); and, of course, Lippmann himself. [6]

Each session was dedicated to a different question. Was the decline of liberalism inevitable, as the Marxists—but also others concerned about the growth of monopoly and economic concentration—claimed? Could liberalism satisfy the social demands of the masses for job security and a reasonable standard of living? Could liberalism be maintained even when a nation was preparing for or fighting a war? (The meeting had as its backdrop Adolf Hitler's increasingly aggressive stance toward the Czech government over the Sudetenland, so the question was anything but hypothetical.) What were the causes—psychological, sociological, political, and ideological—of the decline of liberalism? Finally, if it were to be revived, what would an appropriate agenda look like?

As might be expected, though most there considered themselves liberals, there was considerable disagreement about what exactly that entailed. Indeed, they had a hard time even figuring out what to call themselves. Some, like Mises, wanted to retain the word "liberal." Others thought that it had been so identified with Manchesterism and laissez-faire that it would do them harm: "Liberalism, for many, is the *laissez-faire, laissez-passer,* and one adds the let suffer (*laissez-souffrir.*)"[7] Some preferred individualism, others freedom, while yet others talked of constructive liberalism or neo-capitalism. In his preface to the published report, Rougier suggested the term "neo-liberalism." Few used this term afterward—until it was revived by critics of liberalism later in the century.

Everyone agreed that a system of free markets in a democratic polity that was embedded within and constrained by a legal framework was the best way forward. But this sort of "agreement" did not take one very far; further debate and discussion were necessary. Toward that end, following the meeting, the Centre International D'Études pour la Rénovation du

Libéralisme was created in Paris. The timing was not propitious; the center was an early casualty of the war. Hayek also hoped that a journal to discuss liberal ideas might be formed, but this failed to materialize. Wilhelm Röpke, though, had shown some prescience when he wrote to Lippmann prior to the meeting and said that he had "some years ago . . . launched the idea of assembling the dozen of Enlightened Liberals in a solitary hotel high up in the Alps and to cross-fertilize their ideas for a week."[8]

As the war approached and hopes for international cooperation faded, Hayek turned to other projects. He began work on *The Abuse and Decline of Reason,* a massive, two-volume tome that would trace the rise and spread of what he called "scientism," the increasingly commonplace (but in his view unscientific) belief that the techniques of the natural sciences could be applied to social phenomena, allowing trained experts to construct new societies just like engineers build new bridges. The engineering mentality implicit in the scientistic worldview held that, if only the failed capitalist system could be gotten out of the way and replaced by rational economic planning, a more prosperous and just world could be created. In Hayek's view, when such centralized systems inevitably fail to deliver on their promises, they become susceptible to takeover by corrupt leaders. His book would show how the spread of such ideas in the nineteenth and early twentieth centuries led to the debacles the West had experienced over the prior two decades, the rise of totalitarian systems, and two world wars.

Hayek never finished his *Abuse of Reason* project, but he did complete a part of it, a little book called *The Road to Serfdom.* Published only a month after his Cambridge lecture, the British edition made him, to his surprise, instantly famous. The fame spread further following the publication of an American edition in September and a subsequent condensation the next year by Max Eastman for *Reader's Digest.* That began a sequence of events that ultimately made possible the meeting at Mont Pèlerin.

Hayek Organizes a Meeting

In spring 1945 Hayek went on an event-packed publicity tour in the United States to promote his book.[9] On that trip, he met Harold Luhnow, the president of the William Volker Charities Fund, a Kansas City–based foundation that under Luhnow's direction increasingly supported free-market scholarship. They discussed in general terms Hayek's idea of forming a liberal society, and Luhnow encouraged him to provide a more concrete proposal. A few months later, Hayek sent him a "Memorandum on the Proposed Foundation of an International Academy for Political Philosophy Tentatively Called 'The Acton-Tocqueville Society.'" The prospectus provided a rationale for the society and then talked about its activities: facilitating contacts among members from different countries through meetings, translating foundational and contemporary liberal texts, establishing an international journal, and perhaps even setting up a permanent home. The focus was on promoting liberalism in postwar Europe and the price tag was steep: Hayek estimated it at $500,000. Luhnow, who was more interested in promoting liberalism in America, turned him down.[10]

Hayek kept up his efforts to spread the idea while on lecture trips to promote his new book. As he would note in his opening address at the conference, in each country he would find a handful of individuals working in isolation who thought as he did and who were eager to interact with like-minded scholars.[11] He was also on the lookout for funding. In October 1945, while in Zurich to give a lecture at the university, he met a Swiss banker named Albert Hunold, who was raising funds for a journal to be edited by Hayek's friend and wartime correspondent Wilhelm Röpke.[12]

Hayek had known the German economist Röpke since their first encounters at meetings of the Verein für Sozialpolitik in the 1920s, and, as noted, he was one of the attendees at the 1938 Colloque Lippmann. Röpke, along with Alexander Rüstow, had left Germany for Turkey after Hitler came to power, but in 1937 he got a call to come to the Institut de Hautes Études Internationales in Geneva. The institute, a child of the League of Nations, had been founded in 1927 by William Rappard, a Swiss diplomat, and Paul Mantoux, a French economic historian, and from 1928 had been directed by Rappard.[13] In the 1930s the institute hosted both Hayek and his LSE colleague and close friend Lionel Robbins for lectures.[14] From 1933 onward, it provided a home for scholars escaping authoritarian regimes of various forms, among them the Austrian economist Ludwig von Mises and jurist Hans Kelsen, both of whom were forced to flee again when the Nazi conquest of France made even neutral Geneva unsafe, at least for the likes of them. Hayek's links to the men who had remained in Geneva were both professional and personal. Röpke had kept him apprised of how friends like Walter Eucken and other liberals who had remained in Germany were faring, and Hayek had sent and received messages from Vienna concerning family members and friends through both him and Rappard during the war.

Like Hayek, Röpke was concerned that the past thirty years of war and depression had everywhere undermined confidence in foundational Western values and principles, and that the world was turning for solutions to collectivism, a trend that in his view posed a lethal threat to Europe's cultural inheritance. Though an economist, he had in his wartime writings focused additionally on the spiritual and moral dangers that he felt were threatening Western civilization at its core.[15] To signal its purpose of reclaiming and reconstituting the Western heritage in all its dimensions, his journal would be called, simply, *Occident*. It would provide a forum for a renewed discussion of alternatives to collectivism for shaping the values and policies of Europe as it rebuilt after the war. But the journal was not to be. Hunold wanted considerable editorial control over its content, and when Röpke refused, the plan collapsed. The money that Hunold had raised, however, was still available, and the next time they met (in fall 1946), Hunold offered it to Hayek for a preliminary meeting of the society.[16]

Having secured a promise of funds for the meeting itself, Hayek tried again with his potential American benefactor at the Volker Fund. Their relationship had improved since his first attempt at fundraising faltered. From the start, Luhnow had wanted Hayek to find someone to write an American version of *The Road to Serfdom* and in 1946 financed a four-month trip to the United States for him to do so. Though there were some missteps, Hayek ultimately succeeded in convincing Aaron Director to move to the University of Chicago to undertake what came to be called the Free Market Study. Director received an appointment at the Law School there in fall of 1946, the same term that his brother-in-law Milton Friedman joined the Economics Department. Though Luhnow would never get the book he wanted out of Director, he would later surely take solace in realizing that his efforts helped to create what would soon be known as the Chicago School of Economics.[17]

Coming off this successful venture, Hayek once again approached Luhnow for support. Noting that certain individuals in Switzerland would finance the costs of the actual meeting, he asked whether the Volker Fund would be willing to cover the traveling expenses, if not for everyone, then at least for the Americans.[18] Only a week later came the very welcome reply: "We would have a definite interest in making a major contribution to defray the expenses of the American representatives to a preliminary meeting for an Acton-Tocqueville Society."[19]

Next came a flurry of letters back and forth between Hayek and a variety of interested parties. Even a cursory reading of them shows that it was a very delicate balancing act; the whole thing could have collapsed at multiple crucial junctures. Hayek was adept at negotiating. He was ever the diplomat but, when it counted, quite willing to make his position clear. Because the meeting would be held in Switzerland, Rappard and Röpke were key participants who needed fully to be on board. He sent a letter to each of them to make sure of their approval and, doubtless recalling Röpke's reaction to Hunold's attempts to control the publishing of *Occident*, assured them that the funders had agreed to go ahead with "no strings of any kind" attached.[20]

That certainly was true when he wrote, but soon enough Luhnow began putting on some pressure. Hayek copied him on the circular letter of invitation that he had sent in late December to fifty-four people.[21] The letter noted the purpose, place, and proposed dates of the conference and the possibility that travel funds would be available for those coming from America, and invited a quick response.[22] In his return letter, Luhnow informed Hayek that he had gotten "a violent reaction" from certain Volker Fund directors about some of the names on Hayek's list. Though he did not identify who was objectionable, he summarized that "some of the reactions that I have had on one or two of your suggestions are such that I know the Directors of the Volker Charities Fund would not be interested in paying their travelling expenses anywhere."[23] To resolve the situation, he proposed that a screening committee of four or five people be formed to vet the recommendations, and the Volker Fund would then pay the travel costs for those from the United States who passed the test. Any others would need to pay their own way.

On January 17, Hayek replied to Luhnow with a cable: "If you could provide travel expenses for the following eleven American members Brandt Director Friedman Gideonse Graham Hazlitt Knight Kohn Machlup Mises Stigler some of whom may not in fact be able to attend Vevey conference would appear secured and important opportunity to discuss Chicago investigation created. Letter follows Hayek." In the follow-up letter, he defended some of the people whom he thought might have met with disapproval and made some recommendations for a potential steering committee, but then made two key points: that the meeting would barely be worth having if the Americans could not come, and that if the April meeting date were delayed, the Swiss funding might disappear. Both points were true, but they also implied that Luhnow needed to make the decision about travel funding now, without the benefit of a steering committee. The tactic worked. In his next letter Luhnow agreed to fund the travel for all eleven people.[24]

Hayek also made clear to Luhnow that he should not expect any quick payoffs from the meeting.

> I neither expect immediate results nor believe that any efforts which aim at immediate results are likely to change the general trend of opinion. What seems to me most urgently needed is that those who are capable of gradually evolving a philosophy of freedom which will appeal to the people of our time, should be able to do so in collaboration and full knowledge of their respective efforts.[25]

Tension between those who wanted the society to maintain a more public presence with respect to policy matters and those who adhered to Hayek's original vision of simply bringing together scholars from many countries who would quietly work to reconstruct the foundations of liberalism would arise again and again in the early years of the society.

As for Luhnow, he was not yet prepared to give Hayek an entirely free hand. He requested that invitations to join the conference be extended to

eight more people, plus Leonard Read and Loren Miller as "observers."
He also conjectured that Jasper Crane, an executive at DuPont Chemical,
would come at his own expense if invited. Hayek was again in a bit of a
jam, because in terms of hotel accommodations, he only had room for
six more people. Luckily, two of the people listed had declined previous invitations, so Hayek sent invitations to six, then as people declined,
added others. In the end, the people on Luhnow's list who ultimately
attended were the journalist Felix Morley; Leonard Read, F. A. "Baldy"
Harper, and Orval Watts, all from the recently established Foundation for
Economic Education (FEE); and Loren Miller from the Detroit Bureau of
Governmental Research. Herbert Cornuelle, also at FEE, was a late addition. Regarding Crane, Hayek let Luhnow know that he was in a different
category. The conference organizers had agreed that invitations should
only be extended to "people who are in the first place scholars and writers,
in order to avoid any impression that the conference has been instigated
by any business interests."[26] But they also allowed that people who were
acquaintances of the organizers (Hayek had met Crane on his 1946 trip
to the States) could be personally invited as observers, and if this suited
Crane, he could come. In the end he did not.

Luhnow was not the only one providing Hayek with critical feedback
on his choice of invitees. Both Ludwig von Mises and Karl Popper took
strong, principled, and diametrically opposed stances on the matter.
Mises sent Hayek a letter in which he noted having reservations about
Karl Brandt, Harry Gideonse, Eastman, and especially Röpke, the last
of whom he considered an "outright interventionist" ("ausgesprochener
Interventionist").[27] Accompanying it was a four-page typed addendum
titled "Observations on Professor Hayek's Plan," which laid out his objections with his usual uncompromising clarity. Attempts to stop collectivism had failed because its opponents had adopted middle-of-the-road
positions that appeared as reasonable compromises but in fact made matters worse. *All* problems attributed to markets by critics were in fact the
result of interference with the market process. Perhaps his most pointed
line was this: "He who wants to preserve freedom . . . must not protest
that he abhors laissez-faire"—which, of course, is just what Hayek had
been doing since 1933.[28] (Hayek's view was not the outlier; for example,

virtually all the liberals who had attended the Colloque Lippmann shared it, though they differed on what a renewed liberalism should look like.) For Mises, "Laissez-faire does not mean: let the evils last. It means: let the consumers, i.e., the people, decide—by their buying and their abstaining from buying—what should be produced and by whom."[29] Mises shared the "Observations" with at least one other person, the journalist Henry Hazlitt, who was sympathetic to his views.[30] On the other extreme, Karl Popper thought that "it would be advantageous, and even necessary, from the very beginning, to secure the participation of some people who are known to be socialists or to be close to socialism."[31] Hayek did not budge. Despite their reservations, both Mises and Popper attended the meeting.

Finally, there were those who expressed concerns about calling the organization the Acton-Tocqueville Society. Having read Hayek's original 1944 piece proposing an Acton Society, Röpke had warned him that the name was barely known on the continent.[32] William Rappard later noted that, for those on the continent who knew them, their names "evoke not only the ideals of liberty . . . but also, perhaps on account of their noble birth and their Catholic faith, something reactionary."[33] The issue would come up again.

Most of the work for the final organization of the meeting was left in Hunold's capable hands. The conference was spread over ten days to allow for interaction outside of the formal sessions. Hunold's choice for the meeting venue, a fine hotel overlooking Lake Geneva, was ideal in many ways. In addition to the stunning views, it was centrally located (for the Europeans) and, being in a country that had remained neutral during the war, was undamaged and itself a sort of "neutral territory" for discussants from many countries. Hunold also arranged outings that have since become an integral part of all Mont Pèlerin Society general meetings. On Thursday the group took cars along the lake to a site of considerable meaning and charm, the Château de Coppet, where Madame de Staël had once held her famous salons in the company of people like the early French liberal Benjamin Constant. One imagines that Hayek took the opportunity to entertain his traveling companions with the story of another famous visitor to Coppet, the "megalomaniac visionary" Comte Henri de Saint-Simon, who went there to propose marriage to Madame de Staël, this because (as Saint-Simon told the wife he left behind) "the first man of the world ought to be married to the first woman."[34] On Saturday the group traveled by train to Schwyz to visit a seventeenth-century palace and the famous monastery and abbey of Einsiedeln, founded in the tenth century. As it was the Saturday before Easter, in addition to a tour, the group listened to a chanting of the *Salve Regina*, witnessed the resurrection service, and was treated to an organ concert.

As the meeting dates approached, there were plenty of last-minute details that required attention. Hayek's recently married secretary, Dorothy Salter Hahn (her husband, Frank Hahn, would go on to teach economics at Cambridge), came along to take notes at the sessions. Hayek worried about the fact that only two women, Hahn and Veronica Wedgwood, would be present (some wives also accompanied their spouses, but they did not attend the working sessions) and asked Hunold if he could think of others to invite, but nothing came of it.[35] Four people who were scheduled to attend were for various reasons unable to do so. The no-shows were Luigi Einaudi, then governor of the Bank of Italy; Jacques Rueff, a Colloque Lippmann attendee who in 1947 was president of the Agence Interalliée des Reparations; Charles Rist, a French monetary economist and critic of Keynes who, with Charles Gide, wrote a text on the history of economic thought; and the German historian Franz Schnabel, author of a massive history of Germany in the nineteenth century. The final total was thirty-nine conferees.[36] Unfortunately, the hotelkeeper in the end only retained thirty-five rooms, four fewer than Hayek expected, and as it was Easter weekend, the place was filled to capacity. The organizers were assisted by Aaron Director's request to share a double room with Frank Knight, this in order to get a bathroom en suite for Knight. Three attendees (Morley, Cornuelle, and de Lovinfosse) had to be accommodated in another hotel.[37]

The Participants

So who were the thirty-nine people who came to the first organizational meeting of the society? Hayek's original list of invitees included (excepting Hunold) only academics and writers, and he knew nearly all of them, professionally, personally, or both. There were in the first instance the

Swiss-based hosts and their compatriots: Hunold, Rappard, and Röpke. Added to this was Hans Barth, a philosopher and sometime journalist from the University of Zurich who was an acquaintance of Röpke. We might also include in the Swiss contingent Bertrand de Jouvenel, a French political philosopher and journalist who had fled France for the safety of Switzerland in 1943 and whom Hayek had first met in London after the war.[38]

Jouvenel had a colorful if checkered past. At age sixteen he began what would turn into a five-year affair with his famous stepmother, the writer Colette, and in the early 1930s he traveled across America with his then lover Martha Gellhorn, the novelist and war correspondent who later would marry Ernest Hemingway.[39] As was all too common of intellectuals in the interwar period, Jouvenel's political journey was similarly peripatetic. A progressive leftist intellectual in the 1920s—an early book was titled *L'Économie dirigée*[40]—like many of his generation he was a critic of the nationalism that had led to the slaughter and destruction of the Great War, and accordingly a great advocate of European cooperation, in his case especially between France and Germany. In the 1930s, he was frustrated by the French government's failure to institute national policies to combat the Depression and became increasingly enamored of the strong leadership of men like Franklin Delano Roosevelt and Hitler, the latter of whom sat for an interview with him. In 1936 he joined Jacques Doriot's Parti Populaire Français, the closest thing to a nationalist French fascist party, but resigned in 1938 in part to protest the Munich agreement that gave Germany the Sudetenland.[41] After the June 1940 armistice divided France in two, he continued to view and write favorably about the prospects of a diminished France living under the tutelage of a robust, youthful, community-minded "New German Order"; as one historian put it, he had been "seduced by the idea of an anti-bourgeois fascist youth revolution."[42] During this period he worked with the German ambassador to the occupied portion of France, his old friend Otto Abetz, to advance the cause of Franco-German reconciliation. Yet in his memoirs Jouvenel claimed that at the same time he was working as an intelligence officer for the Service de Renseignements de l'Armée Française. In November 1942 the Allied landings in North Africa led to the German and Italian occupation of Vichy France, at which point Jouvenel soured completely on his earlier vision and began supporting the local resistance. He was arrested and held by the Gestapo for two days and after his release went into hiding until September 1943, when he and his wife escaped across the border.[43] He apparently had a dry wit. Leonard Read once asked Jouvenel if he understood any German: "He replied that the only thing he fully comprehended was during the war when the Germans said of him, 'He should be shot!'"[44]

So how did Jouvenel find his way to Mont Pèlerin? He did not need to go far: the village of Saint Saphorin, where he settled, is one of the towns at its base. While living there he finished his erudite and provocative tome *Du pouvoir* (*On Power*) and at some point was befriended by Wilhelm Röpke.[45] Jouvenel's remarkable book combined (sometimes speculative) history, ethnography, evolutionary metaphors, political philosophy, and much else, portraying power as an almost metaphysical force. His starting point was the fact that the sort of "total war" that had been waged twice in the past thirty years would have been unimaginable in earlier times. What had changed to make such mass destruction possible? Though he identified many changes, two of the most important were the ability of nation-states to tax and to conscript their citizens, which provided both financial and human resources to exploit. Worse, though still in the hands of a few, power was now spoken of as if it were in the hands of all the people, and therefore that any system of checks and balances was no longer necessary. Hayek would summarize the danger that these developments posed in his laudatory review of the English translation of the book:

> Power has an inherent tendency to expand and where there are no effective limitations it will grow without bounds, whether it is exercised in the name of the people or in the name of the few. Indeed, there is reason to fear that unlimited power in the hands of the people will grow farther and be even more pernicious in its effects than power exercised by the few.[46]

Despite his troubling past, the messages in Jouvenel's new treatise would resonate with those about to gather in Mont Pèlerin.

Returning to the other attendees, the people to whom Hayek was closest were, of course, his old friends from the Vienna days, now living in the

States, Ludwig von Mises and Fritz Machlup. Hayek had taken a job under Mises at a temporary government agency for the clearing of war debts (the *Abrechnungsamt*) in 1921, and Mises had helped facilitate his first trip to the United States in 1923–24. On his return, Hayek became a member of Mises's biweekly seminar (the *Miseskreis*). Later, Mises helped set him up as the director of an Austrian Institute for Business Cycle Research. Machlup had been a peer of Hayek at the University of Vienna and later a member of the *Geistkreis*, a discussion group that Hayek had founded with Herbert Fürth. He had gone to the States on a Rockefeller fellowship in 1933 and ended up staying, but the two friends kept in touch. Machlup was Hayek's main sounding board as he was writing *The Pure Theory of Capital* and was instrumental in finding an American publisher for *The Road to Serfdom*. After the war, Machlup's wife, Mitzi, would regularly send the Hayek family, which was enduring the British postwar rationing regime, packages of food.

Hayek knew almost all the others coming from America as well. Frank Knight, Aaron Director, and Milton Friedman were by then all at the University of Chicago, which had been Hayek's home base for his 1945 trip and half of his 1946 trip. He had known Knight since first meeting him in Vienna, and they corresponded while debating the fine points of capital theory in the 1930s. Knight had been one of the readers of the manuscript for *The Road to Serfdom* for the University of Chicago Press. Director had attended Hayek's seminar when he visited LSE in 1938 and, working alongside Machlup in Washington, DC, during the war, was the one who had suggested that Machlup send Hayek's manuscript to the University of Chicago Press for review. Hayek had first met Friedman during his American visits. Harry Gideonse had earlier been at Chicago as well, though by 1947 he was the president of Brooklyn College. In 1939 he had published an extended version of Hayek's "Freedom and the Economic System" in a public policy series that he edited.[47] They were close enough friends that Hayek had met with him twice when he passed through New York on his 1945 trip. Hayek may have encountered Frank Graham, an international economist based at Princeton, when he visited his friends Oskar Morgenstern and Friedrich Lutz there on his American trips. The only American Hayek definitely had not met prior to the meeting was George Stigler, then at Brown University for a year but moving to Columbia University in the fall.[48] He would teach there until 1958, when he left for the Graduate School of Business at Chicago. Stigler had earned his doctorate at Chicago in the 1930s, writing under Knight, and knew Friedman well from their days together there, during their war work in New York, and from their time together in the Economics Department at the University of Minnesota. So, though not based at Chicago, he was very much a part of their contingent. He, Director, Friedman, and Knight traveled together to the meeting.[49]

There were other scholars who, like Machlup and Mises, had left their own countries in Europe at various points in the 1930s. Hayek was very close to two of them. He had known the Austrian philosopher of science Karl Popper since he had presented an early version of "The Poverty of Historicism" in Hayek's seminar at LSE in 1936. Popper and Hayek had carried on an extensive correspondence during the war, and Hayek had been instrumental in bringing Popper from New Zealand to teach at LSE at war's end. Hayek had first met the Hungarian émigré chemistry professor and polymath Michael Polanyi at the Colloque Lippmann in August 1938, but the two men had the same nemeses among the British intelligentsia, people like the Webbs and such "men of science" as J. D. Bernal, as Polanyi made evident in his collection of essays *The Contempt of Freedom*.[50] Like so many other liberal émigrés, Polanyi had left Germany in 1933, accepting the offer of a chair in physical chemistry at the University of Manchester. Hayek had met Karl Brandt, an economist specializing in agriculture who had left Germany for the New School and later for Stanford, when he visited the latter university in 1946. They discussed the Acton-Tocqueville Society on that occasion.[51] Finally, there was Erich Eyck, a German lawyer and historian who had left Freiburg in 1938, eventually settling in Oxford. Like Hayek, he was an admirer of British liberalism. During the war he had penned a highly critical three-volume biography of Bismarck, one of Hayek's nemeses.[52] Given Hayek's various connections to Freiburg— his student Vera Smith had married Friedrich Lutz, who had earned his degree there, and Hayek would stop in Freiburg to see Walter Eucken when he took trips to Austria before the war—he probably knew Eyck, too, and certainly knew of his work: he was someone whom Hayek had recommended to do an article for Röpke's planned journal back in 1945.[53]

A chief goal of the conference was to introduce liberals from the various European countries not only to their counterparts in America but also to each other. Britain was represented by three economists, all of whom Hayek knew. His closest friend and LSE colleague, Lionel Robbins, was joined by Stanley Dennison of Cambridge, who had offered comments to Hayek on *The Road to Serfdom* prior to its publication, and John Jewkes of Manchester, who would in 1948 publish *Ordeal by Planning*.[54] Robbins, Jewkes, and Dennison had all worked together in the British government's Central Economic Information Service in the early part of the war.[55] France would have been well represented had Rueff (another Colloque Lippmann alumnus) and Rist been able to come, but even without them there was the economist Maurice Allais and law professor François Trevoux. Italy would have had two representatives had Einaudi not canceled; the other was Carlo Antoni, a philosopher and historian. Though more were invited from the area, the Scandinavian countries fielded one representative each. Trygve Hoff, the editor of a liberal magazine named *Farmand* and fervent opponent of planning (Hayek had been working on getting a book of his translated into English just before the war began), represented Norway; Carl Iversen, an economist and political scientist, Denmark; and Herbert Tingsten, a political scientist who had also recently become the editor in chief of the Swedish newspaper *Dagens Nyheter*, Sweden.[56] Hayek had visited both Copenhagen and Stockholm in January 1946 and saw both Iversen and Tingsten on the trip.[57] Finally, there was Eucken, Hayek's friend from the University of Freiburg and the only representative from Germany who had actually spent the war there.

The other category of people on Hayek's original list were "writers," principally members of the press and, again, mostly people he knew. There was Henry Hazlitt, by then an editor at *Newsweek*, whose glowing endorsement of *The Road to Serfdom* in the Sunday *New York Times Book Review* section got the American edition off to a strong start. John Davenport of *Fortune* magazine also attended, and he, too, had written an admiring review.[58] As noted earlier, Max Eastman, who had done the *Reader's*

Digest condensation of Hayek's book, was invited but could not come, so he was replaced by the European editor, George Révay. The Oxford-trained historian and sole female participant, Cecily Veronica Wedgwood, was deputy editor at the British weekly *Time and Tide*, which had been an outlet for a number of contributions by Hayek: in 1945 alone he published seven pieces there. Even though he had written books, Hoff was not a professor, so he, too, belonged in this category. The only person that Hayek did not know among the writers who attended was Felix Morley, who had been suggested by Luhnow.[59] Morley had previously been editor of the *Washington Post* and in 1944 had helped found the magazine *Human Events*.

Someone who was not on Hayek's list and neither an academic nor a newspaperman was Henri de Lovinfosse, the founder of the blanket and cloth manufacturing firm S. A. Manta in Belgium.[60] A friend of Röpke, he had received his invitation from Hunold only in March, probably with the latter's intent of increasing the representation of conferees from European countries.[61] He was the only actual businessperson at the conference.

And what about the men whom Luhnow had recommended be added, either as participants or observers, presumably to keep tabs on the meeting and report back to him? Surely the first among them, on paper at least, was Leonard Read, the president of the newly established Foundation for Economic Education. Read had worked in California throughout the 1930s and by spring 1945 had reached the post of manager of the Los Angeles Chamber of Commerce, the largest in the United States. With the war winding down, he decided to leave there for the National Industrial Conference Board, an institution dedicated to educating Americans about the basic principles of economics, something he deemed essential in postwar America. After eight months he quit, finding their requirement to tell "both sides of the story" when it came to issues of economic policy too constraining. One of his jobs at the board had been fundraising, and he came to know several influential and wealthy industrialists. One of these was David Goodrich of the B. F. Goodrich Company, who put him in touch with others of like mind. Read attracted enough funds to create an organization that would promote the study of economic principles in ways more congenial to his own and his backers' predispositions.[62]

The Foundation for Economic Education opened its doors in March 1946, only a year before the meeting. Its first offices were a couple of rooms in the Equitable Building on Park Avenue in New York City, where B. F. Goodrich was located, but by July it had moved into a mansion estate about half an hour north of the city in Irvington-on-Hudson. Read soon brought in Orval Watts, who had served as his chief economic counsel when he was at the LA Chamber of Commerce, as the chief economist, and Herbert Cornuelle to be his executive assistant. A little later, Floyd Arthur "Baldy" Harper, a marketing professor and economist who had been teaching at Cornell, also joined the group. The story is told that Harper decided to leave Cornell after a trustee of the university had suggested that he remove Hayek's *Road to Serfdom* from his syllabus.[63]

The most intriguing character among the foundation men was Loren "Red" Miller. One of the many hats that Luhnow had worn was that of chairman of the board for the Civic Research Institute in Kansas City. Earlier in his career, Miller had worked there, and soon after they met, Miller began to influence Luhnow to turn the focus of the Volker Charities Fund away from local projects and toward the support of free-market causes. Miller later became the director of the Detroit Bureau of Governmental Research, an agency that was part of the privately funded "good government" municipal reform movement, but he continued to be a key adviser for Luhnow. Even from that rather modest posting, it seems he had his hand in everything.

Thus, Miller had been in the audience when Hayek, on his *Road to Serfdom* tour, spoke before the Economic Club of Detroit. Impressed by the talk, he set up the initial meeting between Luhnow and Hayek. It was Miller who sent Hayek an encouraging letter after the Volker Fund initially declined to support the Acton-Tocqueville Society proposal.[64] He also helped Leonard Read raise the funds necessary to purchase the mansion in Irvington-on-Hudson for FEE. Hayek agreed to let Miller and Read join him on the "advisory committee" overseeing Aaron Director's work on the Free Market Study. Herb Cornuelle, whom Read hired to be his executive assistant and who came to the 1947 meeting, had worked for Miller as a trainee in Kansas City and later at the Detroit Bureau.[65]

Miller had multiple reasons to want to be present at the first meeting. Luhnow could not attend, so he was there to represent him and to see whether the Volker Fund's monies had been well spent. Director would be in attendance, so Miller could also inquire into how the (Volker-funded) Free Market Study was coming along. He also wanted to identify who among the various people there were "sound," the sort who might be worthy of further support.[66] Friedrich Hayek would be among those who passed the test: in a year's time Miller would use his multiple connections to start the ball rolling to bring Hayek to the University of Chicago's Committee on Social Thought.

Hayek's Agenda

Even had the meeting at Mont Pèlerin been a one-off affair, it probably would have been worthwhile simply to introduce liberals, given their fewness in number, from a variety of countries to one another. In his invitation acceptance letter, Milton Friedman remarked on "the number of names on your list that are unfamiliar to us."[67] Making those introductions was one of Hayek's premier goals.

But he also wanted to form a society, which was far more ambitious. Such an organization would require a statement of principles, a set of commitments on which all members would need to agree. Having witnessed the fractious discussion that took place among supposedly like-minded men at the Colloque Lippmann, he could not have been sanguine about the prospects for any sort of quick agreement. It was not that disputes were unhelpful, of course, or something to be avoided. The whole point, after all, was to begin the process of arguing out the finer points of how to constitute a new liberalism for the postwar world. But he did not want things simply to explode. The combination of strong personalities and strongly held beliefs (Mises and Knight come immediately to mind) made the danger a real one.[68] Even were such obstacles overcome, people would need not just to agree to some statement of principles, they would need to commit to carrying out the goals of the organization, whatever they might be. But what should they be? Hayek wanted to get a discussion among leading liberal intellectuals going, but he knew that some people, and not just those from the foundations, wanted to have a more public-facing society, one that would attempt to enter the public forum and shape policy debates. Finally, if a society was formed, there would need to be future meetings. Such gatherings, and international travel to them, would require substantial outside funding, and Hayek had just seen how hard that was to come by.[69] We know that in the end the society was formed, but at the time the outcome was anything but certain. The commitment of the people involved must be credited, but also the direness of the situation they confronted. In the spring of 1947, the prospects for Europe looked very bleak indeed.

War's end had pretty much destroyed what little was left of Central Europe. The intensification of strategic area bombing in the last year and the inevitable carnage and destruction that accompanied final military assaults killed hundreds of thousands and reduced city after city to rubble. There were massive flows of desperate refugees fleeing war zones, soon to be followed by the forced exodus of ethnic Germans from newly liberated countries. Finally, there was all manner of retributive violence—murder, beatings, rape, expropriations, public humiliations—in some places carried out by the conquering military forces (especially in areas taken over by the Russians), in others by fellow citizens eager to punish collaborators. By 1947 things had improved somewhat, but pressing geopolitical concerns, economic insecurity, political instability, and a looming humanitarian crisis created a sense of hopelessness and with it the potential for further upheaval.

Chief among the many problems was: What to do with Germany?[70] The eastern part of that country had been occupied by the Soviet Union, and the west by the United States, Britain, and France. In the immediate postwar period, the mantra that had been established at the Big Three meeting in Potsdam in summer 1945 was the four Ds: denazification, demilitarization, decartelization, and democratization. Reparation payments and demilitarization went hand in hand, especially for the Soviets as German factories in industries that could support war efforts that lay in its zone were dismantled and shipped east. All four powers nominally agreed on the eventual goal of a unified German state that could be treated as a single economic entity, but the four-zone structure evidently undercut any progress in that direction. US attempts to break the logjam led to a joining of the American and British zones on January 1, 1947, but neither the Soviet Union nor France was interested in joining, and the creation of the Bizone had few effects on day-to-day life in Germany. For two years the Allied foreign ministers had been meeting, but they were no closer to agreement over the future status of Germany and Austria. Until those questions were resolved, any sort of postwar recovery would be painfully slow, not just for Germany but also for the rest of Europe, which needed an economically viable Germany to help spur its own recovery.

The situation as it existed in the spring of 1947 was clearly unsustainable. Under the occupation regime, the Allies were responsible for feeding the German people. Prices were controlled and a rationing system set up; it was essentially a continuation of a wartime command-and-control economy. The amount of food provided was insufficient to feed the population, but it was still costly for the Allies. Britain, for example, was spending the equivalent of $80 million a year on the occupation while collecting only $29 million in reparations, causing Hugh Dalton, the chancellor of the exchequer, to observe that the British were paying reparations to the Germans while bread was being rationed at home.[71] The desperate conditions were further exacerbated by the weather. The winter of 1946–47 was brutal, the coldest since 1880. Roads and rail lines across the continent closed for weeks, throttling any sort of nascent recovery. There was a shortage of coal, and even when it was available it was difficult to deliver. The horrible winter was followed by a summer of drought, causing food production to fall in some places by 50 percent and more. The prospect of mass starvation was real.

The potential political consequences of the stalled situation were equally dire. The scholars and writers gathering at Mont Pèlerin were not sanguine, of course, about the nearly universal embrace by European governments of collectivist economic and social policies. But in 1947 their concerns went far beyond this. The communist parties were gaining strength in Italy and France, where the potential for civil unrest grew with each strike and violent street demonstration. Meanwhile, in occupied Germany and Austria, the torpid pace and apparent arbitrariness across zones of the denazification process had become so widely resented that "renazification" was becoming the more likely outcome. It is no wonder that the leaders of the Soviet Union, whose minions were sowing unrest in multiple countries across Europe, were in no hurry to resolve the Germany question. The democracies to their west were under increasing pressure, and the longer they delayed, the greater the chances were that the other Allies would simply pull out, leaving all the spoils to them.

The situation was certainly well understood by the Europeans gathering at Mont Pèlerin. Jouvenel would later put the matter precisely: "Doubtless you feel as I do that we are now hovering on the brink. The Russian menace from the outside, the Communist menace from the inside, and to defend Europe against this double offensive, the Socialists whose every idea tends to disorganize and weaken the Occident."[72] Hayek had witnessed the destruction, but also some hopeful signs, himself. In 1946 he visited Germany to give a talk on *The Road to Serfdom*. He entered the lecture hall through a small opening in a burnt-out pile of rubble, only to be greeted by a room full of eager students. This took place while the German translation of the book was still banned there (the Russians, as one of the four occupying powers, had insisted on this), but on the trip he also discovered that samizdat copies had been circulating. Clearly there was a thirst in Germany for ideas, if only the ham-fisted policies of the occupying forces could be gotten out of the way. Later in 1946 and again in early 1947, he visited Vienna and was again horrified by what he saw. The Americans at the meeting would have been less aware of all this, though as Milton Friedman recounted, the active black market that he and George Stigler encountered as they passed through Paris on the way to the meeting at least made it feel more vibrant than London, where the legal controls on prices were more strictly observed.[73] The conferees may have been meeting in luxurious surroundings, but their purpose was clear enough.

What they did not know was that the logjam was about to break. Soon after their meeting, American secretary of state George Marshall returned from the Moscow meeting of the foreign ministers convinced that the Russians were simply stalling and had little concern about the continued deterioration of Europe. Two months later he would give a speech at Harvard that proposed a European Recovery Program, or Marshall Plan, signaling America's willingness to assist actively in the rebuilding of Europe. Within a year the money was appropriated by Congress and the process begun. That the assistance was turned down by Moscow as well as other countries that would soon be within its orbit is often taken to mark the beginning of the Cold War. But in early April 1947, none of this could be foreseen.

If the main point of Hayek's agenda was to form a society that would provide the intellectual foundation for a new liberalism to confront the many problems besetting the postwar world, there was also an actual agenda of *topics* that he wanted to discuss. In the first week, the group would investigate five subjects that he had chosen. These were "free" enterprise or competitive order; modern historiography and political education; the future of Germany; the problems and chances of European federation; and liberalism and Christianity. Topics for the second week's sessions would be determined by the conferees. If the decision was positive to form a society, a statement of principles would also be formulated.

The First Week

At 9:30 on the morning of April 1, the group gathered for the opening meeting. Both Rappard and Hayek gave welcoming addresses, with Hayek thanking attendees and sponsors, describing how the conference came about, offering the reasons behind his choice of topics for the first week, and proposing procedures for the following days. By modern conference standards, the schedule was exceedingly civilized. Morning sessions did not begin until 9:30, afternoon sessions were at 4:30, and evening sessions at 8:30. Thursday afternoon was devoted to the trip to Coppet, and after the Friday afternoon session the group did not convene formally again until Monday afternoon. Evidently, all the free time was designed to promote interaction outside the formal meetings. Sessions would open with either a paper or remarks by whichever person had been given responsibility for it. Discussion then ensued, details of which were preserved in shorthand notes taken by Dorothy Hahn, transcriptions of which compose this volume. It should perhaps be reemphasized that though remarks are attributed to individuals in her notes, these were not verbatim transcripts but only rough and often incomplete summaries of their contributions.

The afternoon session began with Hayek reading his paper "'Free' Enterprise or Competitive Order." The title was meant to emphasize the choice between a system of laissez-faire free enterprise and his own preferred system, one in which the state and the legal framework work in tandem to make competition as effective and beneficent as possible. To be sure, even under free enterprise there was some minimal role for the state, which provided institutions for the protection of property and enforcement of contracts and for the prevention of violence and fraud. In Hayek's view, these were not enough. Exploring what constituted a proper competitive order was of course a chief goal of the conference, but clearly, and right from the start, by making the distinction he was distancing himself from Mises and other advocates of laissez-faire, which presumably included people like Hazlitt as well as all the foundation people.

The next to speak was Aaron Director. Like Hayek, he felt that liberalism as currently conceived was incapable of responding adequately to real challenges that had arisen in the areas of monopolies and combinations, cyclical instability, and income inequality. Because there was no adequate liberal framework for addressing these issues, ad hoc remedies that caused their own problems were typically offered in their place. If Hayek's talk mostly emphasized remedies that involved altering the legal framework, Director's focused more directly on economics and on specific policy responses. Given that he was supposed to be working on the Free Market Study, a project that Hayek had helped negotiate and itself funded by the Volker Fund, his position in the lineup of speakers was clearly intentional. Hayek wanted to showcase Director and for his remarks to illuminate both his abilities and the direction of his thinking.

Director performed his task admirably. His systematic presentation reads in parts like a summary of a mainstream introductory economics text of today on market failures and their possible remedies, though with a strong normative emphasis on his preferred policies. What will strike a reader of today who is familiar with the Chicago view on monopoly are the changes that have taken place since the 1940s.[74] In Director's talk, monopoly is considered a serious problem, and the policy responses he was prepared to contemplate were numerous. His concern with inequality may also surprise some critics of neoliberalism. To be sure, Director decried certain policies aimed at combating inequality, such as minimum wage laws, price supports in agriculture, protection of specific trades, and the like, but he did so because they were ad hoc in nature and favored specific groups. His opposition to those programs did not mean that he thought that inequality should be ignored. The reduction of monopoly and support of education would help to mitigate it, but these needed to be supplemented by a program to improve the physical well-being of children from poor families, a progressive income tax system, and payments to low-income households to ensure a minimum level of income.

The next two speakers were to have been Walter Eucken and Maurice Allais, but neither of their remarks were recorded by Hahn, and so far no record of what Allais may have said (if he in fact spoke) has been discovered. Eucken's words were preserved, however. While Eucken spoke in German, Hayek translated into English and Hunold took down what Eucken said in the original German.[75] A transcript was later sent to Hayek, who kept it with his other papers from the meeting.[76] An English translation of Eucken's talk is included as an appendix to the session in this volume.

It was a risk, Hayek knew, particularly for the Americans who would have known little about him, to invite to the conference a German who had stayed in Germany during the war.[77] They would not have known that, while in Freiburg, Eucken had been vocal in his opposition to the university rector Martin Heidegger's acquiescence in the policies of the Nazis. They would have been ignorant about his participation in groups that criticized the autarkic economic policies of the Nazi regime and of his circle's links to people like Dietrich Bonhoeffer and Carl Friedrich Goerdeler, who were directly involved in the German resistance. All this had made Eucken's situation increasingly perilous at the end of the war. He was in fact detained for a couple of days by the Gestapo, but unlike his colleagues Adolf Lampe and Constantin von Dietze, he had been spared being tortured.[78] The Gestapo had not been the only worry. In January 1945 Röpke had told Hayek that he had had no news "from W. E. since he cannot dare to write to me, but after the wholesale bombardment of his town I am extremely worried about him." Hayek was greatly relieved when he found out that Eucken, "about whose fate I was more concerned than anyone else's in Germany," had managed to survive.[79]

The risk paid off. The contrast that Eucken drew in his presentation between the willingness of various groups in Germany to discuss competition policy and the reality on the ground confronting them—a heavily controlled economy that was equivalent to a world of monopolies—provided anecdotes and institutional details that nicely supplemented the more programmatic statements of Hayek and Director. It also made clear how harmful the current occupation policy was to the prospects of a revitalized Germany, a theme to which he would return.

General discussion waited until the evening session. That event might have been retitled "free enterprise versus the competitive order," or more simply "Mises versus the rest," though both Hazlitt and Miller made brief comments in support of Mises's positions, and "the rest" did not always agree with one another. Mises had some justification to feel a little prickly. After all, in a session posing a choice between free enterprise and a competitive order, it might have been fitting to have had among the opening speakers at least one person who was willing to defend the former. In any event, Mises's defense of laissez-faire was predictably direct and pithy: most of the problems that had been identified had government actions as their root cause, so their solution was to get it out of the way. For most of those attending the conference, this simple advice was unsatisfactory. People wanted to discuss alternative policies, to find out which ones might best cohere with a liberal vision, not the reasons why policies were unnecessary. Both Hayek and Robbins tried to intervene in various ways, mostly to clarify the various positions under discussion, but at times things got testy. This was probably the session at which Mises "stood up, announced to the assembly 'You're all a bunch of socialists,' and stomped out of the room," though that is not recorded in the minutes.[80]

The second session on "Modern Historiography and Political Education" was chaired by Veronica Wedgwood, who (though then working at *Time and Tide*) by 1947 had established her reputation as a historian with books on the Thirty Years' War, Oliver Cromwell, and William the Silent. Her books were well researched but also well written, attracting a readership far beyond the academy. The title of the session, chosen by Hayek, may seem odd, but he used the word "historiography" idiosyncratically, not to mean the methods of writing history but to denote the more popular sort of history that Wedgwood wrote.[81]

Hayek's complaints against the way history was being practiced were multiple and of long standing. He had argued in his 1933 LSE inaugural address that the German Historical School economists, in their attacks on economic theory, had undermined public confidence in the science of economics, thereby opening up debates on public policy to all manner of proposals by quacks and charlatans. Their legacy was that the quest for scientific truth had been replaced by rampant relativism, which had made their support for the policies of Bismarck all that much easier. When he got to England, Hayek encountered new narratives, many colored by the "scientific" Marxist notion that there were inevitable laws of history, chief among them that capitalism was inevitably doomed to destroy itself. Many advocates of planning argued that this made the adoption of a planned society imperative. Those same critics of liberalism also argued that ideas were unimportant, just ornamentation when compared to the true movers of human history: changes in the mode of production and in the social relations of production. For Hayek this was nonsense; ideas were crucial. The *Abuse of Reason* project, to which he had dedicated his war years, was a critique of all these movements. Hayek alluded to all those concerns in his opening address, but the specific focus of the session was what role history should play in influencing political education. He probably had in mind that the study of history might reintroduce liberal ideas and values, not only in Central Europe but in England as well.[82]

In writings during the war in *Time and Tide* and other outlets, Wedgwood had disparaged German historians for creating myths about German history that were then used for propaganda purposes by the Nazis. She also insisted that historians should not shy away from drawing moral conclusions.[83] In her opening remarks, Wedgwood focused on the question of whether "serious" professional historians should cede the writing of the more popular kinds of history to generalists and propagandists. In her view, a competition among many types of historians would be the best guarantee against the misuses of history. Both Erich Eyck (who spoke of the role of nineteenth-century German historians in glorifying the Prussian crown, promoting the German Empire, and destroying liberal doctrine) and Hayek (who questioned both value-free history and the notion of inevitable laws) joined in to expand the discussion to other themes, but not altogether successfully. Some of the subsequent discussion turned on philosophical issues. Can history tell us what really happened, or does all history require selection and interpretation? What is a historical fact? Though such questions are interesting, they were not what Hayek had in mind. He would have to wait until a later meeting, when the papers that were published in *Capitalism and the Historians* were first presented, to challenge the progressive monopoly on how the past gets portrayed.[84]

If the first session was predictably stormy, and the second vaguely disappointing, the third, on "The Problem of Germany," ended up being the most memorable of the meeting, this due to Walter Eucken. Röpke gave the lead talk, with the more senior, white-haired, and distinguished Eucken speaking second. Both emphasized that the occupation that followed the war essentially substituted one totalitarian regime for another. What made Eucken's comments so powerful, even when read today, was his vivid description, again translated by Hayek, of everyday life under the occupation, made the more poignant because it was delivered in calm and measured tones. His summary was both bleak and memorable: "The German economy is undergoing a progressive primitivization and now corresponds rather to the economic system of the sixth and eighth centuries. . . . At the moment, Germany is half a corpse."

In reminiscences about the first meeting, both George Stigler and Milton Friedman recalled the affecting scene of Eucken taking meticulous care in the peeling of an orange, the first he had seen in years.[85] But in a comment that perfectly summarized Eucken's main message, Friedman went on to add, "More important, he made vivid what it was like to live in a totalitarian country, as well as in a country devastated by war and by the rigidities imposed by the occupying authorities."[86] If the people assembled needed a personification of what they were there for, and a depiction of the world they sought to avoid, Eucken provided it. He quickly became, in Hayek's words, "the star of the conference." Eucken was made one of the vice presidents of the society and would play a key role in recommending who from Germany should be invited to future gatherings.[87]

The fourth pair of sessions devoted to "The Problems and Chances of European Federation" were the least successful of the week. Federation had been a topic of extensive discussion just before the war, driven in part by fears over German territorial aggression, and Hayek and Robbins had been active participants.[88] Hayek raised the topic again at the end of *The Road to Serfdom*, in part because he feared that some sort of planning regime would be imposed by the victorious Allies on the conquered territories and in part because he thought that a federation could serve as yet another check on national governments, especially in the area of trade, e.g., by preventing them from pursuing protectionist policies.[89] In January 1947, at the instigation of Winston Churchill, a United Europe Movement was formed that aimed at political and economic integration, and subsequent transnational initiatives followed.[90] Though some of those assembled believed that some form of federation was desirable—Maurice Allais, who had earlier advocated a federalist Atlantic Union, was perhaps the most enthusiastic—others did not, and virtually everyone (even Allais) agreed that current obstacles to it were formidable, rendering the discussion purely theoretical.[91]

On the morning of Good Friday, the topic turned, fittingly, to "Liberalism and Christianity." Though personally he was agnostic, Hayek felt it was essential for the preservation of liberalism that its traditional antagonism toward Christianity be overcome. As Eucken was to note at the session, in Germany some of the most effective resistance to Hitler had been among active members of the church. Liberal political parties in most European countries were a dead letter, leaving those that had affiliations with the church as the only real alternatives to the socialists and communists. If liberals were to have any hope of building coalitions, some sort of reconciliation was needed.

Hayek had originally planned to have someone more sympathetic to such conciliatory views lead off the discussion, like William Orton (his first choice) or Franz Schnabel, but neither of them ended up coming to the meeting.[92] So he turned to Frank Knight. This was a dicey call. In his letter accepting the invitation to the meeting, Knight had warned Hayek against "snuggling up" too closely to the Catholic church, for "if one says he is a Catholic and a Liberal, he either doesn't know what he is or places some other value or interest above telling the truth!" He then went on to disparage Orton, whose book *The Liberal Tradition* he had recently reviewed, noting, "if he is a Liberal I certainly am not."[93] Was a civil discussion of the topic possible with Knight as the lead speaker?

It turned out to be one of the most interesting sessions. Knight's extraordinary opening remarks, imperfectly captured by Hahn's notes, wandered far and wide. The tensions he identified were well known: that between the scientific search for truth, no matter where it might lead, versus belief that was dictated by faith; and that between the liberals' insistence on tolerance of divergent views versus the propensity of the devout to be intolerant of views they deem heretical. In the discussion, some thought the chances of any easy reconciliation between religion and liberalism were remote at best, while others spoke equally resolutely of its necessity. Eucken once again drew on his own personal experience of life under a totalitarian system, arguing that there was no room for religious belief under such a regime, that only under a liberal system, precisely because of its dedication to tolerance, would Christianity be permitted to survive.

Despite some occasionally fractious exchanges, the first week was deemed sufficiently successful that the assembled group decided to take the next steps. A committee of six was formed to write up a statement of principles. Perhaps predictably, the first try produced a document that was both too long and yet still missing bits that certain people wanted included. At that point, the drafting of the document was turned over to Hayek's great friend Lionel Robbins. It was a wise move. Robbins had very efficiently run the affairs of the economists at LSE before the war, then worked equally effectively beginning in late 1941 as head of the economic section in the wartime coalition government.[94] Asked if he could have a new statement prepared for the group to review at breakfast the next morning, he said no, but by the next afternoon it was ready. The new document was briefer—six points rather than ten—and, with the goal of achieving broad support, quite general. Everyone but Maurice Allais signed it.[95] There were also sessions for discussions of the purposes of the society, its membership, and its name.

The Second Week—Economics and Russia

At the end of the first week, the substantive agenda for the second week was also determined. Given the preponderance of economists at the meeting, and the failure to get very far in the discussion at the "'free enterprise' or competitive order" session, it is unsurprising that four of the five were on economic policy. These were contra-cyclical measures, full employment, and monetary reform; wage policy and trade unions; taxation, poverty, and income distribution; agricultural policy; and the present political crisis. The last topic was suggested by Karl Popper and referred to ongoing concerns with how to deal with Russia. The discussions in the sessions of the second week are fascinating to follow, both for their substance and for the way that they reflected tensions that would repeatedly recur in later meetings of the society.

The first session was straight economics, specifically macroeconomics, and at least some of the discussion would be familiar to economists of today. All agreed that the policy that was being everywhere touted—that governments had a responsibility for producing full employment and should use Keynesian demand management policies to do so—was a dangerous one, especially to the extent that Lord Beveridge's definition of "full employment" (around 3 percent unemployment) was taken as appropriate. That way lay inflation, as well as a temptation for further government overreach—when its unrealistic goal went unrealized—through directing labor, interfering with wage bargains, fixing prices, and so on. Given the group's rejection of Beveridge's approach, the next question was what changes might be made in monetary and financial institutions to reduce uncertainty and minimize the likelihood of a business cycle. A movement to a commodity reserve standard to provide the anchor that gold once provided and the imposition of a 100 percent reserve requirement on banks (the so-called Chicago Plan) to make the banking sector less volatile were among these. A second set of issues was whether a rejection of Beveridge's full-employment policy also implied a rejection of Keynesian demand management policy in a downturn. Robbins (who had turned from a critic to a supporter of Keynesian policy prescriptions during the war) insisted that Keynes and Beveridge were not the same thing, that in addition to pushing for greater wage flexibility the government might time its capital expenditures so as to mitigate the cycle—he did not use the phrase "with shovel-ready projects" but could have. This brought the predictable reply from Milton Friedman that it was difficult to get the timing of such expenditures right, and that getting them wrong could exacerbate the cycle. Friedman argued that a system of monetary rules combined with a rearrangement of the tax system to make responses automatic rather than relying on discretion best reflected the liberal creed.[96] Such debates are familiar territory to economists. The only outlier in the discussion was Röpke, who continued to tout his own unique hybrid of Austrian and Keynesian policy. When a boom is underway, the government should try to restrain it to keep it from overheating the economy. When the inevitable recession occurs, it should be allowed to run its course, unless a secondary deflation emerges, at which point Keynesian demand stimulus should be instituted. There was another way in which Röpke was different from the rest: he wanted to inquire what social philosophy a concept like Beveridge's full-employment doctrine implied. No one responded to that; this was a discussion about economics, and only economics, an implicit limit that surely grated on Röpke's nerves!

Similar sorts of tensions were on display in the session on wage policy, and even more so the one on agricultural policy. In both cases, cultural differences as well as differences in institutional constraints that were seen as blocking possibilities for reform held center stage. Fritz Machlup did a masterful job of introducing the main questions to be addressed regarding wage policy. He noted the contradiction produced when the presence of strong unions is combined with calls for full employment. His proposed liberal policy was to avoid cyclical unemployment via a proper monetary policy, to avoid regional pockets of high unemployment by encouraging labor mobility, and to reduce restrictive entry practices (e.g., closed shop laws) by unions. Other ways to reduce union power—by limiting the size or geographical scope of a union—might also be considered. These proposals immediately brought protests that such steps—though useful in theory—could not possibly work in the speaker's country. There is no labor mobility in Switzerland, Rappard said. Other Europeans were split between simply encouraging dialogue between workers and management—Rappard and Lovinfosse favored this route; Knight, supposedly the great advocate of discussion, thought it unrealistic—and having some neutral party, usually the government, in charge of setting wages. John Jewkes made the interesting point that it was the unions in England that were offering the most effective resistance to the Labour government's attempts to direct labor. No consensus was reached.

There was even more resistance to a "one size fits all" agricultural policy. On one side were those who felt that agriculture was truly different from other ways of making a living, and certainly from industry. For Röpke it represented a way of life, and indeed an end in itself, one that would provide a bulwark against "the proletarian nomads of industrialization." He favored a set of policies that would support the spread of the family farm. Others had less romantic views of the agricultural life but still insisted that the sector was afflicted with special problems that demanded intervention. It seemed both unfair and inefficient that a bad growing season or two could put even good farmers out of business. Brandt, the agricultural specialist, felt that changes in credit policy—higher interest charges in good times, lower ones in bad—could help avoid such problems.

The opposition here included Loren Miller, who in one of the most memorable interventions in the conference put the matter precisely:

> Why shouldn't everyone be insured against the vicissitudes of the market, if farmers can be insured? What would be the sum of *all* the interventions which have been suggested during the conference? Wouldn't that be a planned economy?

Hayek supported Miller, noting that if one considers problems only one at a time, it is hard to keep one's mind on the general principles of liberal policy that they were seeking. And indeed, it was at this session that his plea that the conferees ignore existing political constraints was itself most ignored. Robbins, doubtless reflecting knowledge he had gained in his years of wartime government work, added that sometimes the best that a liberal economist could do, when faced with an illiberal government, is to advise on the least harmful way to achieve the illiberal aim. A Hippocratic oath of sorts for liberals in government, it actually captures rather well the general self-image of economists, if one substitutes in "efficiency" as the desideratum.

The other session on economic policy—taxation, poverty and income distribution—was very much the Milton Friedman show. In his opening talk he reiterated that a rules-oriented monetary policy had the best chance of securing macroeconomic stability and that the remaining problem of poverty could be handled by imposing a progressive income tax with a negative-income-tax (though he did not call it that) feature that kicked in below a certain level of income.[97] This simple change in the tax system was all that was needed; all the other programs that were designed to combat poverty could, and should, be eliminated.[98] Dorothy Hahn's notes recorded a barrage of questions that followed. How would it work? At what income level would people start paying taxes, and who would decide that? What about farmers who didn't keep records of income? Won't those who work and pay taxes resent their money being used to support those who did not? In a classic Friedmanian performance, he answered each objection with a short, crisp reply.

Hayek raised an interesting objection to Friedman's proposal: "Freedom not to work is a luxury which the poor country cannot afford." His solution was to provide a labor service, under semi-military conditions that paid below the prevailing wage, for those who would otherwise be unemployed. We note this because when Hayek sometimes during this period said that he favored a "minimum wage," this is what he was thinking of: not a floor below which the wage could not fall, but a wage that was below the prevailing wage, and hence one that would not have much effect on the wage structure, for the unemployable. In any event, no one took him up on it.

These four sessions bring out the fault lines apparent in later meetings: between economists and the more philosophically minded; between those looking for general principles and those focused on culturally sensitive, country-specific solutions to particular policy problems; between the Americans and the Europeans; between the academics and the foundation representatives. The final session had fewer disagreements, but also fewer answers. What was the appropriate liberal response to the Soviet Union's intransigent postwar stance? Liberals believe in the rule of law, in trade, peace, and tolerance. What to do when facing an uncooperative illiberal regime? With Nazi Germany the answer had been appeasement, with horrible results. Was the West in danger of making the same mistake again? Some—Frank Knight in particular—insisted on the importance of dialogue. But in spring 1947, not many others were prepared to follow him, as the comments by Popper, Robbins, and Polanyi make clear.

On the final day, a Memorandum of Association was adopted and the society formed. Hayek was made president and five vice presidents were chosen: in addition to Eucken, these were Jewkes, Knight, Rappard, and Jacques Rueff. Aaron Director would serve as secretary and C. O. Hardy as treasurer. In November 1947, the society was incorporated in Chicago. This was preferable to London because, as Hayek pointed out, the presence of currency controls in England would have made transacting the business of the society difficult (money could come in, but not go out). And thus ended the inaugural meeting of what would be known, despite Karl Popper's misgivings about the meaninglessness of the name, as the Mont Pèlerin Society.

Attendees of the First Mont Pèlerin Conference, 1947

Maurice Allais	Bertrand de Jouvenel
Carlo Antoni	Frank Knight
Hans Barth	Henri de Lovinfosse
Karl Brandt	Fritz Machlup
Herbert Cornuelle	Loren "Red" Miller
John Davenport	Ludwig von Mises
Stanley Dennison	Felix Morley
Aaron Director	Michael Polanyi
Walter Eucken	Karl Popper
Erich Eyck	William Rappard
Milton Friedman	Leonard Read
Harry Gideonse	George Révay
Frank Graham	Lionel Robbins
F. A. "Baldy" Harper	Wilhelm Röpke
Friedrich Hayek	George Stigler
Henry Hazlitt	Herbert Tingsten
Trygve Hoff	François Trevoux
Albert Hunold	V. Orval Watts
Carl Iversen	C. Veronica Wedgwood
John Jewkes	

Notes

1. Mont Pèlerin is the name of the *mountain,* while Mont-Pèlerin (with the hyphen) is the name of the *village* located on the mountain. The village is sometimes referred to on postcards and the like as "Mont-Pèlerin sur Vevey" to indicate that it lies above the larger town of Vevey. I thank Karen Horn for providing me with this geographical information. In later years some members and some people writing about the society would include the accent in the name, while others would not. At some point the society itself removed the accent, so that on its current website it is simply the Mont Pelerin Society. As this is a historical piece, we have retained the original spelling.

2. During World War II, the London School of Economics had evacuated to Cambridge, and Hayek's closest friend while there was the economic historian Sir John Clapham, who was in the role of chair for Hayek's lecture. Clapham had been supportive of Hayek's idea for an international liberal society, but he died in March 1946 so did not get to attend the first meeting. See F. A. Hayek, "Historians and the Future of Europe" (1978) in *The Collected Works of F. A. Hayek,* vol. 4, *The Fortunes of Liberalism,* ed. Peter Klein (Chicago: University of Chicago Press, 1992), 201–15.

3. Acton's papers were in Cambridge, and Hayek spent some time examining them. Hayek sent his paper to the Cambridge historian Herbert Butterfield, for whom Acton was the exemplar of a Whig historian. See Herbert Butterfield, chap. 6 in *The Whig Interpretation of History* (London: G. Bell and Sons, 1931). In his return letter, Butterfield took issue with Hayek's defense of Acton's view that good history can still contain a moral message (see Butterfield to Hayek, August 1, 1944, Friedrich A. Hayek Papers, box 61, folder 7, Hoover Institution [henceforth FAHP], 61.7). Acton, like Hayek, had criticized German historians of the nineteenth century for their role in enabling Bismarck's rise to power. Hayek put the point directly in his talk: "I cannot see that the most perfect respect for truth is in any way incompatible with the application of very rigorous moral standards in our judgment of historical events; and it seems to me that what the Germans need, and what in the past would have done them all the good in the world, is a strong dose of what it is now the fashion to call 'Whig history,' history of the kind of which Lord Acton is one of the last great representatives. The future historian must have the courage to say that Hitler was a bad man." Hayek, "Historians and the Future of Europe," 209.

4. Walter Lippmann, *An Inquiry into the Principles of the Good Society* (Boston: Little, Brown, 1937).

5. Lippmann, *Good Society,* 374. Lippmann's views were eclectic; in his acknowledgments he listed Mises and Hayek but also Keynes and Graham Wallas as influences.

6. For a transcript of the meeting and more on the Colloque Lippmann, see Jurgen Reinhoudt and Serge Audier, *The Walter Lippmann Colloquium: The Birth of Neo-Liberalism* (Cham, Switzerland: Palgrave Macmillan, 2018). See also Angus Burgin, chap. 2 in *The Great Persuasion: Reinventing Free Markets since the Depression* (Cambridge, MA: Harvard University Press, 2012); and Karen Horn, Stefan Kolev, David Levy, and Sandra Peart, eds., "Liberalism in the 21st Century: Lessons from the Colloque Walter Lippmann," special issue, *Journal of Contextual Economics—Schmollers Jahrbuch* 139, nos. 2–4 (2019). For more on Hayek's correspondence with Lippmann, see Bruce Caldwell and Hansjoerg Klausinger, chap. 25 in *Hayek: A Life* (Chicago: University of Chicago Press, forthcoming). Walter Eucken, who had remained in Freiburg after Hitler came to power, was invited to the meeting but was refused permission to leave Germany.

7. Louis Baudin, quoted in Reinhoudt and Audier, *Walter Lippmann Colloquium*, 111.

8. Röpke to Lippmann, September 14, 1937, quoted in Burgin, *Great Persuasion*, 67.

9. This and subsequent sections draw freely on Caldwell and Klausinger, chap. 33 in *Hayek: A Life*. There currently are two good books in English on the Mont Pèlerin Society that discuss the initial conference: R. M. Hartwell, *A History of the Mont Pelerin Society* (Indianapolis: Liberty Fund, 1995); and Burgin, *Great Persuasion*. Another excellent source, in German, is Philip Plickert, *Wandlungen des Neoliberalismus: Eine Studie zu Entwicklung und Ausstrahlung der "Mont Pèlerin Society"* (Stuttgart: Lucius & Lucius, 2008). Ola Innset's *Reinventing Liberalism: The Politics, Philosophy and Economics of Early Neoliberalism (1920–1947)* (Cham, Switzerland: Springer, 2020), half of which focuses on the 1947 meeting, is rather a disappointment. The author gets numerous facts wrong, tends to view the past through the narrow lens of present-day presuppositions, and though he claims to offer a corrective to more ideologically driven accounts, consistently "contextualizes" liberalism as the ideology of an upper-class elite worried about income redistribution and the loss of power that democracy would bring. Thus, "This fear of 'the masses' demanding a decent life from modern states is a recurring and very important theme in the arguments of early neoliberals" (p. 119), or "Fascism has traditionally been construed as fundamentally anti-liberal, but there were also points of great convergence between some variants of fascism and neoliberalism, notably with regard to the question of democracy" (p. 137). Readers of the transcript to follow may judge for themselves the veracity of such claims.

10. Luhnow to Hayek, September 7, 1945. The correspondence between Hayek, Luhnow, and Loren Miller cited here may be found in FAHP 58.16.

11. See Stephen Kresge and Leif Wenar, eds., *Hayek on Hayek: An Autobiographical Dialogue* (Chicago: University of Chicago Press, 1994), 132–33.

12. Hartwell, *History*, 30, dates the encounter to November 1945, but Hayek's datebook for that year indicates that his trip to Zurich took place in October (FAHP 122.3). Hunold had changed jobs frequently over his career and would be in a new one when Hayek met him again the next year.

13. Rappard had been part of the Swiss delegation at the Versailles Peace Conference and is said to have been instrumental in getting the headquarters of the League of Nations placed in Geneva. From 1920 to 1925 he was the director of the league's Mandate Division, overseeing the administration of colonial territories that had been lost by the Central Powers. The Centre William Rappard (so named in 1977) in Geneva now houses the offices of the World Trade Organization.

14. F. A. Hayek, "Monetary Nationalism and International Stability" (1937), in *Collected Works*, vol. 6, *Good Money, Part II: The Standard*, ed. Stephen Kresge (Chicago: University of Chicago Press, 1999), 37–99; Lionel Robbins, *The Economic Causes of War* (London: Jonathan Cape, 1939).

15. For examples, see Wilhelm Röpke, *Die Gesellschaftskrisis der Gegenwart* (Erlenbach-Zurich: Rentsch, 1942), English translation: *The Social Crisis of Our Time* (Chicago: University of Chicago Press, 1950); Wilhelm Röpke, *Civitas Humana: Grundfragen der Gesellschafts- und Wirtschaftsreform* (Erlenbach-Zurich: Rentsch, 1944), English translation: *Civitas Humana: A Humane Order of Society* (London: Hodge, 1948); Wilhelm Röpke, *Internationale Ordnung* (Erlenbach-Zurich: Rentsch, 1945), English translation: *International Order and Economic Integration* (Dordrecht: Reidel, 1959); for a discussion, see Burgin, *Great Persuasion*, 80–81.

16. Hartwell, *History*, 30; W. W. Bartley III, "Hayek Interview with W. W. Bartley, February 10, 1983," copy in possession of Bruce Caldwell.

17. For a fuller account, see Rob Van Horn and Philip Mirowski, "The Rise of the Chicago School of Economics and the Birth of Neoliberalism," in *The Road from Mont Pèlerin: The Making of the Neoliberal Thought Collective*, ed. Philip Mirowski and Dieter Plehwe (Cambridge, MA: Harvard University Press, 2009), 139–78; and Bruce Caldwell, "The Chicago School, Hayek and Neoliberalism," in *Building Chicago Economics: New Perspectives on the History of America's Most Powerful Economics Program*, ed. Robert Van Horn, Philip Mirowski, and Thomas Stapleford (Cambridge: Cambridge University Press, 2011), 301–34. On his 1945 and 1946 trips to America, Hayek had gotten to know the Chicago economist Henry Simons and discussed the plan to organize a liberal society with him. His death from an overdose of sleeping pills while Hayek was away visiting Stanford during the 1946 trip was devastating for both Hayek's and Simons's Chicago friends, but in the end it was a factor in convincing Director to go to Chicago.

18. Hayek to Luhnow, October 28, 1946.

19. Luhnow to Hayek, November 4, 1946.

20. Hayek to Rappard, November 23, 1946, Mont Pèlerin Society Papers, Hoover Institution [hereafter MSPS], box 5, folder 4.

21. Hartwell, *History*, 31, incorrectly states that there were fifty-eight names on the list.

22. MPSP 5.4

23. Luhnow to Hayek, January 6, 1947.

24. Hans Kohn, a historian from Smith College, was the only one of the eleven named in the cable who did not ultimately attend. Burgin, *Great Persuasion*, 101, states that in response to Luhnow's abrasive letter, "Hayek quietly excised the most offensive names from a subsequent version of the list." This is incorrect. There were six people from America on Hayek's original list whose names were not included in the subsequent cable. Two were journalists, John Davenport of *Fortune* and Max Eastman of *Reader's Digest*. They were not on Hayek's cable because if they came their way would be paid by their employers. This was indeed the case for Davenport, and though Eastman ultimately was unable to attend, *Reader's Digest* sent and paid for its European correspondent, Paris-based George Révay, in his stead. We know from a letter that Hayek sent to Luhnow that two others—Henry Wriston, president of Brown University, and William Orton, an economist from Smith College—turned down the initial invitation (Hayek to Luhnow, February 5, 1947). Hayek attempted a second invitation to both people, but they again declined (FAHP 78.25; 80.22). Friedrich Lutz, at Princeton, declined because coming would conflict with his teaching obligations (Lutz to Hayek, December 28, 1946, FAHP 77.21), and the invitation sent to Howard Ellis of the University of California–Berkeley, got lost in the mail. By the time he heard about the meeting from Fritz Machlup, it was too late for him to rearrange his schedule (Ellis to Hayek, February 5, 1947, FAHP 73.23). Hayek did not excise any names from his original list due to pressure from Luhnow.

25. Hayek to Luhnow, January 17, 1947.

26. Hayek to Luhnow, February 5, 1947.

27. Mises to Hayek, December 31, 1946, FAHP 38.24. Röpke had advocated Keynesian-style responses to "secondary depressions" back in 1931 and would reiterate those views at the meeting. Mises and Röpke had been together at the Institut de Hautes Études Internationales in the late 1930s so were well familiar with one another's positions. In his 1942 book, Röpke had advocated a "third way" in which "everything was balanced." (Röpke, *Social Crisis*, 176–81.) All of this was anathema to Mises. For more on the sometimes fraught Mises-Röpke relationship, see Stefan Kolev, "Paleo- and Neoliberals: Ludwig von Mises and

the 'Ordo-Interventionists,'" in *Wilhelm Röpke (1899–1966) A Liberal Political Economist and Conservative Social Philosopher*, ed. Patricia Commun and Stefan Kolev (Cham, Switzerland: Springer, 2018), 66–68.

28. In his inaugural lecture at LSE, Hayek had chided the classical economists for allowing "the impression to gain ground that laissez-faire was their ultimate and only conclusion." See F. A. Hayek, "The Trend of Economic Thinking" (1933), in *Collected Works*, vol. 3, *The Trend of Economic Thinking: Essays on Political Economists and Economic History*, ed. W. W. Bartley III and Stephen Kresge (Chicago: University of Chicago Press; London: Routledge, 1991), 17–34. In *The Road to Serfdom*, which was first published in 1944, Hayek had gone so far as to say, "Probably nothing has done so much harm to the liberal cause as the wooden insistence of some liberals on certain rough rules of thumb, above all the principles of laissez-faire." See F. A. Hayek, *The Road to Serfdom: Text and Documents*, ed. Bruce Caldwell, vol. 2 of *Collected Works* (Chicago: University of Chicago Press; London: Routledge, 2007), 71.

29. Hayek, "The Trend of Economic Thinking."

30. FAHP 74.34.

31. Popper to Hayek, January 27, 1947, FAHP 78.36.

32. Röpke to Hayek, January 2, 1945, FAHP 79.1.

33. Rappard to Hayek, November 29, 1946, FAHP 45.6.

34. The quotes are from Hayek's article "The Counter-Revolution of Science," an essay published during the war in which he located the origins of scientism and the engineering mentality in the writings of Saint-Simon and Auguste Comte. Madame de Staël quickly rebuffed her suitor. See F. A. Hayek, "The Counter-Revolution of Science" (1941), in *Collected Works*, vol. 13, *Studies on the Abuse and Decline of Reason: Text and Documents*, ed. Bruce Caldwell (Chicago: University of Chicago Press; London: Routledge, 2010), 190, 193.

35. Hayek to Hunold, February 4, 1947, MPSP 5.4. Hayek's concern about the underrepresentation of women goes unreported in Innset's *Reinventing Liberalism*, which nonetheless uses pie charts to emphasize the gender and racial imbalance of the attendees, described as mostly "privileged white men" (p. 93). Readers of that account should perhaps be reminded of how different their world was from ours. Thinking only of England and the United States, in 1947 women could attend but still could not receive degrees from Cambridge, and racial segregation was still de jure under Jim Crow laws in the American South and de facto in many other parts of the country. There were very few female or Black scholars in major universities at this time, and I can think of none who was a liberal.

36. A full list of the participants may be found at the end of this introduction. In a footnote added to the 1967 reprinting of his welcoming address,

Hayek listed only thirty-six, and George Stigler repeated this number: George Stigler, *Memoirs of an Unregulated Economist* (New York: Basic Books, 1988), 143. Presumably, Hayek reduced the number from thirty-nine to thirty-six because four of the people were in the category of "observer": Herbert Cornuelle, Henri de Lovinfosse, George Révay, and Felix Morley. But because of Morley's prominence, Hayek added him back onto the list. To further complicate things, the editor of the 1992 *Collected Works* edition added de Lovinfosse back in, but not the other two, bringing the number to thirty-seven. Innset used the latter number: Innset, *Reinventing Liberalism*, 96.

37. MPSP 5.5.

38. Jouvenel to Hayek, January 1, 1947, FAHP 76.15.

39. Daniel Knegt, *Fascism, Liberalism and Europeanism in the Political Thought of Bertrand de Jouvenel and Alfred Fabre-Luce* (Amsterdam: Amsterdam University Press, 2017), 221–22.

40. Bertrand de Jouvenel, *L'Économie dirigée: Le Programme de la nouvelle génération* (Paris: Valois, 1928).

41. Knegt and Robert Soucy review debates among historians of France as to the nature and extent of French fascism. See Knegt, *Fascism, Liberalism and Europeanism*, 13–34; and Robert Soucy, "The Debate over French Fascism," in *Fascism's Return: Scandal, Revision, and Ideology since 1980*, ed. Richard Golsan (Lincoln, NE: University of Nebraska Press, 1998), 130–51. Jouvenel ended up being a test case of sorts. Accused later of having been a fascist, in 1983 he sued the historian who made the claim for libel. At the trial, Henry Kissinger, Milton Friedman, and Raymond Aron testified on his behalf. The court split the difference by finding in Jouvenel's favor but only awarding him a nominal amount in damages. As they were leaving the court, Aron had a heart attack, dying within hours (Knegt, *Fascism, Liberalism and Europeanism*, 20; Soucy, "Debate," 141). Innset—somewhat predictably—repeatedly emphasizes Jouvenel's fascist period (Innset, *Reinventing Liberalism*, 101, 137, 144, 146).

42. Knegt, *Fascism, Liberalism, and Europeanism*, 225.

43. Knegt, *Fascism, Liberalism, and Europeanism*, 53–58; Daniel Mahoney, *Bertrand de Jouvenel: The Conservative Liberal and the Illusions of Modernity* (Wilmington, DE: ISI Books, 2005), 10–12.

44. Leonard Read journal, July 3, 1949, Foundation for Economic Education [FEE] Archives.

45. Bertrand de Jouvenel, *On Power: Its Nature and the History of Its Growth* (1945), trans. J. F. Huntington (London: Hutchinson, 1948).

46. F. A. Hayek, "The Tragedy of Organized Humanity" (1948), in Klein, *Fortunes of Liberalism*, vol. 4 of *Collected Works*, 249.

47. F. A. Hayek, "Freedom and the Economic System" (1939), in *Collected Works*, vol. 10, *Socialism and War: Essays, Documents, Reviews*, ed. Bruce Caldwell (Chicago: University of Chicago Press; London: Routledge, 1997), 181–211.

48. Stigler stated that he had not met Hayek before the meeting, but Hayek apparently knew of him early on: he was one of the people whom Hayek had recommended to Röpke to serve on the editorial board of *Occident* (Hayek to Röpke, October 14, 1945, FAHP 79.1). See Stigler, *Memoirs*, 142.

49. Milton Friedman and Rose Friedman, *Two Lucky People: Memoirs* (Chicago: University of Chicago Press, 1998), 53–54, 146–49, 158–59.

50. Michael Polanyi, *The Contempt of Freedom: The Russian Experiment and After* (London: Watts, 1940). The Fabian socialists Sidney and Beatrice Webb and the crystallographer J. D. Bernal were prominent public intellectuals who in the interwar years lavishly praised the Soviet Union for its approach to science. Bernal was one of several British natural scientists, the "men of science," who advocated for socialism.

51. Brandt to Hayek, December 31, 1946, FAHP 72.36.

52. Erich Eyck, *Bismarck: Leben und Werk* (Erlenbach-Zurich: Eugen Rentsch Verlag, 1941–44).

53. Hayek to Röpke, December 5, 1945, FAHP 79.1.

54. Richard Cockett, *Thinking the Unthinkable: Think-Tanks and the Economic Counter-Revolution, 1931–1983* (London: HarperCollins, 1995), 80; John Jewkes, *Ordeal by Planning* (London: Macmillan, 1948).

55. Susan Howson, *Lionel Robbins* (Cambridge: Cambridge University Press, 2011), 355–56, 367, 372.

56. For Hayek's plans around translating Hoff, see FAHP 75.7.

57. Hayek to Röpke, January 17, 1946, FAHP 79.1.

58. Henry Hazlitt, "An Economist's View of Planning," review of *The Road to Serfdom*, by F. A. Hayek, *New York Times Book Review*, September 24, 1944; John Davenport, "Books and Ideas," *Fortune*, November 1944.

59. In a letter on February 5, 1947, Hayek told Luhnow that Morley was someone he did not know personally. This implies that he had met the others mentioned in the letter, which included Read, Harper, Watts, and Miller.

60. Lovinfosse to Hayek, March 4, 1947, FAHP 77.19.

61. MPSP 5.5.

62. Mary Sennholz, *Leonard Read: Philosopher of Freedom* (Irvington-on-Hudson: Foundation for Economic Education, 1993), 66–73.

63. As Brian Doherty notes, Baldy Harper in fact had a full head of hair. The nickname had been given to him by fraternity brothers in college, and it stuck. Brian Doherty, *Radicals for Capitalism: A Freewheeling History of the Modern American Libertarian Movement* (New York: Public Affairs, 2007), 651n34. On the histories

of FEE and of Read, also see Sennholz, *Leonard Read*; John Blundell, *Waging the War of Ideas* (London: Institute of Economic Affairs, 2015), 27; Doherty, *Radicals for Capitalism*, 149–69; and George Nash, *The Conservative Intellectual Movement in America Since 1945: Thirtieth Anniversary Edition* (Wilmington, DE: ISI Books, 2006), 27–32.

64. Miller to Hayek, November 10, 1945.

65. Hayek to Luhnow, August 26, 1946; Doherty, *Radicals for Capitalism*, 182–83.

66. Ludwig von Mises started teaching at New York University in February 1945, his salary wholly financed by outside funds. Though the exact sources of the funding are obscure, at least part of it appears to have been paid by the Volker Fund. By 1946, Mises was speaking so frequently at FEE that the foundation was required to list him as an employee. Mises was an ideal academic spokesman for its views. For more on this, see Jörg Guido Hülsmann, *Mises: The Last Knight of Liberalism* (Auburn, AL: Ludwig von Mises Institute, 2007), 845–51.

67. Friedman to Hayek, January 2, 1947.

68. Hayek would not have known of the bad blood that already existed between Leonard Read and Orval Watts of FEE on one side, and Milton Friedman and George Stigler on the other. In September 1946, FEE had published a pamphlet written by Friedman and Stigler that criticized rent controls. Watts and Read had asked them to delete a paragraph in which the authors had stated that one benefit of their proposed policy was to reduce income inequality, which they refused to do. When FEE published the paper, the paragraph remained, but a footnote from FEE was appended to it, without their permission having been sought, that implied that Friedman and Stigler favored equality over liberty and justice. Later, in 1947, "the Read group" at FEE and Aaron Director butted heads over the publication of Henry Simons's *Economic Policy for a Free Society*, a posthumously published collection of his earlier writings that was edited by Director. The people at FEE found some of Simons's proposals collectivist. Director's retort was blunt: "If his work contributes to fostering collectivism he shares this distinction with the author of *The Wealth of Nations*" (Director to Read, November 24, 1947, FAHP 58.16). Hayek took Director's side. Friedman later noted, "For some years we refused to have anything to do with the foundation or Leonard Read." But the two men later reconciled and indeed became good friends (Friedman and Friedman, *Two Lucky People*, 151).

69. As Hayek would mention at the April 4 session "Discussion on Agenda, Etc.": "It was purely accidental that we managed to get funds for this conference."

70. The next few paragraphs draw extensively on part one of Dennis Bark and David Gress, *A History of West Germany*, 2nd ed., vol. 1, *From Shadow to Substance 1945–1963* (Oxford: Blackwell, 1993); chapters three and four of Tony Judt,

Postwar: A History of Europe since 1945 (New York: Penguin, 2005); and Norman Naimark, *Stalin and the Fate of Europe: The Postwar Struggle for Sovereignty* (Cambridge, MA: Harvard University Press, 2019).

71. Judt, *Postwar*, 123.

72. Jouvenel to Hayek, March 9, 1948, FAHP 76.15.

73. Friedman and Friedman, *Two Lucky People*, 159.

74. Rob Van Horn, "Reinventing Monopoly and the Role of Corporations: The Roots of Chicago Law and Economics," in Mirowski and Plehwe, *Road from Mont Pèlerin*, 204–37, traces the changes in the Chicago view on monopoly and antitrust between 1946 and 1956. Cf. Caldwell, "The Chicago School," 317–24, for a different take on the causes of the transition.

75. Eucken understood English but did not speak it well, so Hayek was happy to translate for his friend, a service that he later recalled fondly; see F. A. Hayek, "The Rediscovery of Freedom" (1983), in Klein, *Fortunes of Liberalism*, vol. 4 of *Collected Works*, 192.

76. FAHP 81.4.

77. Hayek, "Rediscovery of Freedom," 192.

78. Heinz Rieter and Matthias Schmolz, "The Ideas of German Ordoliberalism 1938–45: Pointing the Way to a New Economic Order," *European Journal of the History of Economic Thought* 1, no. 1 (Autumn 1993): 95–99.

79. Röpke to Hayek, January 2, 1945; Hayek to Röpke, July 10, 1945, FAHP 79.1.

80. Friedman is the source of the anecdote (Friedman and Friedman, *Two Lucky People*, 161), but he did not say when the outburst occurred. Lionel Robbins wrote his wife on April 3 that Mises "attacked us all calling us Socialists and interventionists" (Howson, *Lionel Robbins*, 662). The topics of the sessions on April 2 and 3 did not lend themselves to such a reaction, which suggests it was at this one on April 1.

81. In "The Historians and the Future of Europe," Hayek distinguished between "historical research proper and historiography, the exposition of history for the people at large" (p. 207). Note that Wedgwood discreetly opened the session by providing the more common definition for the term "historiography."

82. The first chapter of *The Road to Serfdom* is titled "The Abandoned Road," which referred to liberalism. In chapter 14, Hayek lamented, "If one were to judge by the ideas which find expression in current political discussion and propaganda, the Englishmen who not only 'the language speak that Shakespeare spake' but also 'the faith and morals hold that Milton held' seem to have almost vanished" (p. 220).

83. Melinda Zook, "C. V. Wedgwood: The Historian and the World," in *Generations of Women Historians: Within and Beyond the Academy*, ed. Hilda Smith and Melinda Zook (Cham, Switzerland: Palgrave Macmillan, 2018), 123–25.

84. F. A. Hayek, ed., *Capitalism and the Historians* (Chicago: University of Chicago Press, 1954).

85. Stigler, *Memoirs*, 146; Friedman and Friedman, *Two Lucky People*, 160.

86. Friedman and Friedman, *Two Lucky People*.

87. Hayek, "Rediscovery of Freedom," 192; Stefan Kolev, Nils Goldschmidt, and Jan-Otmar Hesse, "Debating Liberalism: Walter Eucken, F. A. Hayek and the Early History of the Mont Pèlerin Society," *Review of Austrian Economics* 33, no. 4 (December 2020), 433–63.

88. Howson, *Lionel Robbins*, 345–54.

89. Both Hayek and Barbara Wootton had participated in the Federal Union, an organization to promote the formation of a democratic federation, but they differed on what that would entail. Hayek's chapter on the international order in *The Road to Serfdom* prompted Wootton to publish *Freedom under Planning* (Chapel Hill, NC: University of North Carolina Press, 1945) as a reply. For more on this, see Or Rosenboim, "Barbara Wootton, Friedrich Hayek and the Debate on Democratic Federalism in the 1940s," *International History Review*, 36, no. 5 (2014): 894–918.

90. As Bark and Gress note (*From Shadow to Substance*, 181), "The year 1946–47 marked the high point of enthusiasm for European federation and for the belief that the 'United States of Europe' was a realistic possibility."

91. In 1943–44, Luigi Einaudi had written two works advocating European federation, the second of these while in exile at Rappard's institute. Parts of each work are translated in Luca Einaudi, Riccardo Faucci, and Roberto Marchionatti, eds., *Luigi Einaudi: Selected Economic Essays* (New York: Palgrave Macmillan, 2006). Had Einaudi been able to attend the meeting, perhaps the discussion would have been more fruitful.

92. Hayek to Orton, February 5, 1945, FAHP 78.25.

93. Knight to Hayek, December 31, 1946, FAHP 76.24; the book in question is William Aylott Orton, *The Liberal Tradition* (New Haven, CT: Yale University Press, 1945).

94. See chaps. 9 and 12 in Howson, *Lionel Robbins*.

95. The text of both the original and the final statement of aims may be found in Sessions 12 and 14 of this volume. Allais disagreed with the group's stance on private property. See Burgin, *Great Persuasion*, 107, 257–58n85; and Arnaud Diemer, Jérôme Lallement, and Bertrand Munier, eds., *Maurice Allais et la science économique* (Paris: Clément Juglar, 2010).

96. The "rules-based approach" that was endorsed by Chicago economists like Director and Friedman at the meeting reflects the powerful influence of Henry Simons's work.

97. Burns, in chap. 3 of *The Last Conservative,* notes that Friedman had come up with the negative-income-tax idea as early as 1939.

98. The similarity to Director's proposals on these topics in his comments in the first session should be noted, though Director also discussed corporations and antitrust there.

Minutes of Discussion at
Mont Pèlerin Conference
April 1st–10th 1947

Note: It was neither possible, nor regarded as desirable by the Conference itself, to keep a full shorthand record of the discussion. Except for a few of the more formal papers of which manuscripts have been provided by the speakers and which are indicated by the symbol (*MS*) appearing after the name of the speaker, the following summary has been compiled from brief notes kept by Mrs. Hahn and has not been seen or revised by the speakers. It is intended mainly to indicate the general trend of the discussion and must not be taken to express the precise opinions of the individual speakers. This record is meant solely to assist the memory of the participants and it is specially requested not to quote from it except with the express permission of the person concerned. Many shorter contributions have been omitted and certain parts of the discussions are entirely unrecorded as a result of the absence or exhaustion of Mrs. Hahn.

F. A. H.

Session I

Tuesday, April 1st, 1947, 9.30 a.m.

Welcoming Address (MS):

Professor Rappard in the chair.

Professor RAPPARD: Our first words should be words of thanks addressed to those who have made possible our meeting here today. First and foremost they are due to our eminent colleague Hayek, without whose constructive imagination, tenacious courage and unflagging efforts over a number of months and even of years, this international meeting of academic liberals would have remained an idle dream. Our very warm thanks go out also to those anonymous benefactors in the United States and in Switzerland whose generosity was almost as indispensable for the fruition of Professor Hayek's plans as the plan itself. I say "almost as indispensable" because if one has ideas but no money, one can do but little, whereas if one has money but no ideas, one can do nothing at all. Our gratitude towards those whose material generosity has allowed us to meet here is enhanced by the fact that it was entirely unconditional in every respect. That moral generosity, most worthy of the liberal cause we are here to serve, has made it possible for even the freest minds amonst [*sic*] us to accept the other without any scruples. May I add a word of warm thanks also to my compatriot Dr. Hunold, from Zurich? He has done us the great service not only of making available the Swiss funds just alluded to, but also of arranging our stay at Mont-Pèlerin and our projected trips to Coppet and Einsiedeln with the greatest care and most thoughtful foresight.

The lingua franca of this gathering is, I understand, to be English. Inasmuch as we are meeting in one of the smallest countries of Continental Europe which boasts of four national idioms of its own, none of which is English, that may be taken as a symptom of the preponderance of Anglo-Saxondom in what remains of liberalism in the world today.

I certainly have no quarrel with English. It will serve our purposes well here, I am sure, as it has well served the cause of political and economic freedom throughout the ages. As an economist I have, however, I admit, one minor quarrel with it. The term of economics I cannot help finding dangerously ambiguous in that it refers both to a science and to a policy or a possible variety of policies.

The purpose of economics as a science is that of all science, i.e. to describe and to explain the outer world and its inhabitants as they are. The purpose of economics as a policy is to propound rules of individual and collective conduct for men, for society and for the state as they should be. Now, whereas in French—science économique, politique économique—or in German—Volkswirtschaftslehre, Volkswirtschaftspolitik—there are two generally accepted terms for two entirely different things, both would seem to be defined by the term of economics in English. Has not that contributed to create and to maintain a confusion of which economics as a science and therefore economists as men of science are the chief victims?

Science cannot be liberal or illiberal. In a sense it cannot be anything but liberal. An economist as a scholar may be learned or ignorant, intelligent or dull, profound or superficial, but he cannot be liberal or illiberal. Rather, if he is illiberal as a man of science, that is if he dogmatically and intolerantly denies the rights of liberty of thought without which there can be no true science, then he is not worthy of being called a man of science.

Policies can however be liberal or illiberal. Most policies all over the world today are in fact illiberal and it is because we believe that they should be liberal that we are assembled here today. It is as economists in the second sense of that equivocal word that we are liberal. Or rather we are liberals by conviction, by faith, while most of us are by profession scientific economists.

The distinction is absolutely fundamental. It alone explains why our friend Hayek, in setting up his list of guests, has not included therein many economists who are not liberals, but has to our great joy admitted certain liberals who are not economists.

Is the confusion between the scientific and the political meaning of economics purely verbal and fortuitous? Certainly not. Many men in the course of the last two centuries have made a name for themselves as economists in both meanings of the term. The greatest of all, Adam Smith, was both a great scholar and a most influential publicist. He was a scholar of the first order in that his inquiry into the nature and causes of the wealth of nations was an illuminating analysis of the mechanism of economic life in his day. And he was a most influential publicist in that the liberal policies which he urged became known all over the world and heeded in at least some parts of it. Now, of course, his policies were not unrelated to his science.

Having discovered that the wealth of nations was everywhere being limited and diminished by policies restrictive of human freedom, he preached the liberation of man and the abolition of restrictive policies. But his liberal doctrine was based not only on his scientific findings, but on two assumptions besides which, as all assumptions however plausible, could lay no claim to scientific validity. The first of these assumptions was that men and nations were and should be engaged in the labours of production with the sole or at least with the main purpose of enriching themselves. The other was the assumption of the homo economicus, of the economic man. For the purpose of his discussion and of the reasons underlying both his science and his policies, Adam Smith assumed that the average man always and everywhere, sought to obtain the maximum of material satisfaction at a minimum cost of effort.

Now can it be said that the economic man is by definition a zealous, an energetic and an effective producer of wealth and that he must therefore be a foe of all restrictive policies? Is the economic man necessarily a liberal?

Let us note that the above definition implies a fixed relation between enjoyment and effort, two entirely incommensurable notions. If a man is much attached to earthly goods or if he is by temperament energetic, he will, by working hard, prove that he is an economic man. But if he is by nature either indolent or ascetic, he will limit his exertions to the utmost. Will he therefore be less of an economic man?

When I happened to be in Algiers at the time of the landing of the Allied forces there in November 1942, I was impressed by the sight of countless Arabs seated on the curb of the sidewalks in all the streets of the city. They seemed quite indifferent to what was going on and they certainly were absolutely idle. A French friend whom I questioned about this striking fact explained to me that the Arabs in Algiers never did any more work than was absolutely necessary in order to earn the wherewithal to keep body and soul together. General Weygand, who had recently been Governor-General there, had been so shocked by the meagerness of the rate of the wages paid and of the rations allowed them that he had doubled that rate and decided that they were to receive the same ration cards as the Algerians of European origin.[1] The result was that their productive effort was still further reduced. Placing leisure above all other good in their scale of values, the Arabs apparently got more enjoyment out of life by working less than they would have secured by producing and consuming more.

Yesterday evening, in conversation with some British colleagues here, I heard that the absenteeism of some of the Welsh miners called for a similar explanation. The commodities which they could buy were at present so limited that they preferred the delights of vacation to the well paid, but sterile, drudgery of underground labour.

Can these Arabs and these Welsh philosophers be denied the right to call themselves economic men? Not, as I see it, by any fair interpretation of the homo economicus.

The fact is that the economic man on whom Adam Smith based his arguments was, like himself, a Scotchman who preferred to work and to save rather than idly to enjoy idleness. For the Scotch brand of the homo economicus, work was a virtue first because the sturdy Nordic mountaineer loved freedom, secondly because he did not shirk effort and thirdly and finally because he was not averse to wealth, his propensity to save being proverbially one of his most characteristic traits.

---

1. French general Maxime Weygand (1867?–1965) served as the governor-general of Algeria from August until November 1941.

Is it therefore not quite natural that Adam Smith's economic man was both an assumption of his economic science and, indirectly but truly also, the inspirer of his economic liberalism? Had he been reared among the sun-baked race of Arabs who prefer leisure to work, security on the lowest scale to the insecurity of initiative and therefore equality to liberty, would his semi-tropical economic man not have led him quite consistently to preach a very different doctrine?

These hasty remarks should not be understood as a flippant criticism of the father of modern economics, in both senses of that term. They are intended merely to point to the fundamental distinction between economics as a science and liberalism as a doctrine and to hasard [sic] the hypothesis of their common ancestry in the economic man of the <u>Wealth of Nations</u>.

Modern economic liberalism, as I see it, is the legitimate offspring of the union between two first cousins: Adam Smith's penetrating and essentially sound scientific analysis of the economic world of his day, and Adam Smith's inborn love of freedom, constructive effort and wealth.

Now why has the contemporary world as we see it, and particularly contemporary Europe, so generally rejected the teachings of economic liberalism? There are, I believe, two main reasons for that unfortunate fact which we are here to study, to deplore and, if possible, to alter. The first is that the economic man of our tragic age has everywhere been obliged to put on a national uniform and to seek national security more than general welfare. And the second is that the European economic man, having become politically his own master by the rise of democracy and being physically exhausted by the fatigues of the thirty years' war, is clamoring for social security and equality much more than for economic progress and freedom.

The socialism of Europe is the policy of a tired race. The partly surviving competitive capitalism of America, that of a still energetically youthful continent. Now it so happens that European socialism is more and more heavily leaning upon and is being more and more generously subsidized by American capitalism. This state of affairs is of course not one that can last indefinitely. Unless the world has become completely mad, it must sooner or later come to realize and to admit the productive superiority of a society based upon the principle of free enterprise.

If there is at least something in this snapshot of the contemporary scene, this timely gathering of American and European liberals should be of particular interest to both. May it prove to be for both continents the starting point of an intellectual, economic and political renaissance without which it would seem wellnigh impossible not to despair of the future.

Address to the Mont Pèlerin Conference[2]

Professor Rappard in the chair.

Prof. Hayek (MS): I must confess that now when the moment has arrived to which I have so long looked forward, the feeling of intense gratitude to all of you is strongly mixed by an acute sense of astonishment at my own presumption and audacity in setting all this in motion, and of real alarm about the responsibility I have taken on me in asking you to give up so much of your time and energy for what you might well regard as a wild experiment. I will confine myself at this stage to a very brief but profoundly sincere thank you.

It is now my pleasant duty, before I step down from the position I have so immodestly assumed and gladly hand over to you the task of carrying on what fortunate circumstances have enabled me to initiate, to give you a somewhat fuller account of the aims which have guided me in proposing this meeting and suggesting its programme. I shall endeavour not to tax

---

2. Hayek published a slightly amended version as "Opening Address to a Conference at Mont Pèlerin" in his 1967 collection *Studies in Philosophy, Politics and Economics,* and this was reprinted in *The Collected Works of F. A. Hayek,* vol. 4, *The Fortunes of Liberalism: Essays on Austrian Economics and the Ideal of Freedom,* ed. Peter G. Klein (Chicago: University of Chicago Press; London: Routledge, 1992), 237–48.

There is in the archives another version of the talk in which Hayek began his address in French (in deference to being in the French-speaking part of Switzerland) and then switched to English, at one point thanking "Guillaume Rappard" for chairing the opening session. When he saw that version, Rappard informed him that, "as no one knows me here under the name of 'Guillaume,' the reference to me would arouse only hilarity!" and that Hayek should just speak in English (Rappard to Hayek, March 28, 1947, Friedrich A. Hayek Papers (FAHP), box 45, folder 6, 45.6, Hoover Institution). Hayek was never comfortable with his command of French, so Rappard's suggestion doubtless came as a great relief.

your patience too much, but even that minimum of explanation which I definitely owe you will inevitably take some little time.

The basic conviction which has guided me in my efforts is that if the ideals in which I believe unite us, and for which, in spite of abuse of the word, there is still no better name than liberal, are to have any chance of revival, a great intellectual task is in the first instance required before we can successfully meet the errors which govern the world today. This task involves both purging traditional liberal theory of certain accidental accretions which have become attached to it in the course of time, and facing up to certain real problems which an over-simplified liberalism has shirked or which have become apparently only since it had become a somewhat stationary and rigid creed.

The belief that this is the situation has been strongly confirmed in me by the observation that in many different fields and in many different parts of the world men who have been brought up in different beliefs and to whom party liberalism had little attraction have for themselves been rediscovering the basic principles of liberalism and been hard at work to reconstruct a liberal philosophy which can fully meet the objections which in the eyes of most of our contemporaries have defeated the promise the earlier liberalism offered.

I have had the good fortune in the last two years to visit several parts both of Europe and America and I have been surprised at the number of isolated men I found everywhere, working on essentially the same problems and on very similar lines. Working in isolation or in very small groups they are however forced constantly to defend the basic elements of their beliefs and rarely have the opportunity of an interchange of opinion on the more technical problems which arise only if a certain common basis of conviction and ideals is present.

It seems to me undeniable that common work on the more detailed outline of a liberal order is practicable only among a group of people who are in agreement on fundamentals, and among whom certain basic principles are not questioned at every step. But not only is, at this time, the number of those who in any one country agree on what seems to me the basic liberal principles small, but the task is very big and there is much need for drawing on as wide an experience under different conditions as possible.

One of the most instructive observations to me was that the further one moves to the West and to countries where liberal institutions are still comparatively firm, and people professing liberal convictions still comparatively numerous, the less are these people yet prepared really to re-examine their own conviction and the more are they inclined to compromise, and to take the accidental historical form of a liberal society which they have known as the ultimate standard. I found on the other hand that in those countries which either had actually experienced a completely totalitarian regime or closely approached it, a few men had through their experiences gained a clearer conception of the conditions and value of a free society. The more I discussed these problems with people in different countries the more I was driven to the conviction that the wisdom is not all on one side and that the observation of the actual decay of a civilisation has taught some independent thinkers on the European Continent lessons which I believe have yet to be learnt in England and America if these countries are to avoid a similar fate. As has recently been said "for the inhabitants of a free country it seems almost impossible to understand the process by which freedom is lost."[3]

Yet it is not only the students of economics and politics in different countries who have much to profit from each other and who by joining their forces across the national frontiers can do much to advance their common cause. I was no less impressed with the fact of how much more fruitful could be the discussion of the great problems of our time between, say, an economist and a historian, or a lawyer or political philosopher, if they shared certain common premises than is the discussion between students of the same subjects who differed on these basic values. And of course a political philosophy can never be based exclusively on economics or expressed mainly in economic terms. It seems to me that the dangers which we are facing are the result of an intellectual movement which has expressed itself in, and affected the attitude towards, all the aspects of human affairs. Yet while in our own subject we may have learnt to discover

---

3. The sentence "For the inhabitants of a free country, it seems almost impossible clearly to understand the process through which freedom is lost" appears as part of an excerpt in *Catholic World* 161 (April–September 1945): 46. It is attributed there to Leopold Schwarzschild's *Primer of the Coming World* (London: Hamish Hamilton, 1944).

all the beliefs which are part and parcel of that movement that leads to totalitarianism, we cannot be sure that, e.g. as economists, we do not as uncritically as any one else accept, under the influence of the atmosphere of our time, ideas in the field of history or philosophy, morals or law which belong to the same movement which we oppose in our own field.

The need for an international meeting of representatives of these different subjects seemed to me especially great as a result of the war, which not only has for so long disrupted many of the normal contacts but also inevitably, and in the best of us, created a self-centredness and nationalist outlook which ill accords with a truly liberal approach to our problems. Worst of all, the war and its effects has created new obstacles to the resumption of international contacts which to those in the less fortunate countries are still practically unsurmountable without outside help, and serious enough for the rest of us. There was clearly a case for some sort of organisation which would help in reopening communication between people with a common outlook. Unless some sort of private organisation was created, there would be serious danger that contacts beyond national frontiers would become increasingly the monopoly of those who were in some way or another tied up in the existing governmental and political machinery and were bound to serve the dominating ideologies.

It was evident from the beginning that no permanent organisation of this kind could be created without some experimental meeting such as this at which the usefulness of the idea could be tried out. But as this, in the present circumstances, seemed hardly possible to arrange without considerable funds, I did little but talk about this plan to as many people as would listen until to my own surprise a fortunate accident suddenly placed this within the range of possibility. One of our Swiss friends here, Dr. Hunold, had raised some funds for a cognate but different project which for accidental reasons had to be abandoned, and succeeded in persuading the donors to turn the amount over to this purpose.

It was only when thus a unique opportunity offered itself that I fully realised what a responsibility I had taken on me, and that, if the chance was not to be missed, I had to take it on me to propose this conference and, worst of all, to decide who was to be invited. You will perhaps sufficiently sympathise with the embarrassing nature of such a task to make it unnecessary for me to apologize at length for the manner in which I have discharged it.

There is only one point about this which I ought to explain: as I see our task it is not sufficient that our members should have what used to be called "sound" views. The old liberal who adheres to a traditional creed merely out of tradition, however admirable his views, is not of much use for our purpose. What we need are people who have faced the arguments from the other side, who have struggled with them and fought themselves through to a position from which they can both critically meet the objection against it and justify their views. Such people are even less numerous than good liberals in the old sense, and there are now few enough of them. But when it came to drawing up a list I discovered to my pleasant surprise that the number of people of whom I knew who would have a title to be included in such a list was a good deal larger than I expected or could be asked to the conference. And the final selection had inevitably to be to a large extent arbitrary.

It is a matter of profound regret to me that, largely as a result of my own shortcomings, the membership of the present conference is somewhat unevenly balanced and that the historians and political philosophers, instead of being as strongly represented as the economists, are a comparatively small minority. This is due partly to the fact that my personal contacts among this group are more limited and that even among those who were on the original list a particularly high proportion was unable to attend, but partly perhaps also to the fact that at this particular juncture economists are perhaps more generally aware of the immediate dangers and of the urgency of the intellectual problems which we must solve if we are to have a chance to direct the movement in a more desirable direction. There are similar grave gaps in the national distribution of the membership of this Conference and I particularly regret that e.g. Holland and Spain are entirely unrepresented. I have no doubt that apart from these faults of which I am conscious there are even more serious blunders which I have unwittingly committed and all I can do is to ask for your indulgence and for your sympathy with the very difficult task I had to perform, and to beg your help so that in future we shall possess a more complete list of all those from whom we may expect sympathetic and active support in our efforts.

It has given me much encouragement that not a single one of all those to whom I sent invitations did not express his sympathies with the aim of the Conference and the wish to be able to take part. If nevertheless many of them are not here this is due to external difficulties of one kind or another. You will probably wish to hear the names of those who have expressed their desire that that [*sic*] they were able to be with us and their sympathy with the aims of this Conference. They are:

Professor Bresciani-Turroni, Rome
Mr. William Henry Chamberlin, New York
Professor René Courtin, Paris
Mr. Max Eastman, New York
Professor Luigi Einaudi, Rome
Professor Howard Ellis, Berkeley, California
Professor A. G. B. Fisher, London
Professor Eli Heckscher, Stockholm
Professor Hans Kohn, Northampton, Massachusetts
Mr. Walter Lippmann, New York
Professor Friedrich Lutz, Princeton
Señor Salvador de Madariaga, Oxford
Mr. Charles Morgan, London
Professor W. A. Orton, Northampton, Massachusetts
Professor Arnold Plant, London
Professor Charles Rist, Paris
Mr. Michael Roberts, London
Mr. Jacques Rueff, Paris
Professor Alexander Rüstow, Istanbul
Professor F. Schnabel, Heidelberg
Mr. W. J. H. Sprott, Nottingham
Mr. Roger Truptil, Paris
Professor D. Villey, Poitiers
Professor E. L. Woodward, Oxford
Mr. H. M. Wriston, Brown University, Providence, R.I.
Mr. G. M. Young, London

In mentioning those who cannot be with us for temporary reasons I cannot help also remembering some of those on whose support I had particularly counted but who will never again be with us. Indeed the two men with whom I had most fully discussed the plan for this meeting have both not lived to see its realisation. I had first sketched the plan three years ago to a small group in Cambridge presided over by Sir John Clapham who took a great interest in it but who died suddenly a year ago.[4] And it is now less than a year that I discussed the plan in all its detail with another man whose whole life, as that of few others, was devoted to the ideals and problems with which we shall be concerned: Henry Simons of Chicago.[5] A few weeks later he was no more. And if with their names I mention that of a much younger man who had also taken a great interest in my plans and whom, if he had lived, I should have hoped to see as our permanent Secretary, a post for which Étienne Mantoux would have been ideally suited, you will understand how heavy were the losses which our group has suffered even before it first had an opportunity to meet.[6]

~~If it had not been for these tragic deaths I should not have had to act alone in summoning this Conference. I confess that at one time these blows had completely shaken my will to pursue the plan any further. But when the opportunity came I felt it a duty to make what I could of it.~~[7]

~~There is another point connected with the membership of our meeting which I should briefly mention. We have among us a fair number of journalists, not because we want to be reported, which is not the case, but because this is a field in which people of our interests have special scope and utilities. But to reassure other members it may~~ be useful to mention

---

4. As noted in the introduction, Hayek delivered his paper proposing forming an international society of liberals before the Political Society at Cambridge in February 1944, and Sir John Clapham was in the chair.

5. As noted in the introduction, Simons died from an overdose of sleeping pills in June 1946. Hayek had visited him in Chicago earlier in the month but was in Stanford when Simons died.

6. The French economist Étienne Mantoux (1913–1945) was the son of Paul Mantoux, who had with Rappard founded the Institut de Hautes Études Internationales. Mantoux *fils* was killed in action on April 29, 1945, just eight days before Germany's surrender. His book criticizing J. M. Keynes's analysis in *The Economic Consequences of the Peace* (London: Macmillan & Co., 1919) was published posthumously; see Étienne Mantoux, *The Carthaginian Peace: or, The Economic Consequences of Mr. Keynes* (London: Oxford University Press, 1946).

7. This paragraph and part of the next were crossed out in the manuscript. It appears to be a mistake, as the paragraphs were retained in the 1967 published version of the "Opening Address." One possibility is that Hayek thought about not mentioning his response to the deaths of his friends, but then reconsidered.

that unless and until you should decide otherwise, I think this should be regarded as a private meeting and all that is said here in the discussion as "off the record" as the American term is.

But let me turn now to the programme I have suggested for this meeting. It is obviously the first thing you will have to consider and I need hardly say that the proposals which I sent out and will now explain are no more than suggestions which this meeting may or may not approve.

Of the subjects which I have suggested for systematic examination of this Conference, and of which most members seem to have approved, the first, the relation between what is called "Free Enterprise" and a really competitive order seems to me to be much the biggest and in some ways the most important and I hope that a considerable part of our discussions will be devoted to its exploration. It is the field where it is most important that we should become clear in our own minds, and arrive at an agreement about the kind of programme of economic policy which we should wish to see generally accepted. It is probably the set of problems on which the largest proportion among us are actively interested and where it is most urgent that the work which has been conducted independently in parallel directions in many parts of the world should be brought together. Its ramifications are practically endless, as an adequate treatment involves a complete programme of a liberal economic policy. It is likely that after a survey of the general problem you may prefer to split it up into more special questions to be discussed in separate sessions. We could probably in this manner find room for one or more of the additional topics which I mentioned in one of my circulars, or for such further problems as that of the inflationary high-pressure economy which, as has been justly observed by more than one member, is at the moment the main tool by which a collectivist development is forced on the majority of countries, including even the United States. Perhaps the best plan will be if, after we have devoted one or two sessions to the general issue, we set aside half an hour or so at the end of one of these discussions to decide on the further course of our deliberations. I propose that we devote the whole of this afternoon and evening to a general survey of this topic and perhaps you will allow me to say a few words more about it this afternoon. I have taken the liberty to ask Professor Aaron Director of Chicago, Professor Walter Eucken of Freiburg and Professor Allais of Paris to introduce the debate on this subject and I have no doubt that we shall then have more than enough to occupy us.

Profoundly important as the problems of the principles of economic order are, there are several reasons why I hope that we will, already during the first part of the Conference, also have time set aside for some or all of the other topics. We are probably all agreed that the root of the political and social dangers which we face are not purely economic and that if we are to preserve a free society a revision not only of the strictly economic concepts which rule our generation is required. I believe it will also help to make us more rapidly acquainted if during the early part of the Conference we range over a rather wider field and look at our problem from several angles before we attempt to proceed to the more technical aspects or more detailed problems.

You will probably all agree that the interpretation and teaching of history has during the past two generations been one of the main instruments through which essentially anti-liberal conceptions of human affairs have spread: the widespread fatalism, which regards all developments however undesirable, as inevitable consequences of great laws of necessary historical development, the historical relativism, which denies any moral standards except those of success and non-success, the emphasis on mass movements as distinguished from individual achievements, and not last the general emphasis on historical necessity as against the power of ideas to shape our future, are all different facets of a problem as important and almost as wide as the economic problem. I have suggested merely one aspect of this wide field, the relation between historiography and political education, as a separate subject for discussion but it is an aspect which would soon lead us to the wider problem.[8] I am very glad that Miss Wedgwood and Professor Antoni have consented to open the discussion on this question.

It is, I think, important that we fully realize that the popular liberal creed, more on the Continent and in America than in England, contained many elements which on the one hand led many of its adherents directly into the

---

8. As noted in the introduction, Hayek used the word "historiography" idiosyncratically to refer to more popular forms of history, rather than to the methods of writing history.

folds of socialism or nationalism and on the other hand antagonised many who shared the basic values of individual freedom but who were repelled by the aggressive rationalism which would recognise no values except those whose utility (for an ultimate purpose which was never disclosed) could be demonstrated by individual reason and which presumed that science was competent to tell us not only what is but also what ought to be. Personally I believe that this false rationalism, which gained influence in the French Revolution and which during the past hundred years has exercised its influence mainly through the twin movements of Positivism and Hegelianism, is an expression of an intellectual hubris which is the opposite of that intellectual humility which is the essence of true liberalism and which treats with respect those spontaneous social forces through which the individual creates things greater than he knows. It is this intolerant and fierce rationalism which in particular is responsible for the gulf which particularly on the Continent has for several generations driven most religious people from the liberal movement and into truly reactionary camps in which they felt little at home. I am convinced that unless this breach between true liberal and religious convictions can be healed there is no hope for a revival of liberal forces. There are many signs in Europe that such a reconciliation is today nearer than it has been for a long time and that many people see in it the one hope of preserving the ideals of Western Civilization. It was for this reason that I was specially anxious that the subject of the relation between Liberalism and Christianity should be made one of the separate topics of our discussion, and although we cannot hope to get far in exploring this topic in a single meeting, it seems to me essential that we should explicitly face the problem.

The other two separate topics which I have suggested for discussion are tests of practical application of our principles to the problems of our time rather than questions of principles themselves. But both the problem of the future of Germany and that of the possibilities and prospects of European federation seemed to me problems of such immediate urgency that no international group of students of politics should meet without considering them, even if we cannot hope to do more on these topics than clear our own minds a little by an exchange of views. They are both questions on which the present state of public opinion more than anything else is the great obstacle to any reasonable discussion and I feel that it is a special duty laid on us not to shirk their consideration. It is a symptom of their difficulty that I have had the greatest difficulty in persuading any member of this Conference to open the discussion on these two subjects.

There is one other topic which I should have liked to see discussed because it seems to me central to our problem, namely the meaning and conditions of the Rule of Law. If I did not actually suggest it it was because, in order to discuss this problem adequately it would have been necessary to extend our membership even further and to include lawyers. It was again largely lack of knowledge on my part which made this impracticable, and I mention the fact merely in order to make it clear how wide we shall have to cast our net if in any permanent organisation we are to be competent adequately to deal with all aspects of our task. But the programme I have suggested is probably already ambitious enough for this one Conference and I will now leave this point to turn to one or two other matters on which I ought briefly to comment.

So far as the first of these, the formal organisation of this Conference is concerned I don't think we need to burden ourselves with any elaborate machinery. We could not have wished for a person better justified to preside over us at this first meeting than Professor Rappard and I am sure you will allow me to thank him on your behalf for having undertaken this task. But we should not expect him or anyone else to carry this burden throughout the conference. I have no doubt that the proper arrangement will be to have this office rotate and if you agree with this one of the tasks of this first meeting will be to elect chairmen for at least the next few meetings. If this meeting will agree on some programme, at least for the first part of the Conference, little formal business should arise till we shall have to consider the Agenda for the second part, which I have suggested we might do at a special meeting on Monday evening. It would probably be wise if in addition we set up, at this meeting, a small standing committee of five or six members to fill in any details of the programme on which we agree now or to make any changes which circumstances may make appear desirable. You may also feel it desirable to appoint a Secretary to the Conference, or perhaps still better, two Secretaries, one to look after the programme and another to be in charge of general arrangements. I believe this would be amply sufficient at this stage to regularise our proceedings.

There is another point of organisation which I should probably mention at this stage. I shall of course see that proper minutes will be kept of the business part of our discussions and for the time being my assistant Mrs. Hahn will help me in this. But no arrangements have been made or seemed practicable for obtaining a shorthand record of our discussions. Apart from the technical difficulties this would also have impaired the private and informal character of our discussions. But I hope that the members will themselves keep some notes of their major contributions so that, if the Conference should decide to embody its main results in some form of written record, it will be easy for them to put on paper the essence of their remarks.

There is also the question of language. In my preliminary correspondence I have tacitly assumed that all the members are familiar with English, and as this is certainly true of the majority of us, it would greatly facilitate our deliberations if English were mainly used. We are, unfortunately not in the fortunate position of official international bodies to command a staff of interpreters. The rule should be that every member should use the language in which he can hope to make himself most widely understood.

The immediate purpose of this conference is, of course, to provide an opportunity for a comparatively small group of those who in different parts of the world are striving for the same ideals, to get personally acquainted, to profit from each others [sic] experiences and perhaps also to give encouragement to each other. I am confident that at the end of these ten days you will agree that this meeting will have been well worth while if it has achieved no more than this. But I rather hope that this experiment in collaboration will prove so successful that we shall want to continue it in one form or another.

However small a minority the people of our general outlook may be, even the competent students among them are of course much more numerous than the small number of us who are here assembled. I could myself have drawn up a list two or three times as large, and from the suggestions I have already received I have no doubt that together we could without difficulty compile a list of several hundred men and women in all countries who share our general beliefs and would be willing to work for them.

I hope we will compile such a list, selecting the names rather carefully, and design some means of continued contacts between these people. A beginning of such a list I am placing on the table and I hope you will add to it as many names as you think desirable, indicate by your signatures which of the other proposals you wish to support, and also perhaps let me know privately if any of the persons appearing on the list seems to you to be unsuitable to be included in the membership of a permanent organisation. We should probably not include any names unless it receives the support of two or three members of our present group and it may be desirable later during the conference to set up a small scrutiny committee which would have to edit the final list. I assume that all those who had been invited to this conference but were unable to attend will as a matter of course be included in this list.

There are of course many forms in which such regular contacts might be provided. When in one of my circulars I employed the somewhat high-flown expression of an "International Academy for Political Philosophy" I meant to emphasize by the term "Academy" one aspect which seems to me essential if such a permanent organisation is to fulfil its purpose: it must remain a closed society, not open to all and sundry, but only to people who share with us certain common convictions. This character can be preserved only if membership can be acquired only by election and if we take this admission into our circle as seriously as the great learned academies take admission into them.

But beyond this one essential point, that whatever permanent body we form it must be a closed society, I have no strong views about its form. Much is to be said for giving it, at first at least, the loosest possible form and make it, perhaps, no more than a kind of correspondence society in which the list of members serves no other purpose except to enable them to keep in direct contact with each other. If it were practicable, which I fear it is not, that all the members volunteered by means of sending reprints or mimeographed copies of their relevant writings to each other this would in many ways be a very good solution. It would avoid the danger, which a specialised journal would raise, that we would talk only to those already converted and yet keep us informed of the parallel or complementary activities of others.

But the two desiderata that the efforts of the members of our group should reach a great variety of audiences and not be confined to those who are already converted, and that at the same time the members of our group should be kept fully informed of each others [*sic*] contributions from which they might derive assistance, are not easily combined, and we shall at least seriously have to consider the question whether sooner or later a separate journal or some series of separate papers may not be needed.

But it may well be that for some time to come such a loose and informal arrangement as I have suggested before is all that we can achieve since more would require greater financial means than we can raise from our midst. If there were larger funds available all sorts of possibilities might open up. But, desirable as this would be, I personally should rather be content with such a modest beginning if that is all we can do without in any manner compromising our complete independence from any outside groups. There are of course many more ambitious tasks which in themselves would be very worth while and which not only a much more definitive form of organisation could achieve but which would also require much more substantial funds than we could hope to raise from the membership fees of a group of scholars.

This Conference is a good illustration of the kind of functions which require considerable financial means and we cannot expect to be often so exceedingly fortunate as we have been this time in securing the necessary funds for a specific purpose mainly from Swiss, and so far as the travelling expenses of the American members are concerned, from American sources, without any strings or conditions of any sort being attached to the offer. I wanted to take the earliest opportunity explicitly to re-assure you on this point and at the same time to say how grateful to my friend Dr. Hunold who has raised the Swiss funds, and to Mr. W. H. Luhnow of the William Volker Charities Trust in Kansas City, who has made possible the participation of our American friends, for the readiness with which they have come forward. To Dr. Hunold we are further indebted for taking on himself all the local arrangements and all the delights and comforts we are now enjoying we owe to his efforts and foresight.[9]

I feel that it will be best if we do not turn to any discussion of this practical task until we are much better acquainted with each other and have more experience of the possibilities of collaboration than we have now. I hope there will be a good deal of private conversation on this question during the next few days and that in the course of this our ideas will gradually crystallise. When after three days of work and another three days of more informal companionship we resume our regular business meetings, one of those meetings should probably be set aside for a systematic examination of the possibilities. I will defer till then any attempt to justify the name which I have tentatively suggested for the permanent Society or any discussion of the principles and aims which would have to govern its activity.

For the time being we are just the Mont Pèlerin Conference to which you will have to give your own laws and whose procedure and destiny is now entirely in your hands.

Discussion: The rest of the morning was devoted to a discussion of the programme and timetable of the Conference. Messrs. Allais, Dennison, Friedman, Hayek and Hunold were elected as standing committee, with Messrs. Hayek and Hunold to act as Conference Secretaries.[10]

---

9. For more on Hunold and Luhnow, see the introduction.

10. As noted in the Note to the Reader, all italicized portions of the text indicate handwritten additions.

Session 2

Tuesday, April 1st, 1947, 4.30 p.m.

"Free" Enterprise and Competitive Order[1]

Professor Rappard in the chair.

Professor HAYEK (MS): If during the next few years, i.e. during the period in which practical politicians are alone interested, a continued movement towards more government control is almost certain in the greater part of the world, this is due, more than to anything else, to the lack of a real program, or perhaps I had better say, a consistent philosophy of the opposition groups. The position is even worse than mere lack of programs would imply: the fact is that almost everywhere the groups which pretend to oppose socialism at the same time support policies which, if the principles on which they are based were generalised, would no less lead to socialism than the avowedly socialist policies. There is some justification at least in the taunt that many of the pretending defenders of "free enterprise" are in

---

1. In the conference program that was distributed before the meeting, the title was "'Free Enterprise' or Competitive Order." That was the more accurate title, given that Hayek is contrasting the two in his paper. A slightly different version of the paper in which the "and" was retained appeared in the collection *Individualism and Economic Order*. This was reprinted in *The Collected Works of F. A. Hayek*, vol. 18, *Essays on Liberalism and the Economy*, ed. Paul Lewis (Chicago: University of Chicago Press; London: Routledge, forthcoming). If one compares that version with the one that appears here, it is evident that all changes were stylistic; there were no changes in substance.

fact defenders of privileges and advocates of government activity in their favour rather than opponents of all privilege. In principle the industrial protectionism and government supported cartels and the agricultural policies of the conservative groups are not different from the proposals for a more far-reaching direction of economic life sponsored by the socialists. It is an illusion when the more conservative interventionists believe that they will be able to confine these government controls to the particular kinds of which they approve. In a democratic society, at any rate, once the principle is admitted that the government undertakes responsibility for the status and position of particular groups, it is inevitable that this control will be extended to satisfy the aspirations and prejudices of the great masses. There is no hope of a return to a freer system until the leaders of the movement against state control are prepared first to impose upon themselves that discipline of a competitive market which they ask the masses to accept. The hopelessness of the prospect for the near future indeed is due mainly to the fact that no organized political group anywhere is in favour of a truly free system.

It is more than likely that from their point of view the practical politicians are right and that in the existing state of public opinion nothing else would be practicable. But what to the politicians are fixed limits of practicability imposed by public opinion must not be similar limits to us. Public opinion on these matters is the work of men like ourselves, the economists and political philosophers of the last few generations, who have created the political climate in which the politicians of our time must move. I do not find myself often agreeing with the late Lord Keynes, but he has never said a truer thing than when he wrote, on a subject on which his own experience has singularly qualified him to speak, that "the ideas of economists and political philosophers, both when they are right and when they are wrong, are more powerful than is commonly understood. Indeed the world is ruled by little else. Madmen in authority, who hear voices in the air, are distilling their frenzy from some academic scribbler of a few years back. I am sure that the power of vested interests is vastly exaggerated compared with the gradual encroachment of ideas. Not, indeed, immediately, but after a certain interval; for in the field of economic and political philosophy there are not many who are influenced by new theories after they are twenty-five or thirty years of age, so that the ideas which civil servants and politicians and even agitators apply are not likely to be the newest. But, soon or late, it is ideas, not vested interests, which are dangerous for good and evil."[2]

It is, as I suggested this morning, from this long run point of view, that we must look at our task. It is the beliefs which must spread, if a free society is to be preserved, or restored, not what is practicable at the moment, which must be our concern. But while we must emancipate ourselves from that servitude to current prejudices in which the politician is held, we must take a sane view of what persuasion and instruction are likely to achieve. While we may hope that as regards the means to be employed, the methods to be adopted, the public may in some measure be accessible to reasonable argument, we must probably assume that many of its basic values, its ethical standards are at least fixed for a much longer time and to some extent entirely beyond the scope of reasoning. To some extent it may be our task even here to show that the aims which our generation has set itself are incompatible or conflicting, and that the pursuit of some of them will endanger even greater values. But we shall probably also find that in some respects during the last hundred years certain moral aims have firmly established themselves for the satisfaction of which in a free society suitable techniques can be found. Even if we should not altogether share the new importance attached to some of these newer values, we shall do well to assume that they will determine action for a long time to come, and carefully to consider how far a place can be found for them in a free society. It is, of course, mainly the demands for greater security and greater equality I have here in mind. In both respects I believe very careful distinctions will have to be drawn between the sense in which "security" and "equality" can and cannot be provided in a free society.

Yet in another sense I think we shall have to pay more deliberate attention to the moral temper of contemporary man if we are to succeed in canalizing his energies from the harmful policies to which they are now devoted to a new effort on behalf of individual freedom. Unless we can

---

2. J. M. Keynes, *The General Theory of Employment, Interest, and Money* (London: Macmillan, 1936), 383–84.

set a definite task to the reformatory zeal of men, unless we can point out reforms which can be fought for by unselfish men, within a programme for freedom, their moral fervour is certain to be used against freedom. It was probably the most fatal tactical mistake of many nineteenth century liberals to have given the impression that the abandonment of all harmful or unnecessary state activity was the consummation of all political wisdom and that the question of <u>how</u> the state ought to use those powers nobody denied to it offered no serious and important problems on which reasonable people could differ.

This is of course not true of all 19th century liberals. About a hundred years ago John Stuart Mill, then still a true liberal, stated one of our present main problems in unmistakable terms. "The principle of private property has never yet had a fair trial in any country", he wrote in the first edition of his Political Economy (II/I/ss5, p. 253).[3] "The laws of property had never yet conformed to the principles on which the justification of private property rests. They have made property of things which never ought to be property, and absolute property where only a qualified property ought to exist . . . if the tendency of legislators had been to favour the diffusion, instead of the concentration of wealth, to encourage the subdivision of the large unions, instead of striving to keep them together; the principle of private property would have been found to have no real connection with the physical and social evils which have made so many minds turn eagerly to any prospect of relief, however desperate." But little was in fact done to make the rules of property conform better to its rationale and Mill

---

3. The sentences quoted by Hayek may be found in John Stuart Mill's *Principles of Political Economy*, 1st ed., vol. 1 (Boston: Charles C. Little & James Brown, 1848), 255–56. As implied by Hayek's remark that Mill was "still a true liberal" at the time he wrote the first edition of the *Principles*, Hayek believed that Mill's views shifted over time, away from the liberalism of his early years toward a more socialist outlook. See F. A. Hayek, *Studies on the Abuse and Decline of Reason: Texts and Documents*, ed. Bruce Caldwell, vol. 13 of *Collected Works* (Chicago: University of Chicago Press; London: Routledge, 2010), 56–57, 71, 238–39, and F. A. Hayek, *The Constitution of Liberty*, ed. Ronald Hamowy, vol. 17 of *Collected Works* (Chicago: University of Chicago Press; London: Routledge, 2011), 82, 121–22. Hayek's views on Mill are analyzed in detail by Sandra J. Peart, "Editor's Introduction," in F. A. Hayek, *Hayek on Mill: The Mill-Taylor Friendship and Related Writings*, ed. Sandra J. Peart, vol. 16 of *Collected Works* (Chicago: University of Chicago Press; London: Routledge, 2014).

himself, like so many others, soon turned his attention to schemes involving its restriction or abolition rather than its more effective use.

While it would be an exaggeration, it would not be altogether untrue to say that the interpretation of the fundamental principle of liberalism as absence of state activity rather than as a policy which deliberately adopts competition, the market and prices as its ordering principle and uses the legal framework enforced by the state in order to make competition as effective and beneficial as possible—and to supplement it where, and only where, it cannot be made effective, is as much responsible for the decline of competition as the active support which governments have given directly and indirectly to the growth of monopoly. It is the first general thesis which we shall have to consider that competition can be made more effective and more beneficent by certain activities of government than it would be without them. With regard to some of these activities this has never been denied, although people speak sometimes as if they had forgotten about them. That a functioning market presupposes not only prevention of violence and fraud and the protection of certain rights, such as property, and the enforcement of contracts, is always taken for granted. Where the traditional discussion becomes so unsatisfactory is where it is suggested that with the recognition of the principles of private property and freedom of contract, which indeed every liberal must recognise, all the issues were settled, as if the law of property and contract were given once and for all in its final and most appropriate form, i.e. in the form which will make the market economy work at its best. It is only after we have agreed on these principles that the real problems begin.

It is this fact which I have wished to emphasize when I called the subject of this discussion "Free" Enterprise and Competitive Order. The two names do not necessarily designate the same system and it is the system described by the second which we want. Perhaps I should at once add, although this is probably not necessary in this circle, that what I mean by "competitive order" is almost the opposite of what is often called "ordered competition." The purpose of a competitive order is to make competition work, that of so-called "ordered competition" almost always to restrict the effectiveness of competition. Thus understood this description of our subject at once distinguishes our approach as much from that of the conservative planners as from that of the socialists.

In this introductory survey I must confine myself to enumerating the main problems we shall have to discuss and must leave any detailed examination to later speakers. Perhaps I should begin by emphasizing more than I have yet done that while our main concern must be to make the market work where it can work, we must of course not forget that there are in a modern community a considerable number of services which are needed, such as sanitary and health services, and which could not possibly be provided by the market for the obvious reason that no price can be charged to the beneficiaries, or rather, that it is not possible to confine the benefits to those who are willing or able to pay for it. There are some obvious instances of the kind, like the one I have mentioned, but on closer examination we shall find, that in some measure this kind of case shades somewhat gradually into those where the whole of the services rendered can be sold to whoever wants to buy them. At some stage or other we shall certainly have to consider which services of this kind we must always expect the governments to provide outside the market and how far the fact that they must do so will also affect the conditions on which the market economy proceeds.

There are two other sets of problems which concern preconditions of a competitive order rather than what one might call market policy proper and which I must mention, although if we wish to discuss them we should probably do so in special meetings set aside for these topics rather than as part of the present discussion. The first is the question of the kind of monetary and financial policy required to secure adequate economic stability. We are probably all in agreement that any mitigation of cyclical unemployment depends at least in part on monetary policy, but I hope we shall for to-day at any rate avoid the technicalities into which a further examination of these problems would at once lead. When we turn to these problems one of our main concerns will have to be how far it is possible to make monetary management once more automatic or at least predictable because bound by fixed rule.

The second major problem on which we shall have to assume some definite answer without going into detail at this stage is that in modern society we must take it for granted that some sort of provision will be made for the unemployed and the unemployable poor. All that we can usefully consider in this connection is not whether such provision is desirable or not, but merely in what form it will least interfere with the functioning of the market. Even this question, though of the greatest importance, I feel we had probably better reserve for separate consideration—perhaps in a meeting devoted to the whole complex of employment and unemployment policies and to all the problems of social insurance or "social security."

I have mentioned these points mainly in order more sharply to delimit the proper subjects of to-day's discussion. Before I proceed to the bare enumeration with which I must content myself, I will only give expression to my hope that we shall strongly disagree on these topics, the more the better. What is needed more than anything is that these questions of a policy for a competitive order should once again become live issues which are being discussed publicly and we shall have made an important contribution if we succeed in directing interest to them.

If I am not mistaken the main headings under which the measures required to ensure an effective competitive order ought to be considered are the law of property and contract, of corporations and associations, including, in particular, trade unions, the problems of how to deal with such monopolies or quasi-monopolistic positions which would remain in an otherwise sensibly drawn up framework, the problems of taxation and the problems of international trade, particularly, in our time, of the relations between free and planned economies.

They are not adequate answers because their meaning is ambiguous. Our problems begin when we ask what out [sic] to be the contents of property rights, what contracts should be enforceable and how should contracts be interpreted or rather what standard forms of contract should be read into the informal agreements of everyday transactions.

Where the law of property is concerned it is not difficult to see that the simple rules which are adequate to ordinary mobile "things" or "chattel" are not suitable for indefinite extension. We need only turn to the problems which arise in connection with land, particularly with regard to urban land in modern large towns in order to realise that a conception of property which is based on the assumption that the use of a particular item of property affects only the interests of its owner breaks down. There can be no doubt that a good many at least of the problems with which the modern town planner is concerned are genuine problems with which governments or local authorities are bound to concern themselves. Unless we can provide guidance in fields like this about what are legitimate or necessary government activities and what are its limits we must not complain if our views are not taken seriously when we oppose other kinds of less justified "planning."

The problem of the prevention of monopoly and the preservation of competition is raised much more acutely in certain other fields to which the concept of property has been extended only in recent times. I am thinking here of the extension of the concept of property to such rights and privileges as patents for inventions, copyright and trademarks and the like. It seems to me beyond doubt that in these fields a slavish application of the concept of property as it has been developed for material things has done a great deal to foster the growth of monopoly and that here very drastic reforms may be required if competition is to be made to work. In the field of industrial patents in particular we shall have very seriously to examine whether the award of a monopoly privilege is really the most appropriate and effective form of reward for the kind of risk-bearing which investment in scientific research involves.—(May I take this opportunity to say that I hope that the whole problem of the relation of government to scientific research and of the freedom of science in the modern state is one which I hope that, if not this meeting, at least the permanent organisation which may emerge from it, will take a definite interest in.)

But, to return to the question of patents: they are so particularly interesting from our point of view because they provide so clear an illustration how it is necessary in all such instances not to apply a ready made formula but to go back to the rationale of the market system and to decide for each class what the precise rights are to be which the government ought to protect. This is a task at least as much for economists as for lawyers. Perhaps it is not a waste of your time if I illustrate what I have in mind by quoting a rather well known decision in which an American judge argued that "as to the suggestion that competitors were excluded from the use of the patent we answer that such exclusion may be said to have been the very essence of the right conferred by the patent" and adds "as it is the privilege of any owner of property to use it or not to use it without any question of motive."*4 It is this last statement which seems to me to be so significant for the way in which a mechanical extension of the property concept by lawyers has done so much to create undesirable and harmful privilege.

Another field in which a mechanical extension of the simplified conception of private property has produced undesirable results is in the field of trade marks and proprietary names. I have myself no doubt that legislation has important tasks to perform in this field and that securing adequate and truthful information concerning the origin of any product is one, but only one aspect of this. But the exclusive stress on the description of the producer and the neglect of similar provisions concerning the character and quality of the commodity has to some extent helped to create monopolistic conditions because the trade mark came to be used as a description of the kind of commodity, which then of course only the owner of the trade mark could produce ("Kodak", "Aspirin"). This difficulty might be solved, e.g., if the use of trade marks were protected only in connection with descriptive names which would be free for all to use.

The situation is rather similar in the field of contract. We cannot regard "freedom of contract" as a real answer to our problems if we know that not all contracts ought to be made enforceable and in fact are bound to argue that contracts "in restraint of trade" ought not to be enforceable. And once we extend the power to make contracts from natural persons to corporations and the like, it can be no longer the contract but must be the law

*Continental Bag Co. v. Eastern Bag Co., 210 U.S. 405 (1909) [sic].

---

4. Continental Bag Co. v. Eastern Bag Co., 210 U.S. 405 (1908) was a case that came before the US Supreme Court in 1908, not, as Hayek states in his asterisked footnote, in 1909. The Eastern Paper Bag Company sought to prevent one of its competitors, the Continental Paper Bag Company, from duplicating its patented design for a "self-opening" paper bag. In its counter, Continental argued that Eastern was guilty of suppressing competition because it was not itself currently employing the patented technology. The Supreme Court rejected this argument, maintaining that patent holders enjoy an unlimited right *not* to use the technology in question and that patents entitle their holders to prevent others from using a design irrespective of the patent holder's motivation for doing so. The words quoted by Hayek come from the Supreme Court's ruling on the case.

which decides who is liable and how is the property to be determined and safeguarded which limits the liability of the corporation.

"Freedom of contract" is in fact no solution because in a complex society like ours no contract can explicitly provide against all contingencies and jurisdiction and legislation evolve standard types of contracts for many purposes which not only tend to become exclusively practicable and intelligible but which determine the interpretation of, and are used to fill the lacunae is [sic], all contracts which can actually be made. A legal system which leaves the kind of contractual obligations on which the order of society rests <u>entirely</u> to the ever new decision of the contracting parties has never existed and probably cannot exist. Here as much as in the realm of property the precise content of the permanent legal framework, the rules of civil law, are of the greatest importance for the way in which a competitive market will operate. The extent to which the development of civil law, as much where it is judge-made law as when it is amended by legislation, can determine the developments away from or towards a competitive system and how much this change in civil law is determined by the dominant ideas of what would be a desirable social order is well illustrated by the development of legislation and jurisdiction on cartels, monopoly, and the restraint of trade generally, during the last fifty years. It seems to me that no doubt is possible that this development, even where it fully maintained the principle of "freedom of contract", and partly because it did so, has greatly contributed to the decline of competition. But little intellectual effort has been directed to the question in what way this legal framework should be modified, to make competition more effective.

The main field in which these problems arise and the one from which I can best illustrate my point is of course the law of corporations and particularly that concerning limited liability (the incorporation in the American or the société anonyme in the French sense). I don't think that there can be much doubt that the particular form legislation has taken in this field has greatly assisted the growth of monopoly, nor that it was only because of special legislation conferring special rights—not so much to the corporations themselves as to those dealing with corporations—that size of enterprise has become an advantage beyond the point where it is justified by technological facts. It seems to me that in general the freedom of the individual by no means need be extended to give all these freedoms to organised groups

of individuals, and even that it may on occasion be the duty of government
to protect the individual against organised groups. And it seems to me also
as if historically in the field of the law of corporations we had a situation
rather analogous to that in the field of the law of property to which I have
already referred. As in the law of property the rules developed for ordinary
mobile property were extended uncritically and in full to all sorts of new
rights, thus the recognition of corporations as fictitious or legal persons
has had the effect that all the rights of a natural person were automatically
extended to corporations. I can see strong arguments for so designing corporation law as to impede the indefinite growth of individual corporations,
and the ways in which this could be done without setting up any rigid limits or give the government undesirable powers of direct interference is one
of the more interesting problems which we might discuss.

I have so far deliberately spoken only of what is required to make competition effective on the side of employers, not because I regard this as of
such exclusive importance, but because I am convinced that there is politically no chance to do anything about the other side, the labour side, of the
problem until the employers have themselves shown their belief in competition and demonstrated that they are willing to put their own house
in order. But we must not delude ourselves that in many ways the most
crucial, the most difficult and the most delicate part of our task consists in
formulating an appropriate programme of labour or trade union policy. In
no other respect, I believe was the development of liberal opinion more
inconsistent or more unfortunate or is there more uncertainty and vague-
ness even among the true liberals of today. Historically liberalism first
far too long maintained an unjustified opposition against trade unions as
such, only to collapse completely at the beginning of this century and to
grant to trade unions in many respects exemption from the ordinary law
and even, to all intents and purposes, to legalize violence, coercion and
intimidation.[5] That if there is to be any hope of a return to a free economy the question how the powers of trade unions can be appropriately
delimited in law as well as in fact is one of the most important of all the

---

5. Hayek here is alluding to the 1906 Trade Disputes Act, which provided British trade
unions with immunity from liability for damages arising from strike action. On this and other
examples of granting special privileges to labor, see Hayek, *Constitution of Liberty*, 385–86.
Hayek's views on unions are set out in detail on pp. 384–404 of that book.

questions to which we must give our attention. I have many times already in the course of this outline felt tempted to refer you to the writings of the late Henry Simons, which, as those of one who ought to have been one of the members of this Conference, I have placed among our little collection in the other room, but I want now especially to draw your attention to his "Reflections on Syndicalism" which state this problem with rare courage and lucidity.[6]

The problem has recently of course become even bigger by the assumption by most governments of the responsibility for what is called "full employment" and all its implications, and I do not see how we can, when we reach these problems any longer separate them from the more general problems of monetary policy which I have suggested we should, as far as possible, keep separate. The same is true of the next set of major problems, which I can now only briefly mention, those of international trade, tariffs and foreign exchange control, etc. While on all these our long run point of view ought to be clear, they do of course raise real problems for the immediate future, which, however, we had probably better leave on one side as belonging to the questions of immediate policy rather than long run principles. The same, I am afraid, we should probably not be entitled to do with regard to that other problem I have already mentioned, the problem of the relation between free and planned economies.

If I am to keep my promise and confine myself to the enunciation of the main problems I must now hurry to a conclusion and just touch on one more major field, that of taxation. It is, of course, by itself very large. I want to pick out only two aspects of it. The one is the effect of progressive income taxation at the rate which has now been reached and used for extreme egalitarian ends. The two consequences of this which seem to me the most serious are on the one hand that it makes for social immobility

---

6. Henry C. Simons, "Some Reflections on Syndicalism," *Journal of Political Economy* 52, no. 1 (March 1944), 1–25; reprinted in his *Economic Policy for a Free Society* (Chicago: University of Chicago Press, 1948), 121–59. In the original essay, Simons contended that the "essence" of liberalism "is a distrust of all concentrations of power": "The government must not tolerate erection of great private corporate empires or cartel organizations which suppress competition and rival in power great governmental units themselves. . . . Most important for the future, it must guard its powers against great trade-unions, both as pressure groups in government and as monopolists outside" (3–4).

by making it practically impossible for the successful man to rise by accumulating a fortune, and that it has come near eliminating that most important element in any free society, the man of independent means, a figure whose essential role in maintaining a free opinion and generally the atmosphere of independence from government control we only begin to realise as he is disappearing from the stage. Similar comments apply to modern inheritance taxation, and particularly estate duties as they exist in Great Britain. But in mentioning this I ought at once to add that inheritance taxes could, of course, be made an instrument towards greater social mobility and greater dispersion of property, and consequently ought to be regarded as very important tools of a truly liberal policy which ought not to stand condemned by the abuse which has been made of it.

There are many other important problems which I have not even mentioned. But I hope that what I have said will be sufficient to indicate the field which I had in mind when I suggested our present topic for discussion. It is too wide a field to treat the whole of it adequately even if we could devote the whole of these ten days to its discussion. But, as I have said before, I hope these discussions will be only a beginning and it does not matter a great deal where exactly we start. It will be the next speakers who will have to suggest to which points in this field we ought first to direct our searchlights and it will be for you to decide which of the points you want to take up.

Free Enterprise or Competitive Order[7]

Professor Rappard in the chair.

Professor HAYEK: It is the second name which describes the system which he would regard as desirable.

---

7. The crossed-through section appears to be Dorothy Hahn's summary of Hayek's paper, prepared as he was delivering it. It was rendered unnecessary given that the manuscript for the address was preserved. The roughness of her notes relative to the address is another reminder to the reader of this volume that her transcripts provide at best an incomplete picture of what was said at each session.

Competitive order: to make competition work

Competitive order: to make competition work
Ordered competition: to restrict competition from working.

Main concern is to make the market work where it can work, although there are some other services which cannot be made subject to the market mechanism.

1. Monetary and financial policy. (e.g. full employment) How can monetary policy be automatic, and outside the range of politics?

2. It must be taken for granted that there must be some provision for the unemployed, and the unemployable. But it must interfere as little as possible with the market mechanism.

Problems of market policy proper:

Law of property and contract. Corporations and associations. Problem of how to deal with monopolies. Problems of taxation. Problems of international trade, particularly of trade between liberal countries and non-liberal countries.

1. Law of property and contract: We must beware of the error of believing that private property and freedom of contract solve any problems.

How should contracts be interpreted.

2. Monopoly, trade marks, patents, etc.

Very drastic reforms may be required if competition is to work again.

Patents provide clear-cut illustration of why it is necessary to go back to the rationale of property rights.

We probably all agree that contracts in restraint of trade ought not to be enforceable.

Labour and trade union policy.

Impossible, even in the long run, to do anything about these, until the employers have put their own houses in order, and restored some degree of competition.

If there is to be any hope of a return to a free economy, the problem of how far the Trade Unions can limit it seems to be very important.

~~Taxation.~~

> ~~1. Effects of progressive income taxation on the society. Make for social immobility.~~

~~Tendency towards greater equality therefore makes the society more rigid.~~

> ~~2. Also tends to eliminate the man of independent means. Once it is no longer possible for men of independent means to assist causes which run counter to existing government policy, we have taken a backward step.~~

Professor DIRECTOR (MS): For over two generations there has been a steady shift from individualism to authority in economic life. During the first half of this period the shift was gradual and barely perceptible. The presumption against state interference with free contractual relations between individuals as the basis of organizing economic life was well established. State intervention was mainly a response to the humanitarian tradition of liberalism; it was not designed to change our basic form of economic organization but to offset some of the unacceptable consequences of the competitive market. The ultimate implications of the gradual changes introduced were hardly notices [*sic*].

In our own time the shift from individualism to authority has, in some countries been completed, and everywhere it is proceeding at a rapid rate. Moreover, the shift is now in many places part of a definite design to adopt an entirely different type of economic organization than the one to which we have been accustomed.

There are many explanations for the changes which have and are now taking place. I shall mention only three.

We are perhaps witnessing a fundamental change in our basic beliefs. The virtues of individual freedom no longer command the support they once did. Order, security, and a fixed status in life are now the prevailing objectives. From this point of view, the free competitive market is indicted and abandoned because it does its task too well and thus yields results incompatible with our moral values. This aspect of the problem will be discussed at other sessions.

A second explanation stems from the widespread opinion that the competitive market is no longer suitable as an organizing principle. However suitable the competitive order may once have been, advances in technology have so altered the basic data of economic life as to make it unworkable. First is the alleged increase in the efficiency of larger scale enterprise. To maintain competition in a modern industrial society would consequently involve an intolerable loss of product and an intolerable amount of governmental intervention to prevent enterprises from growing to monopolistic size. Second is the alleged exhaustion of private investment opportunities in highly industrialized societies which requires a large and secularly increasing governmental participation in economic life if we are to maintain employment and economic progress. I need not argue here the case against the existence of these technological facts.[8]

A third explanation, and one which I take as the basis of our discussion, is that a substantial and increasing amount of state intervention which tends to destroy the competitive order is a direct consequence of the incomplete character of the theory of liberalism as developed in the nineteenth century. This theory provides no role for the state in economic life beyond that of enforcing contracts, and performing economic functions which cannot be undertaken by individual enterprise. There may have been a time when free enterprise—enterprise free of political intervention—was the equivalent of a competitive order. It no longer is equivalent, and has not been for some time. Since at least the middle of the last century serious conflicts have emerged between what liberals consider the social interests and the results of free enterprise. As each conflict emerged, the liberal had no solution to offer derived from their fundamental philosophy.

The community insisted on doing something; hence conflict after conflict led to <u>ad hoc</u> state intervention which solved none of the problems, created new ones and discredited free enterprise. Liberals either stood by or more often approved. I do not wish to minimize the harm that has been caused by the state intervention we have now. I wish to emphasize that this

8. The first argument in Director's "second explanation" was frequently made by socialist critics of the market system, whereas the second was more associated with Keynes and his followers.

intervention had its root in real problems and that we can eliminate it only by offering better solutions. The theory of liberalism must be extended to include a prescription of the role of the state in making private enterprise the equivalent of competitive enterprise.

It is now apparent that: (1) Free enterprise as we have known it is consistent with a substantial amount of monopoly power deriving from the growth of excessive scale of enterprise and from the growth of combinations among enterprises and workers.

(2) A competitive system can be expected to perform efficiently the task of allocating resources among alternative uses. But in the absence of stable and suitable monetary rules, it cannot be expected to maximize output over time.

(3) A competitive system appears to fall short of meeting the democratic standards of equality.

The founders of 19th century liberalism served the cause of freedom by promoting free enterprise. The task of our day is to promote freedom by promoting the dispersion of power necessary for a competitive order. The founders of liberalism endeavoured to minimize the coercive powers of the state. The task of our day is to redefine the role of the state so as to prevent the assumption of this power by organized minority occupational groups.

There are thus at least three fields in which state action is required to make the competitive order work.

1. The prevention of private monopolies
2. The control of combinations among either business concerns or workers
3. The provision of monetary stability.

In addition to these there is

4. The problem of economic inequality and distress and the possible scope for state activity in the redistribution of income.

I should now like to indicate briefly and tentatively the kind of measures that are consistent with a free market and with other objectives of liberalism.

Industrial Monopoly.

Free international trade is a significant check on the growth of monopoly. Since, however, this is the one issue on which liberals now agree it is not necessary to discuss it further. It is not, however, a sufficient condition and it is unfortunate that overemphasis of the importance of free trade in this connection has contributed significantly to the abandonment by England of the common law opposition to monopoly and restraint of trade. I do not wish to exaggerate the accomplishments of the American tradition and American law against monopoly. At the same time it is all too easy to be overimpressed with the specific failure of the American effort to maintain competition. The difference between the American and European scene is in some measure at least to be ascribed to the effort we made to enforce our anti-monopoly laws.

A study of the American anti-trust cases discloses the crucial importance which patents on inventions have played in creating and maintaining industrial monopolies. The only promising solution is a drastic reduction of the period of the monopoly grant by change of existing statutory rules and existing administrative procedure.

Associations.

Anti-monopoly laws are, however, mere stop gap measures. We must repair the damage caused by 19th century liberalism in failing to define the scope of voluntary associations—corporations and trade unions.

The unlimited power of corporations must be removed. Excessive size can be challenged through the prohibition of corporate ownership of other corporations, through the elimination of interlocking directorates, through a limitation of the scope of activity of corporations, through increased control of enterprise by property owners and perhaps too through a direct limitation of the size of corporate enterprise.

The trade union problem is even more complex. Dicey somewhere characterized the English wealthy classes as suffering from a combination of intellectual weakness and moral strength.[9] This is quite applicable to

---

9. In the introduction to the second edition of his *Lectures on the Relation between Law and Public Opinion during the 19th Century* (London: Macmillan, 1914), the British jurist A. V. Dicey (1835–1922) stated, "The main current of legislative opinion from the beginning

liberal economists' treatment of combinations among workers. The repeal of the combination acts was defended as a means of removing unduly harsh and discriminatory treatment of workers, and ever since then we have condoned and often defended the growth of combinations among workers as a necessary means of equalizing power between workers and employers.[10] Through statutory enactment and the lapse of the common law against restraint of trade in England and through statutory enactment and judicial legislation in the United States, trade unions have been accorded an unusual position. And as a consequence they now constitute the most serious type of monopoly organization.

The removal of government support of trade union activity is of course an immediate requirement. And the subjection of trade unions to the law against monopoly and combinations in restraint of trade appears to be our only long run safeguard against this form of monopoly power.

Monetary Stabilization.

In no field is the weakness of the liberal tradition more obvious than in that of money. There have been almost universal recognition of the principle that the competitive market is not a suitable means of regulating the supply of money. But aside from the Bank Act of 1844 we have had little to offer, except discretionary authorities to offset the actions of private suppliers of money.[11] It is not necessary to argue that a suitable monetary framework for a competitive society will alone assure us stability of output

---

of the twentieth century has run vehemently towards collectivism" (liii). He attributed the lack of resistance to the trend by wealthy Englishmen to "the combination of an intellectual weakness with a moral virtue" (lxi). The weakness was in thinking that changes in the law would only have small effects, and the virtue was in having sympathy for the plight of the poor.

10. Though it was already illegal in England to form trade unions, the Combination Acts (1799–1800) provided quicker judgments (though with less severe penalties) to be taken when the law was violated. The Acts were repealed in 1824, but an 1825 amendment to the repeal legislation—though permitting unions to exist—limited their activities. Legislation at the turn of the century removed many of the obstacles to labor activity.

11. Before the passage of the Bank Charter Act of 1844, British commercial banks could issue their own banknotes. The act prohibited any new banks from doing so, required notes to be backed by gold or government debt, and gave a monopoly on further note issuance to the Bank of England.

and employment. But such a framework is surely a necessary prerequisite for this goal.

An essential prerequisite of monetary stability is definite control of the quantity of money. Some improvement over the results of the past would no doubt result from the establishment of a gold circulation. The more attractive alternative is that of the direct assumption by the state of the responsibility for issuing currency, but of course under precisely defined rules, such as maintaining a constant per capita quantity of money. As between these alternatives, the gold circulation has two advantages. The supply of money would not depend on state action, and we would have fixed international exchange rates. On the other hand such a system would be costly in terms of resources and stability would depend on the fortunes of the gold mining industry.

Both systems would require drastic revision of existing financial institutions so as to preclude the creation of money or money substitutes by private enterprise.

Beyond the minimal monetary objectives we should be considering the possibility of using price stability as a guide to the regulation of the supply of money issued by the state. The prospect of providing monetary certainty for enterprise so that it need no longer gamble on the behaviour of discretionary authorities may accomplish a great deal in solving the problem of variations in aggregate output and employment. Beyond this its importance stems from the escape it offers out of the confusion of fiscal behaviour and from the great dangers of inflation which are likely to accompany alternative solutions of the problem of economic instability.

Equality

It can be and has been argued that effective freedom is impossible if individuals are highly unequal in economic power, i.e., in income and wealth. Whether or not this is so, we cannot escape serious consideration of the appropriate role of the state in furthering one of the original tenets of liberalism—the greatest good of the greatest number. This dogma reflected the strong humanitarian impulses of the founders of modern liberalism. And these humanitarian impulses are even more widespread today. But the wish is not the deed. They have not been matched by a comprehensive conception of how the desired results could best be achieved. Instead, misguided humanitarianism has led to a host of ad hoc interventions to aid special groups, interventions which, in the main, have interfered with the market and have created inequalities to replace those removed. Minimum wage laws, agricultural schemes, social security schemes, protective tariffs, protection of small shopkeepers, are all obvious examples.

These ad hoc interventions, should, of course, be abolished. But the humanitarian objectives which account for much of the disinterested support they have received reflect a genuine social requirement.

The measures for freeing the market and for providing monetary stability already noted will satisfy a part of this requirement. Some of the existing inequality of income and wealth reflects the monopoly power of industry and labour. But elimination of monopoly power takes time and even when successfully completed would by no means either assure a large measure of equality or completely eliminate distress.

Some further contribution to the reduction of inequality can be attained by measures justified in any event as a means of increasing social output. A private enterprise system cannot provide the appropriate amount of investment in human beings. Large increases in the productivity of our working force could be obtained by measures widening the opportunity to obtain technical and professional education as well as by measures devoted to improving the physical wellbeing of the children in poor families.

These measures alone, however, will still leave what must now be considered desperate poverty and excessive inequality of income. The humanitarian impulse pressed this far can be satisfied only at a price—a reduction in aggregate output as a consequence of some impairment of incentives. We should be prepared to pay this price. The way to minimize this price is to place exclusive reliance on progressive income taxation, extended to include subsidy payments to those with low incomes proportional to their incomes but leaving a margin for incentive to work.[12] A guaranteed

---

12. Economist readers will recognize this as "the negative income tax" proposal with which Director's brother-in-law Milton Friedman would later be prominently identified.

minimum income along these lines will meet our humanitarian objectives far more effectively than the proliferation of ad hoc interventions on behalf of special groups, will facilitate the abolition of these interventions, and will minimize the creation and strengthening of occupational groups which, in the United States at least, now constitute the principal political obstacle to the recreation of a free market society.

Professor EUCKEN: Two remarks I would like to make.

First, it is theoretically objectionable if in a market system two different systems of prices exist, but it is not only monopoly prices which are objectionable. Second, the monopolist is not usually afraid of nationalisation. He is more afraid of competition than of government control. What is required is independent supervisory authority guided by law and not by Parliament.

Professor RAPPARD: Interested in a market economy as a condition of a free society. Germany: the occupying forces not "out for a free society". If the main aim is not the re-establishment of a free economy, monopoly is bound to be the order of the day.

~~**Dr. HUNOLD:** Also antimonopolist.~~

~~There are here some who understand neither English nor German. Will therefore translate into English if anyone wants to speak in French.~~
~~**Professor ALLAIS:** Would like a manuscript of the conference, when it exists after the conference.~~

Professor GRAHAM: In almost complete agreement with Professor Eucken except on his notion that natural monopolies are worse handled when taken over by the state. I question whether monopolies could be any worse handled by state than by natural monopolies themselves. Ideologically, the right place for a natural monopoly is in the state. Not necessarily very bad if the state servant tries to charge monopoly prices. Significant thing is then, that if the administration is otherwise honest, profits go to the state.

But it doesn't seem that liberty is as much invaded by a price which is other than a competitive price as when the public is privately taxed by a private monopoly.

Much worse if the private individual taxes the community.

Professor ~~EUCKEN~~

Appendix to Session 2

[As Hayek noted in his welcoming remarks in session 1, at the following session, after he offered a "few words" of his own on the subject, Aaron Director, Walter Eucken, and Maurice Allais would "introduce the debate" on the topic. Director provided a manuscript which was transcribed into Dorothy Hahn's record of the conference. The talks by Eucken and Allais were not transcribed by Hahn, and no record of Allais's talk was found in the archives.

A transcript of Eucken's remarks, which he delivered in German, was preserved. What appears to have happened was that Eucken delivered his comments extemporaneously in German. Hayek translated them simultaneously into English for the group, while Albert Hunold took down a shorthand version of Eucken's words in German. Hunold later had a secretary write them up and sent them to Hayek, who kept them with his other materials from the meeting.[13] What follows is a translation of Hunold's transcript.

With a few exceptions it appears to be a verbatim account. At a few points in the text Hunold wrote "Mr. Eucken then mentions . . ." or something equivalent. Presumably these third-person passages were not an exact transcript of Eucken's words but Hunold's own summary of them.

Though this is not part of the "official" conference record kept by Hahn, it is a valuable contribution to the meeting, so it is included here as an appendix to Session 2. Its proper position in the order of presentation would seem to be right after Director's talk. It was then followed by remarks by Eucken himself, Rappard, and Graham, the last of whom alluded to Eucken's talk in his comment. I thank Stefan Kolev and Karen Horn for undertaking the translation of Eucken's contribution and for providing helpful explanatory footnotes to the text.—Ed.]

---

13. The transcript of Eucken's remarks may be found in Friedrich A. Hayek Papers (FAHP), box 81, folder 4, Hoover Institution.

Mont-Pèlerin Conference
April 1–10, 1947

Statement of Dr. Walter Eucken on
Tuesday, April 1, on the topic
"Free Enterprise or Competitive Order"

[Translated by Stefan Kolev and Karen Horn[14]]

Not only in the Russian zone, but also in the English zone, a concentration in heavy industry is observable to an extent which we would not have thought possible a few years ago. As this is taking place in reality, the idea of the competitive order has remained much more alive among the Germans than ever. So the facts are moving in the opposite direction to the ideas and to the direction which we are pursuing here. I may relate to you two experiences on this point:

In the French zone, we have a central office for the economy (Centre d'organisation économique et sociale). Some time ago, we had a lively discussion, and expert reports were also drafted on the question of corporation disentanglement and cartel dissolution. Four trade unionists were in this commission of eight people in total, and on the basis of an expert report I had prepared,[15] a discussion on economic order took place. We made it clear to the gentlemen of the trade unions that nothing is more dangerous for the workers than a centrally planned economy, and that workers become slaves and lose their freedom. [We explained that] concentration within the power of the state is dangerous and there is only one solution to overcome it: <u>the competitive economy</u>.

---

14. Stefan Kolev, University of Applied Sciences Zwickau, Germany; Karen Horn, University of Erfurt, Germany.

15. Eucken's reports from 1946 as a member of the council "Comité d'Études Économiques" in the French zone have been published; see Walter Eucken, *Ordnungspolitik*, ed. Walter Oswalt (Münster: LIT, 1999).

The gentlemen explained that they could not as a principle drop their program, but that they would be prepared to go along, and that included the Social Democrats. The expert report I just mentioned contains some formulations in favor of a competitive order which were not only accepted, but also signed by the members. One gained the impression that the danger inherent in socialization and nationalization was recognized on the workers' side as well.

As a second example, I want to mention that some time ago the Hamburg Senate set up a commission to study the question of socialization of companies. The resulting majority report was predominantly socialist, while the minority report contained the idea of establishing a competitive order. The report was signed by

5 Social Democrats,

1 Communist,

2 Liberals and

2 Christian Socials.[16]

So the German attitude cannot be characterized by slogans, since the German socialists are also prepared to accept a great deal of what we hold here. However, they must be convinced that positions are held honestly.

This is the situation:

The actual development is moving against us, while in the field of ideas there is a more relaxed attitude[17] towards our views.

And now, to get into the heart of the monopoly program, let me start right away with Germany. You know—we have an anti-trust law.[18] An American, French and English one will follow, the content of which will be similar.

I have closely observed this legislation coming into being. The matter went very favorably exactly in the sense of our aspirations. General Clay

---

16. This most likely refers to the Christian Democratic Party (CDP), which was founded in Hamburg on October 1, 1945. Eucken probably erroneously used the term "Christian Socials" because the Baden Christian Social People's Party (BCSV) still existed in his own region. A few weeks later, that party renamed itself Christian Democratic Union (CDU) Baden.

17. "Auflockerung" in the original.

18. "Anti-Monopolgesetz" in the original.

had sent a reply to the Council of Minister-Presidents (Länderrat).[19] This draft was passed on for review to a German committee which consisted exclusively of people who would actually belong in our circle. These five men first made it clear that anti-trust laws should not be enacted as a punitive measure. They made an anti-trust law which later was not enacted by the military government; and above all, the state monopolies (invested interests of the state [English in the German original]) have not been subjected to monopoly control, especially not in the heavy industry.

Now we ask ourselves: What do these anti-trust laws mean? For the German economy, they mean nothing, nothing at all. Because if the cartels are dissolved today (we do have a planned economy in Germany), what would change in the allocation of iron? of coal? of leather? of cement?— Nothing! There are central offices which one must approach, and at the most the wording on the signs of the offices has undergone a change. So in this respect, nothing is achieved, because behind the doors the concentration process continues rapidly, and the anti-trust law only serves to conceal the actual conditions.

If we want to fight the monopolies, can we do that within the framework of the centrally planned economy[?] A centrally planned economy and monopolized economy are very similar—not analytically—but especially in the staff involved, since nothing has changed regarding the managers. The same chief executives who managed the former cartel are now at the head of the state monopolies. If once in a while a trade union leader is included, this does not change much, because after a year he acts in the same way as if he was a chief executive. In socialist circles in Germany, the idea is growing: elimination of monopolies, economically and politically, elimination of all this power concentration and massification.[20] This can never be achieved by the centrally planned economy, but only by the

---

19. From 1947 to 1949, General Lucius D. Clay was the military governor of the American zone. From 1945 to 1949, the Council of Minister-Presidents (Länderrat) was an assembly of the prime ministers of the provinces that constituted the American zone: Bavaria, Großhessen, and Württemberg-Baden, joined in 1947 by the senate president of Bremen.

20. "Vermachtung und Vermassung" in the original.

competitive order. In Germany an experiment is being conducted, and it has turned out perfectly unambiguous in its results.[21]

In this context, I would like to say a few more things about the experience in the struggle for the competitive order and about reality itself. If one point is very important, as has also been emphasized very much in this circle, it is the currency. The currency question is centrally managed, and I say this with regard to the emergence of power concentration as it gained more and more ground under National Socialism.

First we had foreign exchange control in Germany. It started with the unfortunate Schacht Plan of 1934.[22] The decision was made at that very moment when foreign exchange was allocated centrally. As a result, the labor force had to be managed centrally. The whole thing was actually created with the currency as its origin, without foreseeing at that time the consequences of this disastrous plan. Later, foreign exchange control was used to push performance.

One of my colleagues once expressed it as follows: Because one has planned incorrectly in the field of currency, planning in all other fields is being provoked. Mr. Eucken is aware of the fact that without a somewhat sound currency, it is impossible to eliminate the centrally planned economy, also internationally.

Another point: When we see the emergence of German monopolies and large corporations, cartels and syndicates in their latest evolution, it always becomes clear: We can never eliminate them at the root through anti-trust laws alone. They are the result of fundamentally misguided overall economic policies[23] which go back a long way. Mr. Eucken then also mentions corporate law, patent law and trademarked articles, resale price maintenance, combined with "suggestive advertising,"[24] which have

---

21. Hayek commissioned a paper from Eucken on the German experience with a centrally planned economy which appeared in two parts: Walter Eucken, "On the Theory of the Centrally Administered Economy: An Analysis of the German Experiment," Part 1, *Economica* 15, no. 58 (May 1948): 79–100; Part 2, *Economica* 15, no. 59 (August 1948): 173–93.

22. From 1933 to 1939, Hjalmar Schacht was president of the Reichsbank. In 1934 he also became minister of the economy. The "New Plan" of 1934 aimed at centrally managing exports and imports, one of its goals being the improvement of foreign currency reserves.

23. "Gesamtwirtschaftspolitik" in the original.

24. "Suggestions-Reklame" in the original.

contributed a great deal to the centrally planned economy. So we also have to look at licensing law, corporate law and trademark law, because we cannot succeed here with anti-trust law. As it is now in draft form, Mr. Eucken finds this law to be quite good. The basic idea is this: As a principle, freedom of contract should not be abused as a means for eliminating freedom of contract. If we start from this principle, then any blocking,[25] however it may be applied, must be prohibited in principle and declared unlawful.

And yet the next question is: What about those markets where monopolies nevertheless exist? For example, in the electricity industry, where there is a tendency in this direction for technical reasons? Here I can say on the basis of the German experience: The worst solution is for the state to take over these monopolies, because the state and finance minister[26] will always have a clear conscience in the case of monopolistic pricing, because he does not set the prices for himself, but for the taxpayer. Much better is strict control of monopolies. What guideline should this control follow? In our opinion, the guideline is the following:

The monopolist must be forced to behave, in terms of pricing and production, as if it was in competition.

With this guideline, one can get quite far in the concrete case. It is not easy, but it is possible.

We have had certain experiences in the field of coal, in the Rhenish-Westphalian Coal Syndicate. On the one hand, the state creates the precondition for having markets in which there is complete competition as far as possible; where this is not possible, the state conducts the matter as if there was perfect competition.[27]

---

25. In Eucken's terminology, "Sperre" is a broadly applied term for anticompetitive behavior by powerful market players. It can mean blocking of certain suppliers, distribution channels, credit channels, or customers who purchase from one's competitor. Patents can also have a blocking property. On the labor market, blocking can appear as strikes and lockouts.

26. "Staats- und Finanzminister" in the original. *Staatsminister* usually designates a minister who is in charge of the central administration of a province.

27. In Eucken's terminology, the concept is called "complete competition" (*vollständige Konkurrenz*), as in the first part of the sentence. The assumptions of complete competition are less restrictive than the neoclassical assumptions of perfect competition (*vollkommene Konkurrenz*), a term which he hardly used in his writings.

In the following, I would like to briefly summarize the experiences gained in Germany:

In a centrally planned economy, the state determines the order of the economy. It directs—or tries to direct—the day-to-day economic process. In a free economy, the state takes care of the actual order of the economy only at certain points. There is a danger here that freedom will be abused in order to eventually kill freedom itself.

In the competitive order, the state is very interested in the order of the markets, but the economic process is free. In this way, the right balance of freedom and order is created.

Session 3

Tuesday, April 1st, 1947, 8.30 p.m.

"Free" Enterprise and Competitive Order (continued)

Professor IVERSEN: ~~Could we not~~ *It is impossible to* lay down what the rules are which should be adopted by the state monopoly.

Decisive ~~factor determining~~ *point is to determine* whether one method or another will lead to the most efficiency.

Professor EUCKEN:

1. If it were the question of placing a single monopoly in the hands of the government, would be one thing. But to transfer a number of monopolies to the government would be very different.
2. Government monopoly always a protected monopoly.
3. Government monopoly becomes one in the interests of the persons in charge of the monopoly.

Mr. MILLER: I would like to disagree with the idea that it makes no difference if even one monopoly is only one transferred to Government ownership. There is such a thing as competition for public favour.

~~**Professor ROBBINS:** Comments on the B.B.C.~~

Professor JEWKES: For the most part, we are now all prepared to accept that it is one function of the state to provide ~~some~~ *certain* services. *There* *is greater difficulty with regard to* employment policy *on which no agreement has yet been reached* in the learned journals.

Professor MISES: If it is true as has been suggested, that I am defending orthodoxy of the 18th century, then it is true that I am defending it against the orthodoxy of the 17th century.[1]

Interventionists all wanted different types of interventionism. Therefore they thought they were in opposition.

~~Great official bankruptcy can no longer be avoided.~~

States have monopolies, but a result of their use is not profits, but deficits.

U.S. Post Office, and New York subway, make deficits.

Governments don't want now to undertake more responsibilities and more burdens.

We have now confiscated about 70% of upper class income. Earlier, we used to regard upper class income as a fund from which we could pay for the services which were planned by the government. But now that 70% has been confiscated anyway, we cannot use this any more for new purposes. We are living in loop-hole capitalism.

We are discussing monopolies from the viewpoint that governments are against monopoly. But they are not!

Governments are monopoly-governments.

They don't like cartels if they are not owned by the government. But they are enthusiastic about commodity control agreements. In the case of commodity control agreements, U.S. are the exploited consumers, with the exception of cotton controls. The consumer knows what he buys. He is not influenced by advertising.

Professor HAYEK: Question of whether, when there are monopolies of one type or another, they are better in the hands of the government or not.

Also, question of whether powers of income taxation should be used to bring about a redistribution of income.

---

1. Mises is contrasting the economic liberalism of eighteenth-century scholars like David Hume and Adam Smith with mercantilist writers of the seventeenth century.

Any proposal to redistribute income is in itself an interference.

Is there a point, once you start towards redistribution of income by taxation, where you can stop short of a totally planned economy?

Must distinguish between interfering with wages and with fixing minimum wages within a market economy. This latter is an interference, but leaves relative scales unchanged.

Professor ROBBINS: We agree with Professor Mises that most of the interventions of the state in regard to the working of the market mechanism have been bad. I hope we should agree with Professor Mises also that one of our main tasks is to re-educate the world to understand the functions performed by the market and by free enterprise.

Two questions:

1. It was an essential principle of the idea of a competitive society that freedom of contract should not be allowed to destroy freedom of contract.
2. We recommend to the people of the world a more favourable consideration of the free play of the market.

They reply "your free enterprise tends to coagulate into monopoly". To which we reply, many manifestations of monopoly have been deliberately fostered by the state, and we should like these manifestations to disappear.

Possible at the moment in England for evil conspiracy between employers and trade unions so as to prevent other employers from getting labour, or raw materials.[2]

---

2. Hayek had warned in *The Road to Serfdom* (1944), "The recent growth of monopoly is largely the result of a deliberate collaboration of organized capital and organized labor where the privileged groups of labor share in the monopoly profits at the expense of the community and particularly at the expense of the poorest, those employed in less-well-organized industries and the unemployed." See F. A. Hayek, *The Road to Serfdom: Text and Documents*, ed. Bruce Caldwell, vol. 2 of *The Collected Works of F. A. Hayek* (Chicago: University of Chicago Press; London: Routledge, 2007), 207. The intense winter of 1946–47 and widespread manpower and material shortages, particularly in coal, may have prompted instances of the behavior of which Robbins complained. See Susan Howson, *Lionel Robbins* (Cambridge: Cambridge University Press, 2011), 656–58.

Professor MISES: All the trouble with monopolies springs from the way in which government policy is fostering monopoly. Why do people attack the monopoly, and not the patent law, the tariff, etc?

Professor GRAHAM: I fear that Professor Mises is 100% wrong in his answer to Professor Robbins.

Perfect freedom exists in the jungle.

There is no law there.

I think if we carry out the suggestions of Professor Mises we shall be in the jungle.

We are here met to find the middle road between the jungle and the jail. It seems to involve a very careful consideration of what the government ought to do, and how much it ought to do.

It seems to me that unless the government takes the active role to maintain competition, competition will not be maintained. Function of the government to see that nobody is able to coerce anyone else.

So far as we must give some powers to the government, we must make them 100% powers, e.g. government says how much money shall be worth so much gold.

Our task to see that we extend the realm of individual freedom just as far as we can, and curtail individual freedom which results in jungle conditions.

Professor POLANYI: Certain collective needs are satisfied by the state, and individuals have to pay. Are there ~~are~~ any principles of the market by which principles of taxation can be determined? Or are the social considerations right in determining types of taxation?

Professor FRIEDMAN: We are all opposed to the government-created monopolies. ~~But t~~Those things are only passed over because we are <u>all</u> opposed to them.

However, where we differ:—

1. in finding out the truth
2. in the best way of presenting the matter to the public.

Mr. HAZLITT: The biggest problem of monopoly is of government-created monopoly.

What are the specific rules going to be for government-created monopoly?

Problem is much simpler in dealing with labour unions.

What we have in the United States is an administrative law which is capricious, and sometimes actually malicious.

Professor RAPPARD: What are the limits to the rights which Professor Mises thinks essential?

Mr. DE JOUVENEL: Should the corporation be treated as an individual?

Professor MISES: Should society be based on public ownership, or private? There is nothing between them which is possible for a permanent society.

I am in favour of private enterprise. If consumers buy something, so that a firm increases in size, I don't want someone to come along and prevent them from enjoying the results of this.

Taxes: In a capitalist country where state expenditure is low, it doesn't matter very much about principles of taxation.

Professor GIDEONSE: I think Professor Mises has only answered the questions he wanted to answer, not the questions he was asked.

Professor TINGSTEN: I think it would be better to discuss a more reasonable type of liberalism. And I don't think it is right to say that we are all opposed to state monopolies.

Professor MISES: We are discussing the limitations of the size of business. There is only one privilege possessed by the corporation—the rights of the creditors are limited. Corporations are at the root of a great deal of progress, so why should we be against them?

Professor DIRECTOR: I don't think we shall ever get anywhere in defining what the rules of the game should be, if we don't know whether there should be any rules at all. Professor Mises seems to think that past rules are good rules. I should like to know "How far back".

~~References to why Ford may go out of business: — new firm is in the field. But it may not stay in, because of the distributive problems in normal times (Problems which are not operative at the moment).~~

Session 4

Wednesday, April 2nd, 1947, 9.30 a.m.

Modern Historiography and Political Education

Professor Robbins in the chair.

Miss WEDGWOOD (MS): I understand that after the animated argument of last night, this morning's session is to be a colling [*sic*] off process. I do not know whether that hope, expressed yesterday evening, has anything to do with what I take to be my status in this Conference. Professor Hayek in his opening words told us that he had assembled, as a kind of general leavening of this body, as well as many economists who were liberals, some liberals who were not economists. That certainly goes for me. But it would be a mistake to get the idea that history cannot generate as much passion as economics. It can generate as much, or even more. Indeed its power to generate passion is one of the cardinal points that I feel this Conference should consider this morning.

The subject before us is Historiography and Political Education. Before going any further I must follow the practice of the best philosophers and define my terms. By historiography I mean, in this context, the practice of the writing of history, and I shall extend the writing of history to take in every sort and kind of historical writing, from the most learned to the most superficial, from the rigidly academic to the frankly propagandist.

By "Political Education" I mean the instruction and persuasion in the widest possible sense of the literate and—in democratic countries—the voting population.

I am interpreting the title of this morning's discussion thus widely so as to make as broad a base as possible on which I hope that many others will build up something more detailed and concrete in the next two hours.

Generalisations, though they are usually very poor history, are useful in acting as spring-boards for ideas and discussion. That must be one reason for this form of approach. Another, and perhaps a better one, lies in the nature of my own recent experience. Seven years of interruption in serious historical work somewhat inhibits me from talking about the technical details of historiography; <u>en revanche</u> experience inside publishers' offices and newspaper offices, and with the much abused B.B.C. has taught me a great deal of value about the average capacity and—more important—the average incapacity of human minds to absorb facts, to understand facts, and to make deductions from facts.

Now Historiography and Political Education—in the end—means simply this: the way in which past facts have been presented to the public, and the way in which the public, in its various sections, has received and used these facts, absorbed them, understood them, and made deductions from them.

I need hardly dilate on the apalling [*sic*] effects of the use of history as propaganda over the last century and in particular in the last generation or so, effects which made H. G. Wells speak of the "poison of history" and in the moments when he wasn't writing Histories of the World (or of the Roman Catholic Church) suggest that it ought to be eliminated altogether.[1]

---

1. Though remembered today for his science fiction, H. G. Wells (1866–1946) was also famous in his time as a progressive public intellectual and for his popular historical writings. Revised multiple times over his lifetime, his *The Outline of History: Being a Plain History of Life and Mankind* (New York: Macmillan, 1920) recounted then known scientific facts about the origin and development of Earth and mankind. A similar work whose title gave rise to Wedgwood's comment was his *A Short History of the World* (New York: Macmillan, 1922). In 1939 Wells gave an address before the Education Section of the Australian/New Zealand Association for the Advancement of Science titled "The Poison of History" in which he derided the nationalist emphasis in most historical teaching and promoted an approach that

I would not myself even go so far as this because great as is the harm done by some sorts of history it yet remains a great humane study, possibly the great humane study, and the best school of politics and political psychology.

But in any case it cannot be eliminated because people <u>will</u> have it. You can eliminate the historian but not the interest and fascination of the past. If people are not given history they will invent it, and they may invent it badly, or at least fall victims to bad inventions. This indeed is one of our dangers, not the forcible elimination of the historian, but the voluntary elimination of the historian by himself. For there is a strong tendency of scholars to withdraw from the public and popular field. This has two effects: 1. that it raises the standards of research, and 2. that it has a very bad effect on the public. Growing public for history, its particular charm, distinction between fiction and non-fiction in the lending libraries. Growing public for history in the form of non-fiction works from the lending libraries, and for historical novels. Publicists and propagandists have seen and taken advantage of this. But historians naturally remain shy. They hesitate to take advantage of the means at present to hand for two reasons: 1. because of their misuse by vulgarisers and political enemies, and 2. because they necessitate compromises with the standards of care which we need.

But should I not talk more of historians? What has historiography to do with these wretched vulgarians? The historiography which interests us here has much to do with it.

The first reason for hesitation is understandable but untenable, and the second is a challenge, and which constitutes a duty for <u>some</u> historians.

The place of the scholar, <u>pur sang</u> is of course essential.[2] But the publicist-historian must come back.

I speak of history as a vehicle of propaganda—but <u>it always is</u>. There is a danger of not recognising this. The only safeguard is free competition between historians and pure propagandists—the historian will tend to win. Conscience and moral values.

---

would focus on the human species as a whole. During the war he penned the polemical *Crux Ansata: An Indictment of the Roman Catholic Church* (Harmondsworth: Penguin, 1943) which, in addition to being highly critical of Pope Pius XII, contained a biting history of the church.

2. *Pur sang* is French for "pure-blooded."

There is no guarantee of historians' political views—these dangers are always present—but they are minimised by the presence of <u>many</u> writers giving the public a choice. Then the public must see that there are different ways of looking at questions. And this is the greatest value of history in political education. (Connection with liberal ideas). Not only two sides to questions but several different ways of looking at events—interpreted in masses, movements, statistics, or individuals.

Emphasis on the individual, dangers and advantages.

Before ending—one word about historical myths, legends and mis-understandings—there is room for much study here. The method and reasons for growth of these myths.

These legends <u>will</u> come; and historians are responsible for them. They must recognise that responsibility however distasteful and minimise its dangers by taking (but only those who have the temperament) a full share in it. Modern historiography has an immense part to play in political education, but it must accept the challenges of a situation which is distasteful to scholars. All historians should have the courage of their convictions, liberals most of all, because liberals put moral and conscience values first and these are the only just criteria.

Professor Antoni: Manuscript not received[3]

Dr. Eyck: I agree that the learned historian has a duty to the public, and that although there must be historians who write for other historians only, there must also be others who write for the public. The danger of the distortion of history was never greater than in the last few generations. How much history has to do with political education I think the political history of Germany in the 19th century shows quite clearly. The struggle which filled the 19th century in Germany, the struggle between Prussia and Austria, was determined largely by the historians of the two parties. They ~~Heuser Züber, Dreusen. F~~filled the minds of the German public with the doctrine of the German mission of Prussia since 1848, when the question of Austria or Prussia was put for the first time.

---

3. The intervention by Tingsten below indicates that Professor Antoni did provide some opening remarks but that they went undocumented.

This historical doctrine has brought with it exaggeration, especially the glorification of the Prussian crown, and in this way has enforced one of the forces in German public life which has done much to destroy liberal docrine [sic] in Germany. It is one of the great arts of Bismark [sic] that he built up himself that legend of the Prussian crown to use it for his own political purposes. Most people know now that Bismarck was the originator of the Franco-Prussian war. But Bismarck had played with such an almost superhuman skill that at the time of the war not only the Germans but also many Frenchmen believed that the real originator was a Frenchman.

Bismarck used for political purposes what he knew was historically untrue.

Harnack—"The Legend is the curse of history."[4]

Historiography's task: to show how things really were. The historian who tries to show that will always find a public among the simple men and women who read history only for his or her own information.

I agree with Miss Wedgwood in stressing the need to bring out the moral values in history. The real value of history is in showing the reader the importance of freedom in the past, the present and in the future.

Professor TINGSTEN: I don't agree with Professor Antoni. I think we have better historians now than in the 19th century. But we haven't the same number of brilliant generalisations of history. Study of detail, with truth as the only criterion, is much better now. I think this is of some importance. I think there is a lot of good popular history, in Sweden, England, and U.S.A.: Trevelyan, Becker, Nevins, etc.[5]

---

4. Adolph von Harnack (1851–1930) was a German theologian and church historian who sought to use historical criticism to strip away the myths and legends associated with Christianity to reach its true essence. The final sentence of his *History of Dogma*, vol. 1, makes the point well: "In point of fact, actual history is often more wonderful and capricious than legends and fables." See Adolph von Harnack, *The History of Dogma*, trans. Neil Buchanan, vol. 1, 2nd ed., app. 3 (London: Williams and Norgate, 1897), 362.

5. George Macaulay Trevelyan (1876–1962), grandnephew of Thomas Babington Macaulay, was a Whig historian in the tradition of both his relative and of Lord Acton, with whom he studied at Cambridge and to whose chair he later succeeded. Trevelyan defended a more literary approach to his subjects over the academic "scientific history" of his day and reached a wide audience: his *England under the Stuarts* (London: Methuen, 1904) was the most popular

It has been said that "If myths are not put forward by philosophers, then they will be put forward by other people, and then they will be worse myths. Therefore they should be put forward by philosophers."[6] But I don't think this is true.

It is not always so simple to combine history as truth plus moral values. I think it would be better to concentrate on truth, and not on moral values.

Professor HAYEK: I question whether strict adherence to truth and scientific principles is enough. There are two major dangers which have existed for a very long time. Both are due to ~~error:~~ *two mistaken ideas:*

1. idea that there are inevitable laws of development which history is out to discover

2. ~~result of an attempt~~ *belief that it is possible* to keep value judgments out of historical writing.

This would lead to criterion purely of success or non-success. Citation of Carlyle and John Stuart Mill[7]

---

volume in Methuen's History of England series, reprinted twenty-two times. For more, see Joseph Hernon Jr., "The Last Whig Historian and Consensus History: George Macaulay Trevelyan, 1876–1962," *American Historical Review* 81 (February 1976), 66–97. Carl Becker (1873–1945) was an American historian who was propelled into fame with his *The Heavenly City of the Eighteenth-Century Philosophers* (New Haven, CT: Yale University Press, 1932). In his presidential address before the American Historical Association, he, too, criticized the nineteenth-century penchant for "scientific history." See Becker's "Every Man His Own Historian" in *Everyman his Own Historian: Essays on History and Politics* (New York: F. S. Crofts, 1935), 233–55. Allan Nevins (1890–1971) was an American historian and journalist who won Pulitzer Prizes for his well-crafted biographies of Grover Cleveland and of Hamilton Fish, the US secretary of state in the Grant administration. Nevins created the first oral history program in the United States at Columbia University.

6. The quotation is evidently a paraphrase. It is suggestive of Socrates's words in *The Republic* regarding the education of future Guardians, where he insisted that rather than let them "hear any casual tales which may be devised by casual persons . . . the first thing will be to establish a censorship of the writers of fiction, and let the censors receive any tale of fiction which is good, and reject the bad; and we will desire mothers and nurses to tell their children the authorized ones only"; Plato, *Republic*, Book 2, 377, in *The Dialogues of Plato*, trans. B. Jowett, vol. 1 (New York: Random House, 1937).

7. Dorothy Hahn's rendering of Hayek's comment is opaque, but regarding Mill, in his essay "The Counter-Revolution of Science," first published in 1942–44 and reprinted in *Studies on the Abuse and Decline of Reason*, ed. Bruce Caldwell, vol. 13 of *The Collected Works of F. A. Hayek* (Chicago: University of Chicago Press; London: Routledge, 2010), Hayek blamed him

Professor TINGSTEN: I think there are two quite different things we have talked about. History <u>should</u> make value judgments. But historian should not make history other than as it really was.

Dr. POPPER: I think Professor Tingsten leads us away from our problem, and to the problem of what is history.

There is one Aarrow pointing from history to political education. But I think the arrow runs mainly in the opposite direction. We cannot be historically educated without being politically educated. Political education is needed in order to select the problems of history which we want to study. It is not possible to study history, just seeking truth, and then to derive one's political views from the truth of history. There is no clash between truth-finding and selectivity in history. But the principle which Dr. Eyck mentioned, i.e. to tell history as it really happened, is just impossible. We would have to take about twenty times as long to tell it as is possible. We must tell it in a short time, and therefore we must be selective. Therefore we must have views on the subject. We must therefore pay attention to historical myth, but not imposing our opinions on history without saying that we are doing it.

Professor MISES: Real problem of history is that to tell things as they really were is impossible in an <u>objective</u> way. I want to say that it is not the problem of value judgments, but the problem of relevance, which is important. "History of America in the last 50 years has clearly proved that a protective tariff is needed for industrial development." This is what all the economic historians outside the U.S.A. say about the problem.

As soon as you have a difference in social philosophy, you have a difference in interpretation of the facts.

---

for helping to spread to England the positivist doctrines of Auguste Comte, among them the idea that there are natural laws governing the development of the human race: "Mill himself, in the sixth book of his *Logic* [*A System of Logic* (1843)], which deals with the methods of the moral sciences, became little more than an expounder of Comtean doctrine" (p. 278). In his *On Heroes, Hero-Worship, and the Heroic in History* (London: James Fraser, 1841), Thomas Carlyle (1795–1881) developed a "great man" approach to historical writing that celebrated the heaven-inspired seer or hero who by understanding the eternal laws of the universe could take transformative action.

Not a problem of partiality and propaganda—it is impossible to derive from history an a posteriori theory. You must have the theory a priori.

Professor ROEPKE: I want to locate our discussion and to stress its general significance. We want to find a general theory of liberty. There is the problem of the relation between economic liberalism and general liberalism. I think there is a very close relation. I think it is an [sic] relationship between ends and means. What we discuss under the heading of economic liberalism is a matter of means, rather than of ends. History in terms of a whole significance has been brought home to us today. What we mean in the liberal idea is that first of all we want to find out the truth, including the truth about ourselves.

Professor RAPPARD: One of the many reasons why I so profoundly enjoyed listening to Miss Wedgwood was that she was a historian talking about history. I agree very strongly with her division of historians into two classes. I think good historians should join battle with bad historians, but not by using the same bad methods, of which the good historian disapproves. It would of course be impossible to give a complete history of everything that happened. You must choose. I don't think there are conflicting loyalties between truth and anything else. The historian is perfectly free to decide the question he wishes to discuss. For the academic administrator, he also must see in history an element of political education. The history of countries other than one's own should be taught. There is a very great virtue in the honest writing of history. But the example of the honest historian who is honestly seeking for truth is the essence of a liberal education. History for truth, not history for use.

Professor BARTH: What is a fact?
A fact is a result, not a beginning of exploration, but only an end. The interference of subjectivity here cannot be put away. The text only speaks to us if we ask it something, and if we put the answer into a larger context.
Our values decide what we ask from the text (as Dr. Popper has pointed out).

Professor EUCKEN: I should like to make some remarks on the acquisition of historical knowledge. The facts are not the beginning but the result of historical search. How do we interpret documents or texts? We ask definite questions and these questions are determined by definite values and subjective views. It is only thus that we can get definite answers. Are there any values which are above question? There is always the problem what is the ultimate value which all accept. We are forced to assume that there is something unconditional. This leads us inevitably to the problem of religion.

Three stages are essential in every interpretation of history. Every philosophy does in fact pass through these three stages. The most difficult problem is what we can do with regard to the unconditional. It evades formulation in words. All we can speak about are the human needs.

Ranke's conception of eliminating the self is impossible.[8] In a sense a maximum of subjectivity guarantees a maximum of objectivity.

Professor KNIGHT: Economic history needs to be written by people who know more about economics, than is common at the moment.

To make anything interesting to a large public, you have to put in much more order than is really there in the facts. You have to use humanistic approach also.

Reviving theory of natural law. Natural law is very important. But with the revival of natural law it is still perfectly possible to have a dynamic theory of natural law.

Dr. EYCK: I don't deny the truth of what Dr. Popper said. But that doesn't change anything in the quotation of Ranke's which I gave—"Wie es eigentlich gewesen ist".

---

8. Leopold von Ranke (1795–1886) was perhaps the most influential historian of the nineteenth century. In seeking to describe "how things actually were," which is how his famous quotation (repeated by Eyck) may be translated, he emphasized the use of primary-source archival materials. He taught for fifty years at the University of Berlin and in his seminar trained many later important historians.

It is not true that all historians go for the same goal, and only differ in the interpretation of the facts. It is an absolute sin for a historian to leave out relevant facts.

Professor ANTONI: Need for political toleration.

The historian's work is always subjective.

One cannot believe in the work of a great historian, if one doesn't share his faith.

Miss WEDGWOOD: I didn't mean to imply that liberals should sit down and make up a liberal myth of history.

"Die Legende ist der Ungluck der Geschichte"[9]

I agree with Professor Rappard on the subject of the liberals using the "same weapons". I don't want the liberals to use the same bad methods which they condemn others for using.

---

9. "The legend is the misfortune of history." This appears to be a restatement of Adolph von Harnack's warnings that were noted in footnote 4.

Session 5

Wednesday, April 2nd, 1947, 4.30 p.m.

The Future of Germany[1]

Professor Iversen in the chair.

Professor ROEPKE: The horizontal distinction, in the war, apart from the vertical distinction going through national frontiers.

The problem of Europe is Germany, and the problem of the world is Europe.

The German problem ~~is~~ *must be seen* in terms of the most elementary needs. We may therefore be forced to define liberalism, for Germany, purely as being the state of non-totalitarianism, and of decentralisation. Dissolving the lumps of power.

I must say first that the famous Stuttgart speech of Mr. Byrnes of last autumn unfortunately did not bring about results which had been expected on all parts.[2] The main thing that happened was the merger of

---

1. A thirty-eight-page paper by Röpke titled "Some Notes on the German Problem" appears to have been distributed at the conference, but its substance is different from the remarks here so has not been reprinted.

2. US secretary of state James F. Byrnes delivered a speech, "Restatement of Policy on Germany," in Stuttgart on September 6, 1946. It became known as "The Speech of Hope" because it signaled the US desire for a unified self-governing democratic Germany, emphasized the importance of reconstruction to achieve the goal (thereby softening the previous stance that focused on reducing industrial capacity, particularly in industries that could allow

the American and British zones. Danger that the Moscow Conference is just one big red herring, and that it distracts attention from what ought to be done.[3] The cost of reviving the German economy is increasing in geometrical progression. Germany economy suffers from pernicious anaemia. I believe in federalism, but the present division of power is the reverse of a training for federalism. Any price policy is made almost impossible.

Purely a matter of chance whether the worker gets enough to live on or not. Will the Russians let down their barriers? I think that the Russians want to do so, but want to get the highest possible price for doing so.

If Germany were allowed to produce, the situation would be much better. But without industrial Germany being allowed to produce, the situation is disastrous.

Immediate problem is to make western zones a going concern again. Once this has been done, no further problem for western Germany.

The question is whether integration with the Eastern Zone under the Russians, is necessary or not. My answer is that it is not necessary.

Germany will still need help for a long time. But this help should now be put on a sound basis. It should be in terms of an investment. Therefore any help which only prolongs the illness of the patient is only wasted.

Drastic monetary reform, in the form of a drastic deflation, is needed. Then you can ask the French whether they would like to join in with the policy. Establish industrial activity, and "normalcy." Then ask the Russians whether they would also like to join, but invite them on your own terms.[4]

---

a revival of military capabilities), and assured Germans that the United States would not withdraw its own troops so long as any occupation army (this was clearly aimed at the Soviet Union) was present. Röpke was distressed that, aside from the subsequent joining of the British and American zones, Byrnes's insistence that "zonal barriers should be completely obliterated" to allow "the free exchange of commodities, people and ideas throughout Germany" had not happened.

3. The Moscow Conference refers to the meeting of the Council of Foreign Ministers (representing the Soviet Union, England, France, and the United States) that was then taking place to determine the terms of the peace treaties for Germany and Austria. The meeting would end in a stalemate, prompting Secretary of State George Marshall, in a speech at Harvard on June 5, 1947, to call for a program to rebuild Europe. The European Recovery Program—or Marshall Plan—was passed by Congress the next year.

4. When the Bizone was created, an open invitation to both France and the Soviet Union was tendered, but they declined to join.

Deflation of administrative personel [*sic*], as drastic as the deflation of the currency, is also greatly needed.

Politically, don't wait for the actual peace treaty.

Russians are trying to cajole the Allies into a situation which would deliver to that power the dominant position, and this to be done by the Lublin trick.[5]

Professor EUCKEN: I agree with Professor Roepke on the most essential points except one to be mentioned later. Confining myself to the economic problem, I will begin by supplementing Roepke's remarks with an account of my personal experience. It was very surprising that occupation did not mean the end of the Nazi system. Their price and distribution system was preserved in all detail and with only little change in personel [*sic*]. The only new fact was the division into zones, with the Länder forming sub-zones.[6] In a planned economy, such a division into political zones means something different from what it would have meant under a liberal regime. It means a complete division of the economic system, and creates small separate economic units. The present development shows that the planned economy of the separate states is so inefficient that it decays. The rations are so small that nobody, literally nobody, can live on them. In consequence, side by side with the planned economy, a separate unofficial economic structure is growing up. I will consider its main features in turn.

I. 1. The general growth of barter. The latest development is that employers are required to pay their workers partly in goods. The Military Government of the French Zone requires that in the textile and aluminium industries the workers must get 10% of their wages in products. Sewing thread or pots and pans are generally used in barter, although the farmer who accepts them

---

5. The Lublin trick refers to the Lublin-Brest Offensive, which took place within Operation Bagration, a military campaign fought between the Soviet Union and Germany in the summer of 1944. The Soviets successfully camouflaged where on the front they would attack, repeatedly causing the German high command to misallocate its resources. Röpke was suggesting a similar strategy was being employed by the Soviets at the Moscow Conference, then taking place.

6. "Länder" refers to the federal states of Germany. Such states formed subzones within the ones imposed by the Allies.

for food is punishable. Deliveries of agricultural products still
constantly decline.

2. A new money is gradually springing up, brandy being used in
the larger transactions and cigarettes in the smaller. A car for
instance will be worth 180 bottles of brandy.

3. The home production of potatoes and vegetables on allotments
is expanding, but this use of labour is very inefficient.

To compress all this in a slogan, the German economy is undergoing a
progressive primitivisation and now corresponds rather to the economic
system of the 6th and 8th centuries. Trading is limited to narrow locali-
ties, which in a highly industrialised economy must result in very low
productivity.

II. Full employment prevails, and an enormous amount of work is
done with very little result. In a short conversation I had with
Lord Beveridge in a room below freezing point he asked what do
people do?[7] My answer was that they spend their time going to
the countryside to barter, with the return of an excursion being
infinitesimal, such as single potatoes or half a pound of grain. A
thousand people thus achieve in a day what a single trader could
do in a few hours. People stand for hours in queues, or do repairs
at home. If we regard it as desirable that the pursuit of people's private interest should produce the largest output, it must be admitted that at present in Germany the unavoidable result of people's
endeavour to preserve life is contrary to collective interests.

Concerning the present position of industry, it had for a long time not
been realised that even at the end of the war German industry still com-
manded comparatively large stocks of raw materials which were deliberately preserved for the return of peace. They are now exhausted. A great
deal of work is being done for reparation purposes, but in many industries as for instance in textiles, this is almost all. The commodities thus

---

7. "Full employment prevails . . . with very little result" was an ironic commentary on Sir
William Beveridge's full-employment policy as articulated in his *Full Employment in a Free
Society* (London: Allen and Unwin, 1944).

produced are paid for at unknown official prices which are then credited to reparation account. The only exceptions are orders to work against a fixed remuneration on raw materials supplied by foreign firms. In fact only agriculture works for German needs, but there is nothing which the farmer can be given in return.

Observing the economic policy of the occupying powers as a German, it is obvious that there are many far-seeing individuals who recognise the seriousness of the situation, but it must also be said that there are among them under the name of technical experts, parties representing particular interests which exercise great influence and use their power to obstruct the reconstruction of the Germany economy. This is true also of the British zone where the destruction of particular works is sometimes due to the influence of such special interests. The developments in the iron industry are a good example of this.[8] There exists the clear contrast between the interests of these particular groups and those of the Allied powers as a whole. These special interests obstruct even inter-zonal trade.

What is to be done? The planned economy is evidently collapsing. The only hope is to restore the market economy. How is this possible? The first need is a decision on the reform of the currency. There can be no division of labour without a functioning currency system. Some suggest that this reform must be postponed till there are more commodities available. But postponement only reduces supplies. This reform is urgent, but other measures are required at the same time. The currency reform cannot be an isolated measure. The new money must at once be linked up with foreign currencies, which would rapidly help to restore trade. The consideration of any particular industry as for instance of the machine tools industry in

---

8. In December 1946 an emergency delivery scheme was initiated in the British zone as part of the reparations program. It stipulated that only surplus nonspecialized equipment whose removal would not seriously reduce productive capacity be taken and specified a list of eligible plants. Instead, British officials commonly selected the best and most modern specialized equipment for removal, often from plants that were not on the official list. As Nicholas Balabkins recounted in his *Germany under Direct Controls, Economic Aspects of Industrial Disarmament, 1945–1948* (New Brunswick, NJ: Rutgers University Press, 1964), 141: "Since most of the machinery removed went to Great Britain, the German business community gained the impression that one of the main purposes of the program was the crippling of German industry to eliminate a potential British competitor."

Baden, makes this obvious. Next, foreign credites [sic] will be available, but they need not and ought not to be of an eleemosynory [sic] nature. Purely commercial arrangements are possible, particularly in the form of "Lohnauf träge."9

Finally the small point of difference from Roepke. It concerns the relation of the Eastern zone, where I should be afraid to be as radical as Roepke. At this moment common action may be impracticable. But it is very important, politically and economically, that the East be no [sic] written off or abandoned for good. The East now begins at the Weser. It is necessary to continue negotiations.

The classical economists regarded it as a weakness of the individual that he does not always regard his true interests. They do not recognise their common interest of regaining Germany to the Western system. The present tendency to keep Germany going for charitable reasons is very unhealthy. The Western powers ought to act on their own self-interest. That presupposes however that German industry is allowed to do something on its own initiative. And that she should not be dependent for everything on permits. At the moment Germany is half a corpse.

---

9. Eucken refers here to commercial arrangements in which subcontracting would take place.

Session 6

Wednesday, April 2nd, 1947, 8.30 p.m.

The Future of Germany (continued)

Professor EUCKEN: The monetary problem cannot be separated from the result. A functioning money is required to make the price system effective. But the price economy has broken down, and the present barter economy is insufficient. How can a real exchange system be restored? The first condition for this is monetary reform. At the moment when this reform is effected, confiscation (i.e. compulsory deliveries) must cease. At present, the farmer accepts money only to keep his customers but he cannot get anything for the money. With the appearance of a new money which people trust, it will again be possible to buy things for it. This will bring a great rise in prices of agricultural products. The objection that this will lead to starvation I should have taken much more seriously some time ago, but now bare life already depends upon bartering.

Further, if rationing and the price stop are maintained, the only effect will be that there will be no supplies. The official low prices reduce what is available in the market.

I believe prices must be allowed to rise but only if at the same time a free market and international trade are resumed. This is admittedly a risky policy, but without such an attempt there is no prospect of any improvement, and the only thing which will start the process of improvement is currency reform.[1]

Professor BRANDT: If we were to go in to [sic] Germany, we would all be shocked at what we saw. Decay of the liberal economy in which we are all interested. It would be wrong to say that the responsibility for the decay in Germany is solely that of the occupying powers. But at the moment there is of course a certain amount of this responsibility.

Influx of people being repatriated, bringing with them into Germany nothing in the way of material goods, but only disease. This has, of course, merely made the situation worse. Great gap in the amount of capital equipment, which will take eight or ten years to replace. It would, therefore, have been a miracle for the occupying powers to have brought about a high standard of living within such a short time.

Attempt to prevent a recurrence of war. Fear of the public sentiments still smouldering in those parts of the world. Germans used to have 3,000 calories, of which 600 were imported. Owing to restoration of land to Poland, this was cut by 700 calories per head.[2] Therefore, if agriculture were still in the same state as pre-war, there would be 1,700 calories per head. But yields in Germany have decreased by another 640 calories per

---

1. Eucken's controversial recommendations—a combination of currency reform, which took the form of the replacement of the existing Reich marks with a much smaller supply of Deutsche marks, and the removal of price controls—actually comprised those undertaken in June 1948 that led to the German economic recovery, the so-called *Wirtschaftswunder* or "economic miracle."

2. Following agreements at the Potsdam Conference, after the war all German land east of the Oder-Neisse line was returned to Poland or granted to the Soviet Union, and all ethnic Germans were expelled. The lands included such heavily agricultural territories as the province of Posen. Germany lost huge amounts of arable land and with it the ability to feed its population. Brandt's statements were not exaggerated. President Harry Truman commissioned former president Herbert Hoover to undertake a tour of Europe to judge the food situation there, and in a series of reports in early 1947 he offered the following bleak assessment: "There is the illusion that the New Germany left after the annexations can be reduced to a 'pastoral state.' It cannot be done unless we exterminate or move 25,000,000 out of it." See Herbert Hoover, *The President's Economic Mission to Germany and Austria, Report No. 3, The Necessary Steps for Promotion of German Exports, So as to Relieve American Taxpayers of the Burdens of Relief and for Economic Recovery of Europe* (Unknown publisher: 1947), 12.

head (if you had the full truncated Germany in full production). Another 160 calories lost due to clumsy methods of agrarian reform. Therefore, less than 1,000 calories per head, if you had equal distribution among the various zones. If we could increase yields to 1935–39 level, there would be 1,600 calories per head. If the area east of the Oder is lost for good, will create a problem of exports which will be very great.

45 millions left in the three zones.

The catastrophe which has befallen the industrial country of Germany has no equal whatever in history.

France gets coal from Germany. But pays by crediting marks. This is, of course, no use to Germany whatever. Germany needs iron now, <u>not</u> credits in marks.

An honest attempt <u>is</u> being made to denazify Germany. The proceedure [*sic*] that has been chosen turns out to be against the intentions of those who have shaped them a re-nazification of Germany.

After destruction of physical assets, the Allies' policy brought about the destruction of personal capital. That is, if anyone had invested under the Nazis, it was taken for granted that the person was persona gratissima with the Nazis. Rate at which the tribunals work is <u>very</u> slow. Germans talk of "Hitler's 1000 years' Reich, 14 years of Nazism, 986 years of denazification". By this slow rate, you are not getting rid of Nazis. And they are not permitted to work. Their children suffer. And the system will have a very bad effect on the children, who will have as a result a hatred of the Allies and of their methods.[3]

I think you should decimate, and give the rest an amnesty. If you wish, you could put a special tax on the other people who would have to go through the tribunal.

On currency question, I disagree with Professor Eucken. Unless you feed into Germany food and textile raw materials, and other raw materials, I am convinced that the new currency will have the same rejection by the consumers.

---

3. Hayek had voiced similar complaints about the effects of the postwar occupation in Austria in such pieces as "Austria: Advance Post in Europe," *Commercial and Financial Chronicle* 164, no. 4546 (November 28, 1946): 2745, 2782; and "Re-Nazification at Work," *The Spectator*, January 31, 1947: 134–35.

I would like to ask Professor Eucken what he thinks is the right time for the removal of the price controls.

Professor ROBBINS: I know of no properly instructed person at home who would argue at this point of time that the policy of a price stop was a wise policy.[4] But I do not think the consumption rationing system can be removed. But price stop can only be removed on grounds of politics. The policy of the price stop was inaugurated at beginning of war as a purely temporary measure. Inflation was under way, and it was wanted to prevent further inflation.

Suggestion was made that a central wage control should be introduced. But this was unacceptable to the trade unions. It was at the end of the war that our difficulties of wages and cost of living really began. The various restraints ceased to apply. Cost of living remained constant, but wages rose another 20% during the next year. Present position: wages level 60—65% above level when price stop was introduced, but cost of living is still the same.

Professor BRANDT: I did not intend to comment on the British situation. I would still cling to my notion that the possibility of establishing in Germany a free price market system, particularly with respect to food, without first having replenished the stocks, would absolutely lead to starvation, unless you took a large number of people and fed them on public relief.

Estimated that about 85% of the food produced goes through the official market.

Professor FRIEDMAN: No reason why the shortage of goods should bring about inflation.

Professor STIGLER: Is it misallocation, or *low* productivity, that causes low national income?

---

4. A "price stop" is a price ceiling, where the government places a limit on the maximum price suppliers are permitted to charge for a commodity. During wartime such price controls are often put into effect to prevent inflation, but because they lead to excess demand at the controlled prices, they also typically require the imposition of a rationing system. All this occurred in Britain during the war, and the system of rationing remained for years after the war ended.

Professor HAYEK: ~~In Germany at this moment, any money income which represents purchasing power is substantially in excess of official rations. You cannot on a free market have a money income to produce enough, and yet at the same time to let the lower classes have enough to live on.~~

Professor EUCKEN: The situation would be different if we had a fixed amount of goods to distribute, but the central problem is the effect on current production. At present current production lacks direction. Expensive oak timber is used for fire-wood, and sometimes one brick works gets an enormous amount of coal while there is none available for the most urgent purposes. There is generally a most senseless use of resources, an intense misdirection. Above all, wheat and timber production continue to fall because their prices are controlled and at an unremunerative level.

Professor BRANDT: Miracle is not a black market, but that the farmer supplies anything at all. One day the sense of social discipline may leave the farmer, and then there would be a collapse. For, at the moment, the farmers give away food for nothing.

The question between Professor Eucken and myself is of the time when the new currency is to be established. I cannot see why the start of a new currency should necessarily lead to an improvement of the situation.

Professor FRIEDMAN: I think it a fallacy that a free market is something that rich nations can afford, but that poor nations must do without. I think the U.S. never had any reason to have any rationing or price control at all.

Professor RAPPARD: If it is right that the food is so short, liberalism should not be prejudiced by trying to establish a free market economy.

Professor ROBBINS: If Professor Rappard rests his case on the economics of siege, I beg leave to doubt whether it is possible to go all the way with him. In conditions of siege, you suspend the normal distributive mechanism, and you ration. Initial distribution of money would bring about in these circumstances a politically intolerable situation. But if the distribution of money were equal, there would be no case for rationing.

Professor GRAHAM: I think there are two questions:
of the shortage of commodities
of the relation of money to them.

If money is of no value whatever: farmers will have to get something for their products, if there is to be any exchange at all.

~~**Professor EUCKEN:**~~

Professor STIGLER: What would happen if Germany were excluded completely from trade with the rest of the world?

Professor BRANDT: It would leave no scope: in a few years, 35 millions would be dead.

Professor ROEPKE: ~~I would like to emphasise all that Professor Eucken said on denazification.~~
~~I think there are two problems:~~
~~Russia: solely a question of East and West~~
~~Economic and monetary reform in Germany.~~

Mont Pèlerin Society 1947 Photos

This is a selection of photographs that were in F. A. Hayek's copy of a commemorative album that was given to all of the participants following the first meeting of the Mont Pèlerin Society. Hayek had handwritten individuals' names beneath many of the pictures, and those were used to provide the captions in this section. The selected photographs show many but not all of the people who attended the meeting.

Friedrich Hayek

Wilhelm Röpke

Left to right: Bertrand de Jouvenel, William Rappard, and Karl Popper

Brochure for Hôtel du Parc, 1947

Left to right: Harry Gideonse (*back*), Karl Popper (*front*), Albert Hunold, and Lionel Robbins

Veronica Wedgwood and Frieda Hunold

Left to right: Hayek leading a session, Dorothy Hahn, *and in the first row,* William Rappard, Ludwig von Mises, Walter Eucken, and Carl Iversen (*with unidentified men in back row*)

Left to right: Ludwig von Mises, Walter Eucken, and Carl Iversen

Left to right: Carl Iversen, Frank Graham (*with unidentified man behind him*), Michael Polanyi, Henry Hazlitt, Felix Morley, Henri de Lovinfosse, and Karl Brandt

Left to right: John Jewkes, Leonard Read, Erich Eyck (*with unidentified man behind him*), Milton Friedman, Lionel Robbins, and Veronica Wedgwood

Aboard a train to Schwyz, *seated left to right, back to front:* Frank Knight with John Jewkes, Bertrand de Jouvenel (*with pipe*) with Michael Polanyi, and Loren "Red" Miller (*facing unidentified passenger*)

Front row, left to right: Trygve Hoff, Frank Knight, Maurice Allais, and Wilhelm Röpke. *Second row, the faces fully visible, left to right:* Stanley Dennison, Fritz Machlup, Eva Röpke and her daughter, and Carlo Antoni. *Back row, the faces fully visible, left to right:* Bertrand de Jouvenel, Lionel Robbins, and (*looking to her right*) Veronica Wedgwood.

Left to right: Carl Iversen, George Stigler, John Davenport, and Frank Graham

Left to right: Veronica Wedgwood, Frank Knight, Aaron Director (*with pipe*), Harry Gideonse, and Fritz Machlup

Friedrich Hayek and Dorothy Hahn

View of Lake Geneva from the hotel

Session 7

Thursday, April 3rd, 1947, 9.30 a.m.

The Problems and Chances of European Federation

Professor Allais in the chair.

Professor ALLAIS: Great error not to realise that Liberalism implies an international outlook.

1. Federation can't be accomplished at a single blow. There will still be separate states for some time to come.
2. Principle [*sic*] obstacle to federalism: the irrational attitude of so many people in saying "I am in favour of federalism, but other people are not, and therefore it is impossible."

Mr. DE JOUVENEL: (*Manuscript not received*)[1]

Professor ALLAIS: Not possible to envisage an international system based on national systems. Obstacles to the type of organisation of the U.S.A. Fundamental difficulties to a federation of western Europe.

---

1. From comments below it is clear that Jouvenel delivered opening remarks—Morley and Rappard both refer to them—but as the note indicates, he failed to send in a paper, if indeed a paper existed.

With respect to France: hopes of the mass of the people have profound justification.

Privilege of class. Would not say that public opinion is the <u>cause</u> for the difficulties to federation.

19th century was a century of <u>nationalism</u>, and the growth of nationalism. Growth of monopolies of power. These could not have arisen but for the growth of <u>nationalist</u> feeling.

If states remain sovereign, obstacles to free exchange of goods, men, capital, etc. will remain powerful.

Mr. DE LOVINFOSSE: Two types of union are possible, the economic and the political. Belgium's road is towards economic union.[2]

Union shows way to international development.

We would have to envisage a European union with common laws in two phases, the first phase being economic, when the separate economies would become interdeveloped, and the second phase being political. This division into two phases would be nearer to the practical possibilities.

Professor ALLAIS: ~~Customs union between Belgium and the Low Countries. Impossible to discuss everything at once, in view of the time available.~~

~~Enormous difficulties, however, for economic union between the industrial and agricultural states. Quotas system as one possible measure.~~

Mr. DE LOVINFOSSE: We must not forget that the monetary and capital situation of the different countries has been very badly and very differently affected by the war.

We cannot judge the problem of customs union, ~~in~~ *at* this moment when the countries, differently affected by the war, especially with respect

---

2. The Belgium-Luxembourg Economic Union (BLEU) was a customs union based on a treaty signed in 1921 and put into effect in 1922. A fixed exchange rate between the Belgian and Luxembourgian francs was established, though the rate was revised in 1935 and 1944. The treaty lasted for fifty years, then was extended in 1972, 1982, and 1992, with the exchange rate mechanism remaining in place until adoption of the euro.

to food, ~~constitute~~ *are in* an exceptional situation. Union could only be effected by a war, or by a victory.

I don't think one can bring about an immediate political union.

After Belgium-Holland union, perhaps France, Denmark, etc. might join in, first economically, then politically.

Professor IVERSEN: Economic aspect first. Enormous advantages in abolishing trade walls between the different countries. I do not feel convinced that for purely economic reasons we are justified in insisting on a complete economic union.

It is sometimes true that countries having a common frontier may have very close economic relationship, but on the other hand the relationship may be even greater between one of those countries and another country somewhere else, e.g. low freight rates by water transport. One may almost say that countries surrounding the same ocean are neighbours.

Mr. MORLEY: While all the obstacles that Mr. de Jouvenel stated are all too important to a political union, nevertheless I do think there is a parallel to the development of the U.S.A. customs and political union. It all depends on whether you <u>really</u> want a union. While the American colonies have a common language and partly a common racial basis, you have the enormous advance in communications. It is more a question of whether a will for unity is present, than we seem to have realised. The American coming to Europe has more of a sense of unity than the Europeans seem to realise.

I believe that if the will were there, it would be possible to achieve it. But why start from the economic union? Why not grasp the whole nettle firmly?

Professor RAPPARD: Much as I would like to disagree with Mr. de Jouvenel, I cannot. Much as I would like to agree with Allais, I cannot. Impossibility of defining Europe. Before the war, Pan-Europe without Germany would have been anti-German alliance, but with Germany, would have been

German Europe. Today, there is no Germany, but the problem is the same, though with Russia taking the place of Germany.

For over five centuries Switzerland lived as disunited as are the United Nations. Yet it is rather striking that Switzerland had managed to have no war. But this was partly due to the war-like nature of the Swiss people. Therefore everyone wanted to be friends with the Swiss cantons.

Much more significant: how one century ago exactly, Switzerland became a federation.

1815, Switzerland a confederation of sovereign cantons. Factors which changed opinion against this confederation:—

1. security
2. economic: cantons would not accept a federal trade policy. It was much easier to export goods into Switzerland than to transport goods from one end of Switzerland to the other.
3. political. After 1830, cantons revolted, 10 or 11 cantons had a democratic revolution. Then the same men who had brought about the revolution demanded closer economic alliance between these cantons. But the 1833 attempt was a failure. The Swiss imitated the American constitution quite deliberately. But it was in spite of the fact that America had this constitution, however, that Switzerland adopted it.[3]

It was feared that it would be institutional deadlock.

A considerable reason for success of Swiss unity: all French speaking Swiss are not Catholic, and that not all German speaking Swiss are Protestant.

---

3. Following the Napoleonic Wars, Switzerland, parts of which had long been organized as a loose confederation of autonomous cantons, added a legislative Diet at the federal level. This governmental setup was challenged in 1845 when seven Catholic cantons, to protect their interests against federal legislation that had been promoted by liberal Protestant cantons, formed a "separate alliance" (Sonderbund). This ultimately provoked the month-long Sonderbund War in November 1847. The outcome was the creation of the Swiss Federation that was modeled, to a certain extent, on the American federal republic. Intriguingly, the American founders also invoked the Swiss confederation experience in their deliberations about the constitution and its ratification; see Robert W. Smith, "Swiss Myths: The Swiss Model and the American Constitution," *Early American Studies: An Interdisciplinary Journal* 17, no. 3 (Summer 2019): 377–95.

We were threatened by annihilation. And when you are placed between annihilation and something that is impossible, the impossible sometimes becomes more nearly possible.

Professor ROBBINS: I am particularly in agreement with the closing remarks of Professor Rappard.

Logic of establishing a supra-national authority seems to me to be inescapable. Considerable difficulties of any union of Western Europe including the British Isles. Problem of the British Commonwealth. Britain would not want to do anything which would weaken the bonds with the Commonwealth.

We would also be particularly anxious to avoid a union which would make it any more difficult for any member of the British Commonwealth.

While they are united by bonds of sympathy of interest with the U.K., they are also united by strong bonds to the U.S.A. I fear that such a union would involve not merely political, but also economic associations, and I think these economic associations might prove disruptive to the unity of the Western world. And could they form a block, then go to Washington, and say "Please we want to form a block, so as to reduce your power in the world. Will you please lend us some money with which to do it?"

Canadians would be in an impossible position. I don't think the U.K. would be pleased to join such a block, unless all other hopes had been abandoned. But I agree with Professor Iversen as to why should we form a block in order to bring about a state of affairs which would be essentially liberal.

Professor ALLAIS: In spite of the obstacles, I see no solution other than a federation.

Session 8

Thursday, April 3rd, 1947, 8.30 p.m.

The Problems and Chances of European Federation (continued)

Professor KNIGHT: What held the U.S.A. together in the beginning was the land position. Nothing remotely corresponding to that in the West of Europe today. No wilderness to conquer and exploit jointly. Slavery question, almost disrupted the union. Therefore I don't think anything can be inferred from American experience for European policy.

Europeans don't fully realise the position of America with respect to any European federation. America is neither in Europe nor out of it.

1. Monroe doctrine[1]
2. Freedom of movement of men goods and ideas are fundamental to any federation, and American public opinion firm on the subject of imports and on immigration.

---

1. The Monroe Doctrine, first articulated by US president James Monroe in an 1823 address to Congress, aimed at limiting further intervention by European powers in the Americas. Though the United States would remain neutral toward existing colonies, attempts at further colonization would be viewed as a potentially hostile act toward the United States. It was perhaps referenced here to support the first part of Knight's claim (historically, American policy insisted on a clear separation from Europe) while the Truman Doctrine and the reality of the current American occupation demonstrated that it was not out of Europe, either.

Some of the problems are analogous, however, to the problems that existed in America. Would you simply be institutionalising deadlock? I don't know why that wasn't the case in America, nor even in Switzerland.

Dr. POPPER: If there is in the present moment to be a European federation, it can only arise on the basis of some sort of common policy towards Russia. There are only a few possibilities with regard to Russia.

European federation might be an outer fringe of Russia. Or it might be possible to attempt to emphasise independence towards Russia. Or it might be an attempt to extend the policy at present adopted by America towards Russia, and to carry that into Europe.

I don't think a discussion without these considerations is of any value at the moment.

I do not feel that it is possible to discuss such problems in fundamentally psychological terms, but instead it should be in political terms.

1. There is a certain amount of cultural unity in Europe
2. Main feeling in Europe is insecurity, rather than of nationalism.

Professor POLANYI: As soon as the purpose of the European Federation became apparent, the position would be somewhat different. It could be a union which would form an alliance with the U.S.A. for creating a centre of power to ensure the peace of the world. On the other hand, it could be a union for ensuring neutrality in the war between U.S.A. and Russia. Danger of our time is the disintegration of our civilisation by civil war.

Community of citizens within nations seems to be the only way in which this conflict can be absorbed, or perhaps eliminated.

The Hitler conflict not a nationalist conflict, but one of ideologies.

An achievement of our time that we have today in the West a new kind of nations. Atomic bombs, and nations without them don't lose sleep because of not having them.

Professor ALLAIS: Would federation increase or decrease class conflict?

Professor POLANYI: United Europe would increase it, relatively to politically divided Europe. But federated Europe is somewhere between the two.

~~Professor ROBBINS: What is mediation in this context?~~

~~Professor POLANYI: Would take a long time to discover.~~

Professor KNIGHT: European block need not be between U.S.A. and U.S.S.R. U.S.A. has no direct conflict with Russia. She only wants to stop Russia from swallowing Europe.

Dr. POPPER: It would be a kind of mediation if Europe could help to prevent Russia from swallowing Europe. It would eliminate some of U.S.A.'s problems.

Professor ROBBINS: Will Europe offer to mediate in Greece by offering Greece the money which U.S.A. has offered already.[2]

Professor POLANYI: Russia a threat to U.S.A. via Europe. Atomic bombs. Need for international control of production of atomic bombs.

International control can function only if it has the power to conquer and destroy any Russian government which is defaulting on its obligations. Why Europe would suffer from U.S.A.–U.S.S.R. war:—

1. Campaign would completely ruin Europe.
2. Moment that such a war broke out, there would be civil war everywhere.

---

2. Robbins refers here to the ongoing crisis in Greece, which by then had broken into civil war. In February 1947 the British government, facing its own financial exigencies, requested that the United States take over its role in supporting the Greek government against insurgents in the National Liberation Front, who were backed by the Greek Communist Party. In a speech before Congress on March 12, 1947, President Truman stated that US policy should support free peoples from subjugation "by armed minorities or by outside pressures." In May 1947, that is, the month after the conference at Mont Pèlerin, the US Congress approved $400 million in economic and military aid to Greece and Turkey. The Truman Doctrine became the basis for the US policy of containment toward the Soviet Union.

3. Probability of the army of U.S.S.R. will march into Western Europe.

Professor TREVOUX: Aspiration of the mass towards international, as Prof. Allais has said.

American attitude very nationalistic in not allowing free movement of men capital etc.

We need to create at same time a confederation and a lessening of nationalism. Up to now, a confederation has either been for something, or against something.

There is no unity at the moment.

Economically: no desire towards unity.

Politically: desire for unity is purely against something.

Two sorts of international ideas: communism and liberalism. Weakness of liberalism is that it hasn't a mystique, whereas communism has.

In the world of ideas, sole chance is of preserving independence within the framework of confederation.

Professor ALLAIS: Mass of workers cannot move, but industrialists are opposed to movement of goods.

I don't think a confederation needs to be, in itself, for or against Russia.

There is no doctrine which can provide a solution to all problems.

Professor TREVOUX: But that isn't to say that liberalism has a mystique, it's only an enthusiasm.

Professor HAYEK: Reason why liberalism so attractive in the past the same as that why it is so attractive now. If federalism is to keep together, there must be a transfer of power to the federal power. But European nations would not be prepared to give up more power. But these powers could not be exercised by the national powers themselves. Federalism, if it is to be effectively used, implies a necessary restriction on the powers any of the governments can exercise.

Federation may be a practical solution in a liberal society, but once the liberal society has disappeared, I don't see how the thing is practicable at all unless as a movement towards liberalism again. Quotation from Lord Acton: "Of all checks on democracy, federation has been the most efficacious and the most congenial. . . . The federal system limits and restrains the sovereign power by dividing it and by assigning to Government only certain defined rights. It is the only method of curbing not only the majority but the power of the whole people."[3]

Professor MISES:

1. Unity of civilisation during the Middle Ages, but that didn't prevent war.
2. This federation is considered as an organisation against Russia. It is a fact that in all the countries concerned, France, Germany, Italy, and Great Britain, there is a very powerful intellectual movement in favour of Bolshevism. How it is possible to bring these nations into a federation which is anti-Russia?

Federations which we have considered as ideal were established at a time when nobody thought there could arise any conflicts between the members of the federations. These conflicts only arose later. Therefore there were civil wars. Sovereignty means <u>supreme power</u>. Confusion on the meaning of sovereignty. Lord Acton had in mind static conditions. He didn't take into account conditions in which some serious conflict would require some considerable changes within the federation's organisation.

Swiss cantons, in favour of interventionism, but against Berne. U.S.A. the same, with respect to Washington. Trade barriers grow up in U.S.A., then Supreme Court declares them to be unconstitutional.

Tendency in our age to overestimate importance of offices and institutions, and to underestimate importance of ideologies. If many people

---

3. Hayek here quotes from Acton's "Review of Sir Erskine May's *Democracy in Europe*," 1878, reprinted in John Emerich Edward Dalberg-Acton, First Baron Acton, *Essays in the History of Liberty*, ed. J. Rufus Fears, vol. 1 of *Selected Writings of Lord Acton* (Indianapolis: Liberty Fund, 1985), 84. Hayek began each chapter of *The Road to Serfdom* with a representative quote, and this one headed up chapter 13 on "The Prospects of International Order." Acton actually said, "Of all checks on democracy, *federalism* has been the most efficacious and the most congenial."

believe that wars can improve their position, an office in Geneva will not prevent wars.

Professor HAYEK: ~~Don't ideologies affect institutions to some extent?~~

Professor MISES: ~~No, I think it's the other way round.~~

Professor MACHLUP: One or two speakers have questioned the desirability of a federation. But I think these speakers have taken for granted what such a federation would do, without pointing out what the federation would do. We must first of all know what the federation would do.

Professor GRAHAM: So far as policy as defence against Russia: good deal of truth in saying that W. Europe will be safer if it isn't federated than if it is.

Canada and U.S.A. have never been a threat to each other. A divided Europe into small nations will considerably advance the prospects of diminished agression [sic] on the part of Russia. U.S.A. ought to be more interested in the European union than the Europeans themselves.

Professor Robbins seems to lay some stress on the economic folly of the U.S.A. in promoting an economic union which would more or less be directed against the U.S.A. But he seems to trust us, the U.S.A., not to be foolish. This is historically unjustified. I don't see the European federation would offer the European nations anything that they could not get now without federation. It could get what it wanted by changing into a free trade area.

Mr. DE JOUVENEL: I suddenly wonder whether federalism had any relationship at all to liberalism. Perhaps it bears no more relationship than nationalism was thought to bear to it in the 19th century. I distrust political power.

Session 9

Friday, April 4th, 1947, 9.30 a.m.

Liberalism and Christianity

Professor Eucken in the chair.

Professor KNIGHT: When one speaks of religion one thinks of fools rushing in. I think the opposition to liberalism is religious. Man is a religious animal. Can liberalism be put in such a way as to satisfy man's craving for a religion?

Christianity: any belief or practice held by someone who calls himself a Christian.

Christianity has endorsed liberalism, just as it had endorsed everything else. But whether they are logically compatible, too large a question. But I think they are not compatible. Struggle between Church and state in Europe. When you discuss religion, there is nowhere to start. But once you start, there is so much to be said, you cannot stop. Man a religious animal: next step to a romantic animal: homo sapiens is what he says about himself. Can liberalism be a religion in itself, or has it to establish it in opposition to Christianity?

Communism is much more Christian than liberalism. Christianity arose in a totalitarian Roman world. From the very first, it condoned it. It has always condemned competition and also co-operation. Communism is like it in all things concerned with the social order.

Communism accepts material well-being as one of the codes of life.

Christianity in the first three centuries said nothing about the moral, but only about the salvation. But in modern world, spirit grew up out of science, commerce, and sport. Modern science was from the beginning applied science. Antithesis between religious spirit and scientific in belief by faith and belief by reason.

Historical development.

Development of heresies, then of humanism.

Revolt of Wycliffe, and others.[1] England as a hot-bed of revolt. 17th century Reformation, and counter-reformation. Development of sport. One of the fundamental roots of democracy is behaviour according to consciously made rules of a democratic nature. Business as a sport, but also politics as a sport.

Religion in America: we think of America as settled by religious zealots, but the Pilgrim Fathers were as much adventurers as political zealots. America Protestant. In the new world, tolerance was essential.

America is fundamentally tolerant. In 18th century, there was rather a tendency towards indifference to religion. Dilemma of modern liberalism; Presupposition of liberalism, that man is a rational animal. Well, he isn't. And man is not just.

Ethic of modern liberalism: workmanship and sportsmanship. When people are playing a game, there is no room for charity. The social order rests on the possibility of rational argument, both on the subjects on which they consider agreement to be necessary, and on the matter of determining where they ought to be able to agree.

To call religion the opiate of the people is sound. When we say "truth" in modern times, we always mean "new truth". Mere truth is in itself merely a bore. People can agree on the scope of law, and the drift of law. Need to

---

1. The English theologian and church reformer John Wycliffe (ca. 1320s–1384) was a prominent critic of the wealth and political power of the church. An early advocate of ideas identified with the Protestant Reformation, he saw the Bible as the only source of religious truth and advocated its translation into the vernacular. What came to be called Wycliffe's Bible was undertaken at his initiative, and he is credited with translation of the New Testament. The "hot-bed of revolt" doubtless included the Peasants' Revolt of 1381 that took place a few years before Wycliffe's death. In 1415 he was declared a heretic, for which his corpse was disinterred and burned.

limit the <u>amount</u> of government, although the tendency is in the other direction in modern times. We have to make the best of life, and also have to make the best of liberalism. Essence of truth: to be the same for all. The same is not true for loyalty. Opinions can be just as dividing as truth. The modern world has got a little superstitious about truth.

Under what conditions opinions and loyalties unite and divide people in groups, and what can we do, as liberals, in the way of establishing a sphere of unity and harmony.

We have to find some way of suppressing unnecessary conflicts. We want to have government by discussion.

Professor EUCKEN: Grateful to Professor Knight for his helpful introduction. Briefly supplementing it, I want to raise the problem not in the theoretical but in the practical form. From the experience of a totalitarian system, I am convinced that ~~life~~ under such a system makes it impossible to be a Christian. There is an enormous danger to any independent Christian life, and all theories of Christian socialism have collapsed. The fact is that in a planned economy we are in every respect dependent on authority: work occupation etc. are all determined by political officers. This deprives me of the freedom of obeying my Christian conviction. The problem of the relation between Christianity and liberalism has entered a new phase. The work of Max Weber and others is now antiquated.[2] We face an entirely new situation, in which Christianity if it is to be an active and determining force, can exist only if the ends which unite us here are successful. I have had many discussions with Catholic and Protestant clergymen who still believe that we must have socialism and that the practice of Christian love requires socialism. We are now realising that in fact under socialism there is no opening for it.

I hope that in addition to the questions raised by Professor Knight, this question of Christianity in a collectivist system is considered and that

---

2. Eucken refers to the German sociologist and economist Max Weber's thesis in *The Protestant Ethic and the Spirit of Capitalism* (1920 edition, trans. Talcott Parsons [London: George Allen and Unwin, 1930]) linking the growth of capitalism in Northern Europe to the "work ethic" (e.g., work hard, save, invest, avoid conspicuous consumption) promoted by Calvinism.

we ask whether the reversal of the tendency towards a planned economy is not a precondition for the survival of Christianity. If the movements towards a planned economy and totalitarianism, which are identical, continue, there is no hope for Christianity.

Dr. HOFF: It seems to me that the decline of liberalism ~~is~~ *has* something to do with what we call the cultural crisis. Majority of men in the western world have lost their faith in God. And few have the ability to be agnostics. Then there is a tendency for people to become converts to secular religions, Nazism, Communism, etc.

Trevoux pointed out yesterday that liberalism has no mystique. I agree. And this is a handicap in the fight against secular religions. If we are going to diagnose the causes for the decline of liberalism: the need for faith, the will to believe, and the need for group feeling.

Liberalism has not satisfied that need, but has done the opposite. If that were one of the main causes of the decline of liberalism, chances of a revival would be small indeed. One of the reasons why liberalism has a very difficult time now is that ideas advanced 100 years ago have become virulent. If that were one of the main reasons, the chances for liberalism would be better.

Is it not only right that truth-seekers should try to counter-balance what they consider to be wrong?

One of the few expectations that has not yet been realised here is that I would give here counter-arguments to those put forward against liberalism by the socialists and planners. We might start out from the end of the field where we agree, instead of from the end of the field where all is controversy. When your neighbour's house is on fire, you don't sit down and discuss the causes of fire.

Mr. DAVENPORT: I suppose the morning's discussion is to find out what is the basis of liberalism. A very barren outlook for liberalism if you disregard man's religious nature. Difference between facts and values.

If the market is viewed as an end, not only is life very dull, but I do not think that many men would go along into the liberal standards. If the market is viewed as one of the means, by which men can live a free life, then I think the market comes into its own. There is no conflict. But to go around viewing the market as an end in itself is the best way to defeat liberalism.

America respects man, while Russia respects property.

Professor ALLAIS: Problem for liberals to examine conditions for free discussion.

Discussion of Christianity seems to me no more important than discussion of agnosticism and liberalism, or Buddhism and liberalism. Religion a matter of intuition, and not of reason.

Need to realise the conditions in which division of opinions on religion is possible.

Consideration of conditions for freedom of press.

Professor HAYEK: Does liberalism presuppose some set of values which are commonly accepted as a faith and in themselves not capable of rational demonstration?

Does liberalism need to be antagonistic to existing religions, or can they be reconciled?

So far as Allais is concerned, I might as well have called this discussion the problem of religion and liberalism, rather than of Christianity and liberalism.

Western thought seems to take it for granted that if you discuss anything sufficiently, you will come to some agreement on what policy ought to be taken.

~~Not a coincidence that in England one of the two papers that are always liberal is the Roman Catholic *Tablet*.~~[3]

There is no chance of any extensive support for a liberal programme unless the opposition between liberals and Christians can somehow be bridged. This antagonism is an accidental accretion of liberalism, rather than one of the essentials to liberalism. And are people likely to accept liberalism if they think it is in opposition to their faith?

---

3. The Roman Catholic weekly *The Tablet* carried one of the first (unsigned) reviews of Hayek's *The Road to Serfdom* (see *The Tablet* 183, March 11, 1944: 123–24), and the review was positive. It is unclear why this sentence was struck out.

Professor POLANYI: Ambiguity between freedom for individual desires and freedom to criticise indefinitely holding no opinion by faith.

Obligationist view: to liberalte [*sic*] ourselves from personal desires.

Fight against planning of science during the last 10 or 12 years. First attack which we had to face was that we were only trying for our own desires to discuss science freely. We were acting, however, on <u>duty</u>. We were performing a function for the community. It was alleged that science was determined by needs of society, and that therefore the proper position of science was to be conducted under the aegis of the government of the day. Such is the case in Russia. We could only reply to this on metaphysical grounds. It is not true that science is determined purely by the people who are conducting it. It is merely a transcending of these desires. In reality it makes a demand on scientists, and it is not true that scientists are just enjoying themselves. When we started defending freedom of science, we compiled a list of scientists having religious convictions. Logically coherent that these people were transcending personal desires in being scientists.

Individualist view fairly weak: it is not from this that the Red dangers to our civilisation arise. It is difficult because we cannot say what this spiritual reality is to which we owe allegiance. Therefore we can only define this by adhering to some traditional purpose of science. We are therefore traditionalists to some extent. Uncritical acceptance of underlying premises, which we can hold only on <u>faith</u>. Logically necessary premiss for freedom in that community. We find today that writers who recognise the terrible dangers to which we are drifting, and who are socialists themselves, say they want freedom. Then they become involved in the question of "Are there any values, faith etc., which we can justify."

Professor KNIGHT: I haven't any quarrel with Mr. Davenport at all. Christianity not in opposition to liberalism, providing you let Christianity mean anything you want it to mean.

Question is of freedom of discussion. I think there must be some limit to discussion. We do not discuss public issues in terms of whether they are Christian or not. But when we have freely discussed it, we may, if we want to, call it a Christian matter.

We have to have some faith in the world, in historical process.

Religion should be a private matter, the free action of free groups. We are not facing the facts: maybe we could not. I have doubts how far we should face the facts.

Dr. Popper:

1. Does liberalism presuppose a set of rules?
2. Is there necessary antagonism between liberalism and the various religious beliefs? (Questions raised by Prof. Hayek)

2. Religions are intolerant, or tend to be intolerant. But Liberalism is <u>tolerant</u>. The one thing we do not tolerate is intolerance. I feel that Professor Knight does not <u>respect</u> religion.
1. It does. We probably all agree. I do not intend to question Professor Polanyi's metaphysics. Here I think we are in very grave danger of throwing liberalism overboard altogether.

Liberal is a man who operates things with two values.

On the one hand, he has his own opinions. On the other hand, he wants to tolerate all the other opinions, and to find some common basis of agreement.

We must not be led into a compromise which is really not sound with fascism and communism.

We speak of western problems. Derivation from the Greeks. Problem arose from them originally. The problem of humanitarianism. Communism etc. only really distorted humanitarianism. Faith of liberalism a very strong faith. Responsibility for other peoples' suffering.

Economic liberalism of Mises is I think perhaps not quite enough. We have to realise that this religious and humanitarian faith will mean that in a way we pay for it: we have to pay for a religion in recognition of the need for compromise: it is part of humanitarianism that we have to be equalitarians: 1. It is irrelevant that man includes the genius and the fool, for the political field.

2. recognition by the geniuses that the difference between the genius and the common man is very slight. We are all fools to some extent.

Humility necessary in order to keep rationalism in check. Maximum common basis of values which we have in common with the other religions. We are not all utilitarians: therefore in argument the utilitarian has to realise that all are not utilitarians, and to try to replace it by something rather more acceptable to other people.

Professor KNIGHT: We have to agree on premisses.

Why did the Christians clash with the Roman Empire? The Empire didn't object to the Christians. Christians objected to pagans. The question is whether Christians will allow us to be liberals. I think there are other dangers to modern world apart from Christianity, and the others are more important and powerful, nationalism for instance.

Dr. GIDEONSE: There are so many uses in this discussion of the word religion. There must be a conflict between religion in the sense that you believe what you are told, <u>because</u> you are told it, and liberalism.

Differences between liberalism as an intellectual structure and as a going political movement. As a political movement, it is not a going concern any more.

Calvinist party of the Netherlands: just liberal party when it comes to economic policy.

Tocqueville: "You can't have a loosening of political bonds without a strengthening of moral bonds."[4]

This is one of the weaknesses of liberalism as a going concern as a political movement.

Professor ROEPKE: Complete change of front: many of the things said today are probably obsolete from the viewpoint of the modern world.

---

4. In *Democracy in America*, Alexis de Tocqueville examined the "Principal Causes that Tend to Maintain the Democratic Republic in the United States," and one of these was religious belief strong enough to constrain interested behavior. "Despotism can do without faith, but not liberty.... How could society fail to perish if, while the political bond grows loose, the moral bond does not become tighter?" See Alexis de Tocqueville, *Democracy in America*, ed. Eduardo Nolla, trans. James T. Schliefer, vol. 1 (Indianapolis: Liberty Fund, 2010), 478.

Problem of defining the necessaries in order to say "in necessariis unitas."[5]

Professor BRANDT: Struggle between totalitarians and liberalism and not between Russia and U.S.A.

It runs horizontally through all the countries.

Incredible number of totalitarians in U.S.A.

It is not an accident that you haven't liberalism in Buddhist and Islamic countries. Difference in the attitude towards the individual. But Christianity and liberalism have a common attitude to the <u>individual</u>.

Mr. DE JOUVENEL: I can see no reason for liberty unless it is on account of the idea that it is wrong to have to obey the commands of other people without reason.

Professor GRAHAM: Strong sympathy with Professor Knight's view. A certain fear of religion.

Religion has been a great oppressor of freedom during history, whenever a religious group happened to get into power.

But religious groups in strong favour of toleration of freedom when they happen to be in a minority. But they <u>are</u> now in a minority. Therefore we should try to enlist help for liberalism from religion. We begin to lose economic freedom first, then political, then religious. If we can convince the religious that they will be suppressed if we first let economic and political freedom go, then we may enlist their support.

I therefore find myself growing closer to the people who are interested in religious ideas. They have a faith which can be made to energise liberalism.

---

5. "In necessariis unitas, in dubiis libertas, in omnibus caritas" may be translated as "in necessary things unity, in uncertain things liberty, in all things charity." Recent research suggests it was first used in 1617 by the Archbishop of Split in his anti-Papal text *De Repubblica Ecclesiastica* in defense of freedom of religious thought. Röpke is suggesting that agreement on fundamentals is more difficult in the modern world, but it is unclear whether the fundamentals he has in mind are those of Christianity or those of liberalism.

Mr. MORLEY: I think this morning's discussion has been by far the most important part of the Conference so far.

It is a matter of enlisting ourselves on the side of religion. Not so much a matter of whether Christianity will allow liberals to be liberals, but of whether liberalism will allow Christians to be Christians.

Professor EUCKEN: What Mr. Morley said makes it unnecessary for me to say much. I am in almost complete agreement. It may be useful first to explain my position. I am a Christian, and I want to say that from a purely Christian point of view I regard the competitive order as essential. If we consider what resistance there was in Germany, and the main victims of the Nazi oppression, these men were all liberals, but at the same time also Christians—Christians it is true without any formal dogma, but agreeing on man having an eternal life.[6] It was that conviction which gave them their strength.

---

6. Recalling again that Hahn's notes are only rough summaries, and that Hayek was translating for Eucken, it would appear here that Eucken is simply emphasizing that German resistance to Hitler within Germany was often promulgated by Christians and liberals, some of whom he knew and who paid for it with their lives. The unfortunate phrasing should not be taken as suggesting that he was denying the Holocaust. For more on the relation between the Freiburg circle and the German resistance, as well as the religious background of the participants, see Heinz Rieter and Matthias Schmolz, "The Ideas of German Ordoliberalism 1938–45: Pointing the Way to a New Economic Order," *European Journal for the History of Economic Thought* 1, no. 1 (Autumn 1993): 87–114.

Session 10

Friday, April 4th, 1947, 4.30 p.m.

Discussion on Agenda, Etc.

Professor HAYEK: "Economics the field where people are doing the most harm with the best intentions."—as a subject for discussion.

Mr. HAZLITT: Why not have a committee to draft a set of principles?

Professor ROBBINS: I think it would be a good idea to have a discussion now on our ultimate object.

Professor HAYEK: It was purely accidental that we managed to get funds for this conference. Unless we discuss some method of permanent organisation now, there will be no-one who can do anything at all towards calling another meeting, and nothing further will be done at all.

Professor KNIGHT: Would it be possible to publish a journal in England?

Professor HAYEK: England the worst place for a journal, if we decide to have one. Switzerland or the U.S.A. would be much better.

Mr. HAZLITT: To have a permanent organisation, we must have a purpose. Therefore we must have a statement of principles. A statement would be a necessary part, whether it is published or not.

Professor STIGLER: Can have an organisation of any degreer [*sic*] whatever. Exchange of periodicals could be managed without a great deal of expense. A mimeographed journal would cost rather more.

Professor MACHLUP: Separate journal not advisable: we want out [*sic*] stuff published by organs which will be read by other people.

Professor JEWKES: I have very grave doubts about the advantages of preparing any detailed statement of principles at the moment. If we were to set down in detail those practical policies which we would all want to see put into practice, we would be in the position that we don't know what the aims, in terms of policy, of our colleagues are. I think some permanent organisation, with a <u>small</u> central organisation, should be set up.

Mr. HAZLITT: I didn't say a "detailed" statement of principles. Merely a statement of "very broad principles." Must be broad enough to be meaningful, and not detailed enough to split us up.

Professor GRAHAM: To have a permanent organisation, must have some principles. I personally would be much happier with a declaration of principles.

Professor HAYEK: Extreme difficulty of drawing up a statement. I do want to stress that if we form a society, I do not want to confine it to people who are now present. If we invite other people, we have to write letters which will have to set down our common principles. Otherwise, whoever acts on behalf of the organisation will have no authority to say anything at all about the principles and aims of the group. The statement need makes [*sic*] no statement of means, only of ends.

Professor HOFF: Liberal conference in Oxford, 9th to 14th of April.[1] There was another meeting of that group last year in Norway, and a political manifesto was drawn up.

---

1. The International Liberal Conference that took place April 9–14, 1947, at Wadham College, Oxford, brought together representatives from Liberal parties from nineteen countries. The meeting resulted in the creation of the Liberal International and the issuance of the

Professor ROBBINS: I think it is up to the Conference to decide what type of manifesto is to be drawn up by the committee.

Mr. DE JOUVENEL: I am quite prepared to leave it to Professor Hayek.

Dr. GIDEONSE: Professor Hayek needs it for approaching other people. When you have a statement like that before you, it will help sharpen up choices made of topics for next week's discussion.

Could Professor Graham formulate the motion? Standing committee of 5?

Absolutely necessary to have ends defined.

Bulletin of information about publications.

Agreement on exchange of publications would be very helpful, particularly with respect to France.

Merely information about publications in the bulletin would still be very helpful.

Professor HAYEK: I haven't that much time. Also, difficulties about having the thing centralised in England. A country where you can pay money in, but not get it out, would not be very suitable for central organisation.

I personally have never intended any manifesto for publication. But merely <u>instructions</u> for a secretary seems to me to be <u>too</u> modest.

Professor GRAHAM: I move that we empower Professor Hayek to appoint a committee of five, including himself, to draw up a set of principles to be discussed at our next meeting. Nem. con.[2]

Professor FRIEDMAN: I agree not to include details of policy. This statement will really have a very important part in deciding who will join, and if we will join.

Intellectual meeting.

Oxford Manifesto, a statement of liberal principles. Hayek kept a memorandum regarding the conference in his papers (Friedrich A. Hayek Papers [FAHP], 61.11, Hoover Institution); the text of the Manifesto is available online: https://liberal-international.org/who-we-are /our-mission/landmark-documents/political-manifestos/oxford-manifesto-1947.

2. "Nem. con." stands for "nemine contradicente," that is, with no one dissenting; unanimously.

The statement should not be used by us, nor by others. Liberalism is in a curious position, and on the downgrade. It is at times used as a defence of the status quo, instead of being dynamic and progressive.

We want to make sure that our manifesto is concerned in the progress of man's welfare. We have to distinguish between the negative and the positive approach. Broad statements on which we can very easily agree are negative in nature.

We ought to agree on the necessity for a positive approach. Statement must be designed so as to let potential members know whether they really want to join or not.

Professor GRAHAM: In the statement we should recognise that in the heyday of liberalism there were very grave social evils, which still persist, and to which we ought to address ourselves to do something towards their elimination. Totalitarian principles are necessary in war, but as soon as possible after the war the totalitarian principles should be disposed of.

There is nothing worse than war except losing a war.

We must emphasise that it is up to the individual to establish his own ends.

Mr. HAZLITT: This sort of discussion ought to be held <u>after</u> the committee has presented its draft.

Professor ROBBINS: Great difficulty for the committee to set forth methods of policy rather than general aims. What do we really want this association to do?

I do not want to see it indulging in propaganda, nor collectively putting out manifestos for public policy.

Unity in liberty, freedom, and exchange of ideas. <u>Main</u> purpose, to exchange information with regard to each other's activities, and sometimes to have meetings of this nature. Optimal size of the <u>meeting</u> this time.

If this be the case, not necessary that this statement should go into questions even of <u>broad</u> policy.

We only want a statement of aims which unite us.

Dr. Popper: Professor Hayek had something like a study group in mind, and I don't want that to be forgotten.

Professor Polanyi: I don't see precisely what we want. If there are more members, we can't select among them for meetings. Therefore, if there are more members, our meetings will have to be larger.

Professor Hayek: I think it important that we should be able to determine our own membership. If you want in future either to study a particular problem or a general conference I think it very desirable that the person acting should have some authority from the group, and that the membership of study groups, for instance, should be determined by the whole group. If any group is not fixed, danger that the donor of funds, of good will, might influence the direction of the meeting.

Professor Dennison: I think that has an important effect on the type of draft. It would not be a draft to which any prospective member would be required to subscribe.

Professor Jewkes: Do we defer consideration of whether there is to be a permanent organisation until we see what would be the aims?

Professor Knight: Yes.

Professor Hayek: For the committee, I appoint Professors Jewkes, Eucken, Iversen, Dr. Gideonse, and Mr. Hazlitt.

Dr. Popper: I should like to suggest for one of the discussions "The Present Political Situation."

Friday, April 4th, 1947, 4.30 p.m.

Aims and Organisation of Permanent Body

Professor Antoni in the chair.

A general discussion took place on the aims and organisation of any permanent body which might emerge from the present conference. After a
brief introductory statement by Professor Hayek and remarks by Messrs.
Dennison, Friedman, Graham, Hazzlitt [sic], Hoff, Jewkes, Jouvenel,
Knight, Machlup, Polyanyi, Popper, Robbins and Stigler, a committee
was set up consisting of Messrs. Eucken, Gideonse, Hayek, Hazzlitt [sic],
Iversen and Jewkes to draft a statement of aims of such a permanent body.

Session 11

Monday, April 7th, 1947, 4.30 p.m.

Contra-cyclical Measures, Full Employment, and Monetary Reform.

~~Professor~~ *Mr.* Hoff in the chair.

Professor STIGLER: I think there will be a wide split between the American and Continental economists here.

U.S.A. concerned with full employment.

Continent concerned with reconstruction.

Main aim of the gold standard was to combat major inflation. Concern with gold standard has declined very greatly in recent times. Any automatic features of the gold standard have disappeared. Also, our problem is much more one of deflation, on which the gold standard has very little to say. Can we all agree that the first step should be to bring all money-making institutions under the control of the state? I throw this question open.

Alternative policies:—

1. Diminution of monetary uncertainty.
2. Combatting changes in the economy by monetary measures.

Will we have to choose between them?

1. Government has to work in a framework of law.
2. We are still unsure of the results of the contra-cyclical measures.

Professor GRAHAM: The commodity reserve money system.[1] Theory of commodity reserve money is the same as the idea of the gold standard.

To make a representative group of standard materials the unit of money. No essential difference between Marshall's symetallism [*sic*] and commodity reserve money.[2]

Government under <u>obligation</u> to buy commodity and sell warehouse receipts.

Objections to gold standard, while almost perfect theoretically:—

1. it didn't cover a wide enough field, and
2. it was slow in operation.

Stabilising effect of gold in the 19th century operated only over long cycles of 25 years.

Change in the level of gold didn't have any relationship to the change in the level of production in other goods. But with the commodity reserve system you affect a much larger part of the economy.

Not desirable to accumulate stocks under this system and <u>as part of this system</u>, for purposes of war.

Mr. HAZLITT: What about credit?

---

1. A commodity reserve monetary system would involve the creation of a composite unit consisting of a weighted group of basic commodities that would be awarded monetary status by its two-way convertibility with paper currency. It was viewed as an alternative to the gold standard. Graham had promoted the new system in his "Transition to a Commodity Reserve Currency," *American Economic Review* 31 (September 1941): 520–25. For some background and a contemporaneous critique, see W. T. M. Beale Jr., M. T. Kennedy, and W. J. Winn, "Commodity Reserve Currency: A Critique," *Journal of Political Economy* 50 (August 1942): 579–94.

2. In his quest to provide a stable standard of value, the British economist Alfred Marshall (1842–1924) proposed a form of symetalism, a plan in which a fixed weight combination of gold and silver, rather than a fixed ratio, would serve as the monetary base. His plan also called for a standard unit of purchasing power to be used for longer-term contracts that would be based on a periodically updated price index covering a variety of important commodities. The major features of the plan, which he submitted to the Gold and Silver Commission in 1888, may be found in his 1887 paper, "Remedies for Fluctuations of General Prices," reprinted in A. C. Pigou, ed., *Memorials of Alfred Marshall* (London: Macmillan, 1925), 188–211. For context, see Peter Groenewegen, chap. 11, *A Soaring Eagle: Alfred Marshall 1842–1924* (Hants: Edward Elgar, 1995).

Professor GRAHAM: Either 100% system, which I would prefer, or a system such as we have in the Western hemisphere at the present moment. Commodity reserve the criterion however, and not the supply of gold.

Professor ROBBINS: What about the international position?

Professor GRAHAM: I prefer a <u>national</u> monetary system. If it were introduced as a national system I see no grave difficulties through international complications. If any national unit adopted such a system it would be open to any other nation to get stable exchange rates by adopting the same unit. If other nations didn't adopt it, you could have perfectly free exchange market. Any country that had anything to sell would be able to sell it, by way of buying currency on the free market.

Internationally: international monetary authority would be able to issue this currency money.

This system would seem to be an energiser of the economy, as well as a stabiliser.

Professor ROBBINS: Could we have some information on the 100% plan?

Professor DIRECTOR: I am not aware of any improvement on the original 1933 proposal.[3]

Proposal is to remove anomaly with respect to the commercial banks. Banking system is an extreme: some banks have little or no capital. But they have large fixed demand obligations. Therefore very serious banking derangements when anything untoward happened in the economy.

---

3. The 100% Plan or Chicago Plan refers to a proposal put forth in a six-page memorandum on banking reform and signed by eight University of Chicago economists, among them Frank Knight, Aaron Director, and Henry Simons, and distributed to members of the Roosevelt administration when they came into office in March 1933. The plan called for, among other reforms, the strict separation of the deposit and lending functions of banks. Instead of operating under a fractional reserve system, deposit banks (whose role would be to accept deposits and transfer funds) would face a 100 percent reserve requirement. Their lending and discounting functions would be taken over by separate lending companies. For more, see Ronnie J. Phillips, *The Chicago Plan and New Deal Banking Reform* (Armonk, NY: M. E. Sharpe, 1995), which also includes as an appendix the text of the original memorandum.

Monopoly: nothing can happen to banks, just <u>because</u> they <u>are</u> a monopoly. Widespread idea that the government must prevent anything from happening to the banks.

Tendency for volume of bank money to fluctuate.

But with 100% system, banks would no longer have any demand obligations except in so far as they were covered by assets. It would be a matter of indifference whether people ever wanted to convert one type of money into the other.

How should we carry on the function now provided by the commercial banks?

Develop institutions which would collect savings of individuals and distribute these savings to various other activities. These proposals don't go far enough. What about insurance companies?

Professor Roepke: Why are we discussing this problem?

1. Unemployment.
2. We are divided upon this question.

Some say that full employment is one of the essential prerequisites of our time. There are others who say that the influence of Keynes and his whole school has been dangerous.

Why are we divided?

Problem could be discussed on two levels: a lower level of technicalities, the higher level of social philosophy.

But it is difficult to separate these levels.

Necessity of a social philosophy which goes beyond materialistic, positivistic doctrines.

One is able to accept full employment doctrine fully only if one is prepared to accept a certain social philosophy.

We can consider the task of the problem facing us here as a technical problem of steering, controlling, the total <u>quanta</u> of economic life. We are all acquainted with the business cycle engineer. He looks at the problem from the point of view of quantities, not qualities. We need an outlook which goes beyond the quantitative approach which merely considers society as a machine.

What should we suggest instead? Personally I would favour

1. rational business cycle policy, controlling the boom in time.
2. rational policy would attempt, after the depression has run its course, and when there is danger of secondary depression, the need for Keynesian measures.

Problem of instability of our time: a highly institutionalised, proletarianised, society, where most of the people live on salaried income. Full employment policies usually run in terms of money income.

The bumpier the road, the better the springs we need.

I.E., need for <u>resilience</u> in the system.

Dr. HOFF: <u>Danger</u> of monetary expansion and unwillingness to face the consequences of the credit expansion.

Professor ALLAIS: I agree with Professor Roepke that unemployment is inevitable in the free economy without controls. Resiliency needed. But this is distinct from the problem of the cycle.

I agree with the proposal for 100% money. Reform towards total cover is absolutely necessary. This would remove the large fluctuations in monetary income. But even this is not enough. Total volume of money - 100% would establish stability of the credit money. But there would still be circulating money, which could fluctuate, and which could still cause instabilities. Therefore, need to reconsider the function of circulating money.

In the Middle Ages, money was used as a medium of exchange and as a standard of measure, and there was a difference between the two. But by the 19th century, there was no longer a difference of money of account and as a measure.

Professor KNIGHT: 100% plan essentially does away with a perfectly idiotic feature of our monetary system, that is, that money values are determined by the amount redeemed.

Seems diabolically designed to increase instabilities as things are now.

A circulating medium also used as a store of value, and therefore held for speculative purposes.

Professor Graham's system tries to put an automatic standard into the monetary system.

Would the 100%, or commodity reserve system, eliminate instability?

Professor ROBBINS: I find myself in the reverse position to Professor Roepke, who was Keynesian, and is so no longer. There was a time when I thought Keynesian stabilisation schemes utterly reprehensible, but I have gradually been forced to believe that these ideas were not so wrong.[4]

In all probability the discussion of this problem in terms of the ideas of Lord Keynes is a thoroughly undesirable thing today.

I think we should beware of identifying the theories of Keynes with the theories of Beveridge.[5] Full employment in the <u>General Theory</u> permitted existence in British economy of perhaps 3/4 million, which is a figure far above that suggested by Beveridge. Keynes suggested a reasonably high level of global demand.

Is it not perhaps better to devote ourselves to the consideration of the concrete problem? The essential problem, to which we must have an answer, is the problem of <u>preventing severe deflation</u>. It is very difficult to escape the conclusion that there is a problem of stabilising the aggregate aspect of the economy.

---

4. Though Lionel Robbins was a severe critic of Keynes in the 1930s, he changed his mind during the war. In lectures delivered at Cambridge in spring 1947, he announced his change of view. "Whatever we may think of the virtues of the price system as a mechanism of allocation, whatever views we may hold of the alleged automatism of the price and private enterprise system as regards *relative* demand and *relative* supply, I am quite clear that as an instrument for maintaining reasonable constancy of *aggregate* demand it has most profound limitations. . . . I owe much to Cambridge economists, particularly to Lord Keynes and Professor Robertson, for having awakened me from dogmatic slumbers in this very important respect" (emphases in the original). See Lionel Robbins, *The Economic Problem in Peace and War* (London: Macmillan, 1947), 67–68.

5. The distinction that Robbins was drawing was between Keynes's emphasis on using government spending to offset a downturn or deflation, a policy of which he approved, and William Beveridge's endorsement of using Keynesian demand management tools to attempt to maintain a permanent state of full employment at a very low rate, which he opposed. See William Beveridge, *Full Employment in a Free Society* (London: Allen and Unwin, 1944), 128, where the author stated, "3 per cent appears as a conservative, rather than an unduly hopeful, aim to set for the average unemployment rate of the future under conditions of full employment."

The onus of proof is with those who say that you can explain global aspects while concentrating attention on the relative. Some will say that the theory of wages will provide an answer. I am not one of those who wish to dispense with flexibility in the labour market. Much more difficult to give a satisfactory relationship between total employment and level of wages than I used to believe. I think the classical theory of wages holds between industries. But even in a closed economy, the problem is still enveloped in confusion. I say nothing against the importance of flexible wage rates as a stabiliser in the system as a whole. But I don't think flexible wage rates are the complete answer to a drop in aggregate demand.

Possible remedy:

Timing of public investment. Especially difficult point for those professing liberal viewpoint. If this is pushed too far, may change type of society in which we live. It might swallow up the private sector by the public sector of the economy. If we are content with merely stating and emphasising the dangers, we are in danger of ignoring some quintessential facts of the liberal society. There are certain acts of public expenditure which state <u>must</u> carry out. Therefore timing does command serious attention.

I always tended to assume that people in charge of public treasuries could hardly be so silly as to plan their expenditure without any regard to the state of the cycle. But it is not so. The state tends to go the same way as the herd. Even within the limits of the most classical view, we would still do well to point out to states that they should not aggravate the situation.

I think examination of public investment reveals that there is a margin of expenditure which is essential, over a period of years, but not essential in any one year, which can be used to counteract the cycle. But I think this has its limits. We should favour some degree of automatism, and those policies which interfere least with the usual market mechanism.

Unsolved problem for the future of liberalism: to discover automatic stabilisers which will work for the system as a whole. Essential if we are to persuade the peoples of the world that liberalism has something to offer them. We are obliged to admit that there have been sins of omission before.

I think there is nothing to lead us to believe that Say's law, or anything like it, operates in the modern world.

Mr. DE JOUVENEL: I would like to make sure that we agree: it is a fact that in the present world there is no longer a means of <u>international</u> exchange. Plans of managed currency have a tendency, or some of them have, of making money lose its quality as an international means of payment. I think money <u>should</u> still be a means of international payment.

Professor GRAHAM: I think we ought to consider what Prof. Simons thought about monetary policy, especially his insistence that the state should confine itself to two instruments, the issue of 1. money and 2. securities.[6] Extent of arbitrary action would be very much limited. It seems to me very attractive as a monetary mechanism, pure and simple. Its effects on employment are by no means sure, but could not be easily adverse.

Borrowing, as it is done by states, is a contradictory measure, although often without the contradiction being realised.

Professor ROEPKE: When all is said concerning Keynes, there is still the problem of emphasis. Even if I believed in most of Keynes, I would hesitate to say so publicly. I believe with Rueff that the great danger is not deflation, but <u>inflation</u>.

Keynes has been accepted by the popular writers <u>pecar [*sic*] fortiter.</u>[7]

Professor FRIEDMAN: Much of the complexity that Professor Robbins attributes to this problem arises out of our attempt to make adjustments to maladjustments. By examining the monetary system, however, we may be able to set the whole house in order. If we go beyond, we get the problem of rules versus regulations. Great caution called for by the facts of the world. Attempts to time public investment—great chance that they will end up making the system more unstable than before. Law of Large

---

6. Simons's views on monetary policy incorporated the banking reforms of the Chicago Plan, of which he was an author, with the insistence that the monetary authorities follow a simple, easily articulatable rule rather than discretion. See Henry Simons, "A Positive Program for Laissez Faire: Some Proposals for a Liberal Economic Policy" (Chicago: University of Chicago Press, 1934), and "Rules versus Authorities in Monetary Policy," *Journal of Political Economy* 44, no. 1 (February 1936), both reprinted in Henry Simons, *Economic Policy for a Free Society* (Chicago: University of Chicago Press, 1948).

7. The correct Latin phrase is *pecca fortiter*, often rendered "sin boldly."

Numbers: Adding random numbers, average is stable, but total is more unstable. For timing to be of any good, there must be a system where the errors are less than in the random sample. But there are time lags before your public investment measure comes into effect.

I would prefer a fiscal system where we had relatively stable government expenditure.

Stability of tax structure and tax rates. We need systems which are <u>automatically</u> active in response to stimuli.

We ought to concentrate on getting the fundamental framework in order.

Session 12

Monday, April 7th, 1947, 8.30 p.m.

Statement of Aims

The following draft of a statement of aims, prepared by the Committee appointed on April 4th, was submitted for discussion by the Conference:

A group of students of society met at Mont Pèlerin, Switzerland, on April 1 to 10, 1947 to discuss the foundations for the preservation of a free society. For fruitful collaboration in working out these principles they feel that means for maintaining closer contact should be maintained among all those who share in substance the following convictions:

1. Individual freedom can be preserved only in a society in which an effective competitive market is the main agency for the direction of economic activity. Only the decentralization of control through private property in the means of production can prevent those concentrations of power which threaten individual freedom.
2. The freedom of the consumer in choosing what he shall buy, the freedom of the producer in choosing what he shall make, and the freedom of the worker in choosing his occupation and his place of employment, are essential not merely for the sake of freedom itself, but for efficiency in production. Such a system of freedom is essential if we are to maximize output in terms of individual satisfactions. Departure from these individual liberties leads to

the production not only of fewer goods and services but of the wrong goods and services. We cannot enrich ourselves merely by consenting to be slaves.

3. All rational men believe in planning for the future. But this involves the right of each individual to plan his own life. He is deprived of this right when he is forced to surrender his own initiative, will and liberty to the requirements of a central direction of the use of economic resources.

4. The decline of competitive markets and the movement towards totalitarian control of society are not inevitable. They are the result mainly of mistaken beliefs about the appropriate means for securing a free and prosperous society and of the policies based on these beliefs.

5. The preservation of an effective competitive order depends upon a proper legal and institutional framework. The existing frameworks must be considerably modified to make the operation of competition more efficient and beneficial. The precise character of the legal and institutional framework within which competition will work most effectively and which will supplement the working of competition is an urgent problem on which continued exchange of views is required.

6. As far as possible government activity should be limited by the rule of law. Government action can be made predictable only when it is bound by fixed rules. Tasks which require that authorities be given discretionary powers should therefore be reduced to the indispensable minimum. But it must be recognised that each extension of the power of the state gradually erodes the minimum basis for the maintenance of a free society. In general an automatic mechanism of adjustment, even where it functions imperfectly, is preferable to any which depends on "conscious" direction by governmental agencies.

7. The changes in current opinion which are responsible for the trend toward totalitarianism are not confined to economic doctrines. They are part of a movement of ideas which finds expression also in the field of morals and philosophy and in the interpretation

of history. Those who wish to resist the encroachments on individual liberty must direct their attention to these wider ideas as well as to those in the strictly economic field.

8. Any free society presupposes, in particular, a widely accepted moral code. The principles of this moral code should govern collective no less than private action.

9. Among the most dangerous of the intellectual errors which lead to the destruction of a free society are the historical fatalism which believes in our power to discover laws of historical development which we must obey, and the historical relativism which denies all absolute moral standards and tends to justify any political means by the purposes at which it aims.

10. Political pressures have brought new and serious threats to the freedom of thought and science. Complete intellectual freedom is so essential to the fulfilment of all our aims that no consideration of social expediency must ever be allowed to impair it.

Professor BRANDT: Statement contains <u>almost</u> everything. But the idea that liberals believe in the solidarity of human beings is missing.

Human dignity should be emphasised, and if possible somewhere near the beginning of the statement.

Professor GRAHAM: It would be as well for us to recognise that we do not want a "planless" system. We want the individual to be able to plan as he thinks best.

Professor FRIEDMAN: I think you need to add the idea that liberalism has a humanitarian aim and is a progressive philosophy.

Professor ROBBINS: I think the draft would be more effective if the larger cultural and moral issues were put first, and the economic later on. I think that paragraph 10 should include the idea that it is no duty of the tolerant to tolerate the intolerant.

Professor KNIGHT: Religious toleration needs to be included.

Freedom of association: people never act as individuals, but as members of a group.

Mr. DE JOUVENEL: I don't think decentralisation is achieved by personal property if for instance it is by small-holding in a large corporation.

Mr. WATTS: I protest against Jouvenel's disapproval of concentration of economic power in private hands.

Mr. MORLEY: Freedom is more important than efficiency of production. Therefore change things around in a particular system, so as to be in ascending order of importance. Liberty and freedom are not the same thing. Freedom is a social condition.

Professor ALLAIS: The statement should emphasise the international aspect. Limitation of sovereignty.

Economic means as a technique of organisation, relatively to the political ends.

Professor BRANDT: One of the ways to get things circulating as quickly as possible is to mark them confidential. Therefore we should have reference to public opinion.

Professor RAPPARD: Distinction between our friends and the public is hardly valid. I think the statement should be made capable of withstanding criticism from our worst enemies. "Moral code"—some may say we are thereby using a way out of our difficulties. We should not avoid discussion by referring to the "moral code". I don't see how "moral code" and expediency can be in opposition.

I don't think it a criterion of government to be predictable. More necessary to consider whether it is equitable.

Dr. EYCK: Predictability refers to the rule of law, and to the action of the government with respect to the action of the individual.

Professor KNIGHT: Don't we need something on humanitarianism?

Professor HAYEK: Concentration of economic power, as distinguished from monopoly: on this there is no chance of agreement at all, so we have kept it out of the statement.

Humanitarian aims: to be specific, we would need a lengthy statement of humanitarian aims alone.

Mr. HAZLITT: Committee had to limit expression of its own opinions, and try to deal with the presumed opinion of the meeting.

Professor ROBBINS: I'm disquieted by the suggestion that this may be published, disquieted by the idea that we are making a <u>detailed statement</u> of beliefs to be discussed in great detail so as to achieve the maximum of agreement. If the statement is for our friends, why not write <u>as though</u> we were writing personally? But I do <u>not</u> wish to disparage in any way the results of the committee's efforts.

Professor HAYEK: Extreme difficulty of putting our beliefs into a very short statement. Are we wasting our time? Does the meeting want a statement at all?

Professor FRIEDMAN: No statement either means no extension of the society, or alternatively a personal letter by the secretary, whoever that may be.

Mr. DE JOUVENEL: I was not criticising concentrations of <u>economic</u> power only, but of concentrations of power.

We in France have the position whereby all the parties have objections to private property.

Professor ROBBINS:

1. We recognise dangers to liberty.
2. We believe this to be connected with the decline of private property and the market.
3. We believe we should explain to the public these dangers.

Mr. MORLEY: Problem is that a good number of individuals are a little reticent about putting their names to any general statement. Why shouldn't the Secretary write a letter, including the statement, and saying that it was drafted with the aid of a drafting committee?

Professor MACHLUP: Could Professor Robbins write out a statement over-night, and present it at breakfast?

Professor ROBBINS: Not overnight, but I'm prepared to dictate one after breakfast tomorrow morning.

Professor HAYEK: Some things seem to me absolutely essential. Private property as an essential. It's just too bad that private property is not practical politics in France. It's merely that liberalism is impossible in France.

Professor STIGLER: I don't think we should defer drafting this. If we can't agree on a fairly general scheme of ideas, then it seems that there would be very little purpose, or reason, in forming a society.

Professor ROBBINS: How could there be adequate liberty in a society in which there is only one property owner and one employer?

Professor ALLAIS: Control by democracy is better than by State planning. It has not yet been proved that competitive controls are impossible under collective ownership.

Professor ROEPKE: I think that if Professor Allais proved anything about private property, I think he proved that we must retain it.

Mr. LOVINFOSSE: Impossible to have private property when you have State control over capital.

Professor Robbins was requested to submit a revised draft of the statement of aims for discussion at a later meeting.

Session 13

Tuesday, April 8th, 1947, 9.30 a.m.

Wages and Wage Policy

Professor Graham in the chair.

Professor MACHLUP: Wage determination, trade unions, and certain state legislation regarding trade unions, the main serious obstacles to the working of a free order in the U.S. Position probably similar in England and France, though different in Germany.

John Stuart Mill always considered the legislation against trade unions would be a government interference "in which the ends and the means are alike odious."[1]

Labour's natural disadvantage in bargaining.

One argument that holds: there might be <u>restricted</u> competition among employers in getting labour.

1. Tacit oligopsony.
2. Some labour markets are geographically or occupationally isolated.
3. Chronic unemployment makes labour immobile.

---

1. John Stuart Mill, *Principles of Political Economy with Some of their Applications to Social Philosophy*, 1871 edition, in *Collected Works of John Stuart Mill*, vol. 3, ed. J. M. Robson (Indianapolis, IN: Liberty Fund, 2006), 929. Mill utilized the singular "end" rather than "ends" in his sentence.

1. I don't think tacit oligopsony a very frequent case in our times.
2. Isolated labour markets a more frequent case. Is this a case for strong labour monopolies to combat this, or is it a case for increasing the mobility of labour, so as to reduce the isolation of those isolated markets? I think the latter.
3. If it is true that we have <u>chronic</u> unemployment, then mobility <u>is</u> reduced. There is then no real competition among several employers for the labour. If there is unemployment, and therefore immobility, if we then allow trade unions, we <u>prevent</u> full employment from coming about. I don't think full employment is compatible with a strong monopoly power of labour.

Solution: good monetary policy to <u>prevent</u> mass unemployment, and at the same time a policy <u>reducing</u> the monopoly power of unions. But how?

1. Appeal to the labour leaders
2. Remove all state aid to the trade unions. I don't believe that removal of state aid to unions will effectively reduce the monopoly power of the unions.
3. Flagrant acts of restriction of entry to unions should be combatted. BUT effective restriction of supply lies quite simply in the <u>wage contract</u>.

My own view: to restrict the size of unions either geographically or with respect to one single plant. Must also exclude combination <u>between</u> the different unions.

Professor RAPPARD: Professor Machlup's conclusions strongly affected by U.S. policy.

Common law period. U.S.: optimistic view of the mobility of labour. Mobility just does NOT exist in a country like Switzerland, for instance. No point in analysing economic soundness of his conclusions if it leads to policy which he admits himself to be politically impossible.

Swiss war experience: instability, but <u>no</u> labour troubles, because the labour leaders closely tied up with the whole economic process. They were shown and convinced that wage rises, for instance, would be bad for the country as a whole, and in the long run for the workers themselves.

Educate the trade union leaders, and members, to conception of solidarity of employers' and employees' interests. Not to weaker [*sic*] the unions, but to adapt them to the needs of the modern society. Professor Brentano favoured unions, because they helped the workers to get the <u>fair</u> distribution of the results of their labors.[2] Modern liberals take the opposite view. Why? Change in the fundamental objectives of the trade unions. Formerly—long strikes, embarrassing to the employer, therefore higher level of wages. Now—strikes calculated to harm the community, therefore <u>state</u> will have to intervene, therefore higher wages.

Professor ALLAIS:

1. Not possible to defend free competition in the labour market without provision for sub-marginal workers whose product is inferior. I think economic minimum wages a mistake. But minimum wages essential for the free working of the labour market.
2. I do not think organisation of labour market possible in France without cooperation of the trade unions.
3. Right to strike incompatible with a free order. Wage rates should be fixed by arbitrary body.

Mr. DE LOVINFOSSE: Tendency to discuss firm's interests with the workers themselves is becoming practically universal. Interests of employers and employees converge, and both sides realise it. Labourers naturally aspire to be a privileged class. But they are in the majority, and privilege can only apply to the minority, and they realise this. Labourers becoming more aware of the relation between prices and costs:

1. Agreeable labour conditions
2. Maximum of freedom and dignity

---

2. The German economist Lujo Brentano (1844–1931) was a founding member of the Verein für Sozialpolitik and in various works advocated the establishment of labor unions to improve the position of the working class.

3. Wages: <u>a</u> Establishment of a general <u>scale</u> of wages. In Belgium at
the moment, this does not apply. I would favour a central organisation to fix the scale of wages.

<u>b</u> the state of <u>real</u> wages. Steady increase of earning power
of labour. Couldn't it be automatic, rather than as a result of
bargains.

Workers come to see the advantages of cooperation.

I find workers on the whole not disinclined to serve the consumers by
cooperating. This applies not only in the production of consumers' goods,
but also in the production of producers' goods.

The alternative to the free market, i.e. collectivism, cannot but be bad in
its results to the workers, as well as to the community as a whole. Further,
it would conduce to monopoly, and therefore have further worse effects.[3]

Professor GRAHAM: We're failing to recognise fundamental principles.
I don't know about political feasability. [*sic*] I don't think we <u>can</u> know
anything about political feasability [*sic*]. Fundamental disagreement with
Professor Rappard. No sense in preaching to the various groups that they
must all be good. They <u>won't</u> all be good. All groups are united about volume of production. But problem is of <u>distribution</u>. No such thing as a <u>Just</u>
price. Nearest to a just price is the price ruling on a competitive market.
Concentrations of power are inevitably enemies of freedom.

Essential to have sufficient people <u>outside</u> your combination whom
you can exploit, otherwise your combination doesn't stand to gain much.
Function of the state, and primary function, to monopolise power in a
narrow field, in order to keep power dispersed in the rest of the field.

Professor MACHLUP: When I said "political feasability [*sic*]", I meant "at
this moment."

---

3. It should be noted that Henri de Lovinfosse, as the founder of a blanket and cloth manufacturing firm that employed 1,300 workers, may have been the only one there to have actually
participated in management-labor negotiations. Karl Brandt visited Lovinfosse in Belgium on
his way back from the conference and praised him in a subsequent letter to Hayek: "He is a real
liberal of the very best caliber; a progressive employer who has the most satisfied employees
I have ever seen anywhere, because he uses his imagination and leadership for their benefit"
(Brandt to Hayek, June 6, 1947, Friedrich A. Hayek Papers (FAHP), 72.36, Hoover Institution).

Professor DENNISON: Incompatability [*sic*] of full employment and monopoly in trade unions. In Great Britain, maldistribution of labour, resulting from the war. Insistent demands for a wages policy in Britain. But people won't way [*sic*] what wages policy should be. Difficulties of control of wages appear almost insoluble. But anyway, trade unions will have none of it. We had compulsory arbitration in Great Britain in the war. Strikes were illegal.

1914–18: no wage increases, led to serious unrest. But at present, instructive case of demand for higher wages in building. National Arbitration Board has given no award, and this is for the first time in its history. Serious trouble. I think <u>national</u> negotiation has come to stay in Britain.

Full Employment White Paper:

1. Government would take steps to encourage mobility of labour.
2. Government would control location of industry.

These two are quite incompatible. At the moment, government is concentrating on the second.

We are suffering from the legacy of the Great Depression. Government officials tend to say either

1. labour is immobile, or
2. if it <u>is</u> mobile, well, it oughtn't to be!

Government controlling the location of industry. Factories in development areas won't be ready for a year or two. Therefore government says, if you move to an area where labour is short, we'll move you back to this area when the new factory is built.

Professor POLANYI: Solidarity between employees can be established. And we want to educate the legislators. Can we do so unless we assume solidarity for instance in the belief in government by discussion?

Excesses due to remarkable tolerance by community of violence imposed on it by the unions.

We must in one way or another reunite peoples of Europe on the fundamentals, and expectations of what <u>can</u> be achieved, in a free society.

Professor IVERSEN: Influence of price control systems on the employers' attidue [*sic*] in bargaining with labour, in the Scandinavian countries.

Price-fixing authorities should reimburse employers for variable costs. The employers believe that there should be automatic compensation for wage increases. Mere repeal of price control will not change the attitude of the employers. Employers don't want to be the resisting power against the trade unions.

Depreciation in early thirties. But then there were increases in costs. By about 1938, we should have had a further depreciation.

If we are to have anything like a fixed exchange rate, as under Bretton Woods, I don't see how there can be compatability [sic] of full employment and wage bargaining by the unions.

I don't see, therefore, how we can avoid at least some state control of wages.

In Denmark, there is a black market in labour. The small employers disregard the rules of the Employers' Union.

Professor KNIGHT: Idyllic picture of solidarity—inimical to the free society, and free economic order.

Implies orderliness and stability of change, which is just not true.

Mobility that is fundamental is the willingness to move into the unknown to adventure, and particularly the entrepreneurial function.

Adventurous thesis—excessive wages contradictory.

Professor RAPPARD: No such thing of course as a just price and a just wage. You can't expect everyone to be good, but you can try to get them to be more intelligent. You can expect people to see their interests as they really are. Restrictions on immigration. Tariff restrictions. When Professor Graham goes on to speak of the incompatability [sic] of solidarity and full employment, it leads to the jungle, with no solidarity.

There is a maximum above which a wage is unjust—by ruining the employer permanently. Profit margins are low!

But we should certainly not, out of hatred of solidarity, disregard the things which are in the common interest of the employers and employees. Without a minimum of solidarity, no human society is possible.

Mr. WATTS: Problem of cycles has largely been caused by government.

Professor Dennison said that there is a maldistribution of labour in Britain—but this is due to wage controls, and to unemployment relief. Had there been a free market for goods and services, there would have been greater speed in removing maldistribution.

We need to remove the obstacles to mobility. Merely neutralising the violence of the trade unions on the picket line would go a long way towards solving the labour problem. Government has failed to remove violence of trade union power.

Concentrations of economic power are necessary, for incentive purposes and the like. But they must not be acquired by violence, either legalised or not. I think we are forgetting part of the liberal philosophy, about absolute moral codes. They used to speak of natural rights. But there are certain moral principles which people must have, even to have a family.

Has government the moral right to restrict the rights of the individuals to make contracts? Even the sub-marginal worker has the right to work, even if at a lower rate of wages. We should try to get away from the idea that we're dealing with statistics, instead of men.

Why should we say that the amount of unemployment at any one moment is normal? If people don't choose to work at the current rate of wages in a free society, that's normal unemployment.

Professor BRANDT: Rapid decline in the number of people in the German unions. But I don't think this will happen elsewhere.

No longer, in Germany, a question of striking in one industry so as to bring equilibrium within that industry between employers and employees. It is more of a general strike. American citizens think that if different groups are left to battle things out, democracy will perish.

Mr. DE JOUVENEL: Workers tend to get more of the income of the nation. Spirit of Mussolini's corporations reigns.[4] Main problem is the problem of the state.

---

4. After describing the Fascist corporative state variously as "an absolute," "a will and a personality," and "a spiritual and moral fact in itself," Benito Mussolini concluded, "Through the corporative social and educational institutions created by it, its influence reaches every aspect of national life." See Benito Mussolini, "The Political and Social Doctrine of Fascism," in

Mr. Davenport: In U.S., where the tower of labour power has erupted, through Lewis and the miners, there is a peculiar kind of case.[5] Communist element not very important, relatively to France. But importance of the middle group.

It is necessary to convince, but difficult to do so, the people who want to extend the area of the wage contract, and the people who look up to the success of the British experience.

I can't see how the closed shop fits the liberal order.[6]

I think we should use the anti-trust law against the unions, and leave the closed shop where it is, but not let it spread. I think further that we should bring back the concept of the company union, or plant union.

If there were secret ballots in French unions, it might be a great improvement, and a move against the Communists.

Is the church movement, concerning the just price and the just wage, as bad as it seems? Have the Christian parties any specific reforms.

Professor Jewkes: Success of our wage policy during the war largely due to the understanding and restraining influence of the union leaders. I think that has been continued since the end of the war. Revolution in England: working classes have come into power. It might have gone to their head—but people are taking, in the main, the long view about wage increases, and this is largely due to excellent trade union leadership. It has

---

Planned Society: Yesterday, Today, Tomorrow: A Symposium by Thirty-Five Economists, Sociologists and Statesmen, ed. Findlay MacKenzie (New York: Prentice Hall, 1937), 810–13.

5. In response to postwar inflation, from 1945–46 a wave of labor strikes hit the United States. The automobile, electrical, steel, oil, and meatpacking industries were some of the major ones affected, but others included such disparate professions as railroad engineers and film crews. At the time, the most famous and, for some, notorious labor leader was John L. Lewis (1880–1969). President of the United Mine Workers of America, Lewis led his members on a deeply unpopular wartime strike in 1943. Between 1945 and 1950 coal miners engaged in some form of strike or work stoppage activity every year. Many of the labor protections that the Mont Pèlerin Conference attendees viewed as antiliberal (e.g., closed-shop laws, secondary boycotts, wildcat and solidarity strikes) were deemed unfair labor practices and prohibited in the Taft-Hartley Act. The act became law in June 1947, just two months after the meeting.

6. A closed-shop law requires employers to hire only union members and requires workers to maintain their union membership as a condition of employment. Davenport mentions anti-trust laws as a remedy because closed-shop laws essentially give the union monopoly power over who can be employed.

been the trade union leaders who have been largely responsible for getting rid of the direction of labour.[7]

Trade unions are opposed to a National Wages Policy. If government had been able to impose a policy, it would have been used to hand people from one job to another, to cover up one mistake in planning after another.

Allais seemed to urge that compulsory arbitration in industry was desirable to a large extent. But I think it creates chaos on the labour market. Compulsory arbitration removes responsibility from labour. Much easier to bluff an independent tribunal than to bluff the employer. Chief argument against compulsory arbitration is that it doesn't prevent strikes. Fundamental right to starve.

Professor ALLAIS: I didn't say what you allege—less extreme than your interpretation. In a truly competitive society, wages should emerge in such a way that strikes would not arise. There is a wage level for equilibrium between supply and demand.

Professor MACHLUP (summing up at the beginning of the evening session): I want to group together the opinions of Professors Rappard Polanyi and Jewkes, that the unions are here to stay, that we can hope that unions will restrain from making excessive demands, and that we should educate the labour and union leaders and members.

---

7. During the war the British government had the power to direct labor into those areas where its manpower needs were the greatest. It retained this right after the war. As Jewkes noted, the labor unions had until that point successfully opposed government attempts to direct labor and to set higher wages in industries that suffered from manpower shortages. Later in the year, however, the British minister of labour issued the Control and Engagement Order of 1947. Ivor Bulmer-Thomas, in *The Socialist Tragedy* (London: Latimer House, 1949), 104–5, offered this summary: "Under this Order men between the ages of 18 and 50 and women between the ages of 18 and 40 may not be engaged except through an employment exchange of the Ministry of Labour, apart from certain exempted occupations. Workers in coal mining and agriculture are not permitted to leave those occupations. Other applicants at an employment exchange are offered jobs that in the Government's view have the highest priority. If an applicant refuses to accept such a job he can in the last resort be directed, and failure to obey the direction can be punished by a fine or imprisonment." Though on the books, the unpopular order was seldom invoked and was withdrawn in March 1950.

I consider this position to be romantic. I don't see why the labour union with the power to keep its members from starvation should let them starve.

Arbitration is no way out—on this I agree with Professor Jewkes.

Industrial peace is something we should be afraid of, as it can only be bought at the cost of further distortion of the wage structure. I am most afraid of Professor Iversen's proposal for wage determination by the state, and consider it to be the end of democratic government.

Smaller sized unions might be a way of decreasing the monopoly power of the unions. Small amount of poison is better than a larger amount.

Session 14

Tuesday, April 8th, 1947, 4.30 p.m.

Further Discussion of Statement of Aims

The new draft of the "Statement of Aims" prepared by Professor Robbins was discussed and after some further amendments approved by all members except Professor Allais in the following form:

"A group of economists, historians, philosophers and other students of public affairs from Europe and the United States met at Mont Pèlerin, Switzerland, from April 1st to 10th 1947 to discuss the crisis of our times. This group, being desirous of perpetuating its existence for promoting further intercourse and for inviting the collaboration of other like minded persons, has agreed upon the following statement of aims.

The central values of civilization are in danger. Over large stretches of the earth's surface the essential conditions of human dignity and freedom have already disappeared. In others they are under constant menace from the development of current tendencies of policy. The position of the individual and the voluntary group are progressively undermined by extensions of arbitrary power. Even that most precious possession of Western Man, freedom of thought and expression, is threatened by the spread of creeds which, claiming the privilege of tolerance when in the position of a minority, seek only to establish a position of power in which they can suppress and obliterate all views but their own.

The group holds that these developments have been fostered by the growth of a view of history which denies all absolute moral standards and by the growth of theories which question the desirability of the rule of law. It holds further that they have been fostered by a decline of belief in private property and the competitive market; for without the diffused power and initiative associated with these institutions it is difficult to imagine a society in which freedom may be effectively preserved.

Believing that what is essentially an ideological movement must be met by intellectual argument and the reassertion of valid ideals, the group, having made a preliminary exploration of the ground, is of the opinion that further study is desirable inter alia in regard to the following matters:

1) The analysis and explanation of the nature of the present crisis so as to bring home to others its essential moral and economic origins.

2) The redefinition of the functions of the state so as to distinguish more clearly between the totalitarian and the liberal order.

3) Methods of reestablishing the rule of law and of assuring its development in such manner that individuals and groups are not in a position to encroach upon the freedom of others and private rights are not allowed to become a basis of predatory power.

4) The possibility of establishing minimum standards by means not inimical to initiative and the functioning of the market.

5) Methods of combatting the misuse of history for the furtherance of creeds hostile to liberty.

6) The problem of the creation of an international order conducive to the safeguarding of peace and liberty and permitting the establishment of harmonious international economic relations.

The group does not aspire to conduct propaganda. It seeks to establish no meticulous and hampering orthodoxy. It aligns itself with no particular party. Its object is solely, by facilitating the exchange of views among minds inspired by certain ideals and broad conceptions held in common, to contribute to the preservation and improvement of the free society."

Some further discussion was devoted to the question of the form of the organisation of the permanent body and a small informal sub-committee was set up to prepare a draft memorandum of association for submission to the meeting on Wednesday afternoon.

Session 15

Tuesday, April 8th, 1947, 8.30 p.m.

Taxation, Poverty, and Income Distribution

Professor Mises in the chair.

Professor FRIEDMAN: Desire to eliminate povery [*sic*].

Measures to break up unions can bring success only if we have policies to combat the evils which unions were designed to counteract.

Problem of poverty underlies many of the lines of intervention, even though to some extent poverty has been <u>caused</u> by such interventions.

Even if we had completely free access to different employments, and to capital, there would still be the problem of poverty. Sub-marginal workers. Men are not born equal. In a large country submarginal workers are not evenly distributed throughout the population. You can't expect New York charity to help the poor cotton workers of the South, who are hit by the use of artificial fibres.

There <u>are</u> definitely people who cannot earn, in the market place, an income even that we could consider to be a minimum. Other people have to pay for this help. Therefore we have progressive taxation. No democratic society is going to tolerate people starving to death, if there is food with which to feed them.

But what is the best thing to do?

Two alternative kinds of techniques.

1. General techniques, of national minimum type.
2. Poor law type of technique, judging each case on its merits.

If we were starting from scratch, there would be a case for the second type. But we have done too much of poor law type already. Therefore, if we want to do any more, it ought to be of the first type.

I want to propose that we maintain the kind of progressive income tax now in force, but also with progressive negative taxation below the exemption [*sic*] limit.[1] If a man earned nothing, he would be given something by the state.

This would give an incentive to getting additional income. Would make clear how much society would have to pay for helping the poor.

In U.S.A., large cost of living differences between different parts of the country. Therefore if we made figures uniform throughout the country, would give too much to some, too little to others.

This policy is suggested as a substitute, not as an addition, to present social policy. Substitute for unemployment relief, old age pensions, etc.

In any system of progressive taxation, it appears to tax away a minority.

Seems rather fantastic to try and prevent peoples of other countries not to use progressive taxation at all. But it would be easier to persuade them to my policy, and to be restrained in the use of progressive taxation.

In U.S.A., progressive taxation has gone too far in affecting incentives.

Professor JEWKES: In fixing tolerable standards, who will decide what is tolerable, and in particular, in modern times, how will you prevent the "minimum tolerable" from rising too high?

Would you still have social services?

Professor FRIEDMAN: The elected representatives of the people would decide.

---

1. Those familiar with Friedman's thought will recognize this as his negative-income-tax proposal. As Jennifer Burns notes in chapter 3 of *The Last Conservative: The Life of Milton Friedman* (New York: Farrar, Straus, Giroux, forthcoming), he first proposed this idea in 1939.

Of course the entire cost of my policy is not obvious. For there would be some fall in production.

Social services which the community considers essential would of course be maintained. Some funds for orphans, for instance.

Mr. MILLER: Is this offered as a frankly expedient program?

Professor FRIEDMAN: No, merely as a policy which is in accordance with the liberal society.

Expediency is merely an <u>additional</u> advantage.

Even with a completely competitive order, we'd still have the problem of <u>poverty</u>.

Professor POLANYI: Is it the head of the family who pays the taxes?

Professor FRIEDMAN: Yes

Professor DANNISON [*sic*]: I don't think Professor Friedman entirely answered Jewkes's question about the minimum standard.

1934, Unemployment <u>Assistance</u>.[2]

Means test, and <u>needs</u> test.

As a result, some workers are getting more, from assistance, than they would have received from Insurance.

Professor FRIEDMAN: It is a merit of my scheme that it doesn't have <u>that</u> sort of objection to it.

Professor RAPPARD: In most countries, you have taxation on income of the year before. Wouldn't this create hardship?

---

2. Under the British Unemployment Act of 1934, the benefits for long-term workers who had paid into the national insurance scheme reflected their prior payments. For others, the Unemployment Assistance Board determined the amount of assistance based on need, using a means test that took the wages and other assets of family members into account. This led to the possibility of disparities in payments noted by Dennison.

Professor FRIEDMAN: Pay-as-you-go.

Professor ALLAIS: I agree with the purpose, but disagree with the means.

I disagree with progressive positive taxation, and therefore disagree with progressive negative taxation.

Why not the better use of taxation on scarce factors, monopoly rents, land, inheritances, etc.[3]

Mr. DE JOUVENEL: Not easy to find out how much income a man has. Even less easy to find out how little income a man has. Inquisition into amounts of income.

Professor FRIEDMAN: Part of the cost would be paid by increased returns under the present income tax. Administrative difficulties, yes. But otherwise, the administrative difficulties would be even greater.

Professor HAYEK: Ideal of eliminating poverty. But what do we mean by poverty, and how far can you extend the idea from rich countries to poor countries?

I doubt whether I would dare to put the phrase "eliminating poverty" on my programme as a liberal.

Just not practicable not to make some provision for the poor. But I am doubtful whether a certain money income from the State is the right means.

Voluntary labour service, at which anyone who cannot find employment, can find employment at just under market rates, under semimilitary conditions.

Freedom not to work is a luxury which the poor country cannot afford. "Duty to work under direction"?

You can refuse to enter this service, if you prefer to exist on a pittance.

Professor KNIGHT: I think you have to use expedients. But I am going to discuss what I consider to be the least worst expedient.

---

3. Allais's objection to progressive taxation is based on his viewing the taxation of assets inherently fixed in supply, such as land, as a preferred form of taxation.

Natural resources on the whole cost much more than they are worth. Lot of scarcity rents <u>could</u> be taxed, but that would be negligible to the amount of taxes you need. We want natural resources explored further—if they are subject to scarcity rents, this would not really be done.

Even if you tax away future accretions of value, you're still taxing <u>present value</u>.

The bigger the chance that if there is a gain it will be large, the more likely that the amount put into natural resources is greater than the amount received from it.

Professor BRANDT: Farmer hasn't to keep books. Prices of all amenities operate in his favour, from tax point of view. If you have two identical houses, one in town and one in country, there will be a considerable difference in their market values, because there is less demand for the country house. This is to the favour of the farmer for tax purposes. Agriculture holds the largest reservoir of the people with the least initiative and the least incentive to contribute the maximum to the social product. Your system would maintain the large part of the population in a position which should be remedied by incentives as soon as possible.

Dr. POPPER: Professor Friedman's idea is an attractive alternative to socialism. But Professor Hayek's idea is not. But: don't pay just below, but pay the minimum. It would still be less attractive than normal work. Cost of the scheme is in any case dubious. Why should the poor get it in the neck both ways?

Professor HAYEK: As long as it is less attractive to work for the government than the market, the essential is there.

Professor MISES: High rates of allowances in the U.S.A. Ought we to discuss the problem of poverty all over the world? Why shouldn't the Chinese and Japanese ask for this alleviation to be international.

Professor RAPPARD: Not to suppress poverty, but to subsidise the poor. Problem is to avoid acute avoidable distress without creating poverty. An attractive scheme of help to the poor is anti-social.

Professor Friedman's scheme has the worst possible psychological effects: the good citizen, who pays his taxes, has to pay for the poor.

Once you have depression, where majority are receiving, and the minority paying taxes, you are in a position of decadence. Pay-as-you-go would be even more difficult with negative taxes.

Professor ALLAIS: I wonder whether I understood correctly when Professor Knight said there was no such thing as scarcity rent.

Mr. WATTS: I agree with Professor Rappard against Professor Friedman. But I thought the objection could also be applied to Professor Hayek's idea. W.P.A. a political and economic cancer that continued to grow.[4] Only the war, and inflation, allowed us to get rid of it.

Professor FRIEDMAN: This is not a panacea for all evils.

1. Many of the difficulties are inherent in the problem and not in the solution.
2. Many of difficulties are difficulties of our present income tax structure.
3. Income tax implies inheritance taxation.
4. Re Professor Hayek's scheme, you run the risk of private business being afraid of what will happen in the public sector. Also, it would imply minimum standards throughout the whole of the economy.
5. Much depends on your level of allowances.

---

4. The Works Progress Administration was a New Deal program that was established in 1935. Between then and 1943 the WPA employed about 8.5 million Americans to carry out a variety of public works projects, from the construction of roads, bridges, parks, playgrounds, and other infrastructure to the production of plays, music, and artwork. Low wartime unemployment brought the program to an end in 1943. Critics viewed WPA projects as instilling poor work habits (there was little incentive to work efficiently; wags said the acronym stood for "We Piddle Around" or "We Poke Along") and criticized the allocation of projects as politically motivated. Watts's comment that it was both an economic and political cancer reflect such complaints. He also no doubt was unhappy that Hayek's plan would involve the government taking on the role of employer of last resort.

6. International aspects of the problem.

7. Purely in terms of the <u>Elimination of Poverty</u>. But it also has an anti-cyclical effect. If you manage to have a liberal society with this flexibility, it would be very good from a cyclical point of view.[5]

---

5. Regarding the business cycle, a progressive income tax is a form of automatic stabilizer which a negative income tax further strengthens. It supplements incomes in downturns and collects more in taxes in booms, thus reducing recessionary or inflationary pressures at the appropriate points of the cycle.

Session 16

Wednesday, April 9th, 1947, 9.30 a.m.

Agricultural Policy

Mr. Read in the chair.

Professor BRANDT: I think agricultural policy one of the testing grounds of the Liberal philosophy.

Key position held by farmers, more than by any other class. Only a Marxist idea that the key position is held by the proletariat.

Labour unions have long since given up fighting for lower prices of food. Where food is concerned, the outlook is a producers' outlook.

Compromises on food prices likely due to having to import food from abroad. This would apply to England, for instance, having to import at a higher price.

Germany—price of rye began to fall, therefore the farmers said that ~~stage~~ *state* must intervene to raise prices.

Farmers had the assurance in 1933 in U.S.A. on prices. Hoover had the same policy, even before Roosevelt.[1] Limitation of agricultural production

1. Improvements in farming methods and the loss of export markets led to surpluses in production for American farmers following World War I, with consequent declines in prices for agricultural products and farm incomes. Various proposals for federal government intervention during the 1920s were unsuccessful until the Agricultural Marketing Act of 1929 was passed under the Hoover administration. The act established the Federal Farm Board, which

by quotas, and then price-raising. Agriculture makes two chief claims, for equality and security. Equality would lead to the end of freedom. A minimum of security is compatible with a liberal society, although you may distort the whole economic system, and it is very dangerous. Competitive economy has a procedure of reward and penalty, and by loss and bankruptcy those who fail are eliminated. This is accepted by the people by and large.

But this ethic was thought to be wrong, when even the best farmers, for instance, failed to make profits.

Credit structure in agriculture with mortgages is very rigid, making it hard to make adjustments without thousands of families losing their livelihood. Length of time measured in terms of years for adjustments in scale in agriculture. Prevention of collapse needs to begin at the start of the upswing. The more you finance by credit in the upswing, the more rigidities you erect. We have to ask for State regulatory supervision of mortgages. State should decide the policy of the mortgage companies. I'm strictly against any impediment of the rights of the creditors in any other way. Increased interest rates to be paid by farmers in the boom, lower interest rates in the slump. This would diminish the bad effects of the rigidities of the credit structure.

We don't want artificial profits for agriculture, with quotas and restrictionism. We don't want an income parity practice. We do not want, when prices of agricultural commodities go down, to upset the whole economy and set the farmers into revolt.

Plan which would have the feature of automatism, and leave the market entirely free, but where, remote from the market, the government is

---

was provided with $500 million in funds to assist farmers and farm cooperatives in the buying, selling, and storing of agricultural surpluses. Under the Roosevelt administration, the Agricultural Adjustment Act of 1933 was passed. Its goal was to achieve parity of agricultural prices with those from the prewar 1909–1914 period, using price supports, quotas, and other means. Hoover's policy aimed to assist farmers to use their own organizations to manage surpluses, whereas Roosevelt's policy directly intervened in the price system, so Brandt's claim that "Hoover had the same policy" seems unwarranted. See Douglas Bowers, Wayne Rasmussen, and Gladys Baker, "History of Agricultural Price-Support and Adjustment Programs, 1933–1984," Economic Research Service, US Department of Agriculture, Agriculture Information Bulletin No. 485, December 1984.

prepared to underwrite a minimum level of income, based upon commodity prices. Will it be possible to have this minimum low enough to avoid upsetting the rest of the economy?

Insurance company, announcing the level of underwriting, with the goal of no surpluses in the market, but which would also have to make it plain what the maximum risk it underwrites is. That maximum risk would vary from year to year.

There should be some degree of <u>gradualness</u> in the change in agricultural prices—and this also happens to be <u>politically expedient</u>.

Winning the farmers back to the idea of a free economy seems to me <u>very</u> important.

Professor DIRECTOR: There was some hesitation last night on the subject of minimum incomes. In the U.S., challenge to democracy comes from groups organised on <u>occupational</u> lines. Minimum standards can, I think, only increase the pressure of these minority pressure groups.

Fluctuations in the economy as a whole <u>affect</u> agriculture, not the other way round, therefore if you can solve the problem of general oscillations, there is no problem of agriculture at all.

Professor ROEPKE: What is the position of liberalism towards agriculture? Tendency to look at agriculture as at any other industry. More and more liberals, however, are coming to believe the opposite, that agriculture is a way of life. No longer so much interested in agriculture as such, but as the social life of the family farm. This would make it wise to have units smaller than would otherwise be rational for normal business standards. Family farm—thereby we avoid the proletarian nomads of industrialisation. Liberal wants to do justice to the "social way of life" of the farmer, but at the same time does not want to associate himself with reactionary policies.

It is the family farm which provides the optimum form of agricultural production in the industrial countries. We need the diversified form of agriculture, which makes the farmer largely independent of money income. Land policy. Credit policy. Policies of succession, and tenure.

Mr. MILLER: How do you determine tolerable standards, and minimum standards?

How can the state interfere with, without participating in, the mortgage policies?

And why shouldn't everyone be insured against the vicissitudes of the market, if farmers can be insured?

What would be the sum of all the interventions which have been suggested during the conference? Wouldn't that be a planned economy?

The trouble is by using partial equilibrium analysis. It is wrong to say that "a little bit doesn't hurt."

Professor BRANDT: Not the essence of a liberal economy to construct a 100% logical machine purely because the Nazis had a 100% logical machine.

Agricultural depression may be an adjustment depression, as a result of trying to maintain industry.

I did not want insurance to underwrite an absolute minimum standard—only to make the change in prices somewhat more gradual.

Professor ROBBINS: I don't share Brandt's view about practical desirability. Nevertheless, I'd defend its practical possibility.

Two kinds of practical considerations of government policy:—

1. Policy designed to remedy some gap in automatic reaction system of prices and private property.
2. Advising on practical proposals which have in them some elements of political expediency. If there is a government aim, liberal can still advise on policy towards that aim, even if that aim is illiberal. Advise on least harmful way of achieving the illiberal aim.

There is no need for the liberal economists to turn sulky, just because they don't agree on the aims of government. Professor Roepke mentioned that departures from free market and free trade lead almost certainly to a limitation of the national dividend, and that, on the other hand, if we try to maximise the national dividend, we are forfeiting certain social qualities.

But then he said that peasant agriculture gave you farms of optimum size, at which I bridled. I don't think its [sic] a law of nature. Fundamental question: supposing that peasant agriculture universally gave an optimum, even so, if present tendencies persisted, and application of scientific techniques persisted, you would have greater and greater production, and if demand is relatively inelastic, Prof. Roepke would still have his problem unsolved.

Professor HAYEK: Like Mr. Miller, I am alarmed at the aspect of considering our problems one by one. Primary task seems to be to clear our minds on what principles we would like to see applied if we had a free hand. We ought to make it clear what concessions we would regard as desirable and what concessions we consider to be politically expedient at the present moment.

It is already a definite ethical judgment when we say that everyone in a particular country ought to be entitled to a minimum standard.

Also, a definite ethical judgment that if people go into agriculture, knowing all the risks, to say that they ought to be relieved of its risks.

Professor ~~EUCKEN~~:

Professor RAPPARD: I can't help feeling that its [sic] not an accident that the subject of agriculture has been kept towards the end. Agriculture is the great challenge to economic liberalism. Why?

Would there be such a thing as economic liberalism if we didn't live in an industrial age?

Reason why economic liberalism doesn't fit agriculture:

1. aims; economic liberalism aims at producing the greatest social dividend. (if peasant farm were the optimum, it wouldn't need protection.)
2. in rest of industry, equilibrating movements are reasonably quick. But in agriculture the equilibrium can only be brought about in a longer space of time. Biological processes and time. Climatic conditions. It doesn't follow that we have to throw liberalism

overboard. But I don't think we can apply liberalism, for doctrinaire reasons, to agriculture.

Who would be in favour of economic liberalism with respect to agriculture, regardless of security? Majority.

Professor ROBBINS: Would Professor Rappard say we ought to safeguard agriculture against <u>secular</u> change, as apart from cyclical change?

Professor GRAHAM: I shared Miller's alarm, but I could not follow his completely simplistic policy.

Need for definition of aims. There is <u>conflict of loyalties</u> at the basis of our difficulties.

Do we make liberalism our supreme aim, or our unique aim? Supreme yes, but not, I think our unique aim.

Perfectly free migration would be simplistically liberal. But transfers from super-Malthusian situation would bring down the rest of the world.

Would we want freedom above everything, if it meant freedom for us all to be miserable?

John Stuart Mill considered slavery essential for part of the population, so that people would <u>not</u> need to scratch the ground in order to keep alive.[2]

Freedom isn't the <u>only</u> value on which we lay importance. We are not ready to concede that all who are sub-marginal, on a free basis, should be allowed to die.

---

2. This statement mischaracterizes Mill's position. In his "Considerations on Representative Government," 1865 edition, Mill asserted that most currently civilized societies passed through a period when many were held in slavery, seeing it as a step by which "people in a state of savage independence" became accustomed to doing the "continuous labor of an unexciting kind" necessary to develop. See *Essays on Politics and Society*, vol. 19 of *Collected Works of John Stuart Mill*, ed. J. M. Robson (Toronto: University of Toronto Press, 1977), 394. But this was a historical conjecture, not an endorsement, as is evident in his next statement about slavery: "Its adoption under any circumstances whatever in modern society is a relapse into worse than barbarism" (p. 395). In his chapter "Of Slavery" in *Principles of Political Economy with Some of their Applications to Social Philosophy*, 1871 edition, Mill wrote passionately about the "enormity" (p. 250) of the institution, calling it a "detestable . . . constitution of society" (p. 245). He decried those Englishmen who had encouraged the Southern cause in the American Civil War, saying their attitude "will be a lasting blot in English history" (p. 250). See *Collected Works of John Stuart Mill*, vol. 2, ed. J. M. Robson (Toronto: University of Toronto Press, 1965).

If you allow freedom to individuals, they will not provide themselves with insurance. I am therefore in favour of some forms of <u>social insurance</u>.

Constant tendency under free conditions for people without foresight to get themselves into debt to the foresighted. What are the things we really want BESIDE freedom?

Professor MISES: Professor Rappard has a brilliant way of pointing out why industrial countries have protected agriculture in the last 70 to 80 years. But this is only one part of the picture. What causes brought it about that this majority in the industrial countries subsidised the agricultural minority?

Comparative cost doctrine.[3]

Professor ROEPKE: In answer to Professor Robbins, I believe profoundly in peasant agriculture as an end, or as a means rather high up.

~~Whereas in former times to be in favour of agriculture would have involved protectionist outlook, we say that reasoning and experience proves the opposite.~~

Professor BRANDT: I did not elaborate on the attack made against protectionism.

I still want to fight against any monopoly, labour monopoly, protective tariff, government determination of the size of agriculture. To fight for a competitive economy.

But I still want to fight for an emprovement [*sic*] of the credit possibilities open to farmers. But I don't agree with Professor Mises, and I don't think what Professor Rappard imputed is correct.

---

3. The comparative cost doctrine states that countries will do best if they specialize in the production and export of goods in which they have a comparative advantage while importing those goods they are less efficient in producing. Mises is questioning the wisdom of industrialized countries subsidizing agriculture, an area in which they are at a comparative disadvantage.

Session 17

Wednesday, April 9th, 1947, 4.30 p.m.

Meeting on Organisation

Professor ROEPKE: The word "liberal" is associated with different things in different countries. Would it be better to replace "liberal" by "philosophy of freedom."

Mr. DE JOUVENEL: Why shouldn't the society be called the Acton-Tocqueville Society?

Professor HAYEK: Because some have objected.

Mr. DE JOUVENEL: How about Andre Siegfried as a Vice-President, to represent French thought?[1]

Professor FRIEDMAN: Lets [*sic*] subordinate national representation.

---

1. André Siegfried (1875–1959) was a French political scientist who introduced a new approach to studying politics, "political ecology," which used maps to portray the influence of geography as well as other factors on political outcomes. He was widely known for his books on other countries, including New Zealand, Canada, Britain, and the United States and in 1944 was elected to the Académie Française.

Professor IVERSEN: Rather peculiar that the purpose of an international society should be <u>specially</u> to translate into English.

The draft was approved.

What Should Be the Title of the Organisation?

Professor HAYEK: Suggestion for calling it the Acton-Tocqueville Society, with the subtitle of "an international academy of political philosophy".

Professor KNIGHT: Acton and Tocqueville neither stand for anything economic.

Professor MISES: Political mistake with respect to Tocqueville, who held a position under Napoleon, even though he soon discovered his mistake.

Professor BRANDT: I favour the Acton-Tocqueville Society.

Mr. HAZLITT: Might be a case of invidious selection of names.

Professor DIRECTOR: How about Adam Smith-Tocqueville Society?

Professor RAPPARD: Both Acton and Tocqueville were Catholics and noblement.

Professor FRIEDMAN: Incongruous to name it after <u>people</u>. We want it to be named after principles.

Professor ROBBINS: Some of us feel the use of a name has a somewhat pleasing esoteric nature.

Mr. MILLER: I have serious reservations about using anyone's name in the title.

Professor ROBBINS: The Protagonist Society?

Mr. DE JOUVENEL: Alteration of Acton-Tocqueville will be subject to even more difficulties.

Dr. POPPER: The Periclean Society?

Professor GRAHAM: If we name it after people, we might discover parts of their writings which we would not endorse.

Mr. MORLEY: I appoint a committee of Mr. de Jouvenel, Miss Wedgwood and Mr. Davenport to consider the name.

International Society for the Study of Freedom in Society.

John Milton.

International Academy for the study of the requisites of a free society.[2]

Professor BRANDT: The Mont Pèlerin Society.?

Dr. POPPER: That is meaningless.

Wednesday, April 9th, 1947, 4.30 p.m.

Discussion on Organisation of Permanent Body

The draft of the Memorandum of Association submitted by the sub-committee was discussed and after a number of minor amendments approved in the following form:

---

2. In the original typeset manuscript, it is ambiguous whether Mrs. Hahn wrote these notes to indicate the discussion at large or whether these ideas were spoken by Mr. Morley.

Memorandum of Association

Resolved 1. that the members of the Mont-Pèlerin Conference agree to form a society to be called [blank space left for name] for the purposes set out in the Statement of Aims already agreed upon which is to be regarded as an integral part of this Resolution.

2. that the affairs of the Society be directed by an EXECUTIVE COMMITTEE, consisting of the President, Vice-presidents Secretaries and Treasurer, advised by a COUNCIL consisting of fifteen members including the members of the Executive Committee; the first Executive Committee to consist of

President: F. A. Hayek

Vice-Presidents: W. Eucken, J. Jewkes, W. E. Rappard

Secretaries: A. Director, A. Hunold

with the addition of a further Vice-President and a Treasurer to be co-opted by the above. The remaining members of the Council also to be appointed by the Executive Committee.

3. The Executive Committee and the Council to hold office until the next General Meeting of the Society, but for no more than three years from the present date. If no General Meeting of the Society can be held within three years, a new Executive Committee and a new Council to be elected by postal vote after the members have been given an opportunity to nominate candidates.

4. that the Executive Committee be authorised to take the steps necessary to secure the legal existence of the Society.

5. that the Executive Committee, with the advice of the other members of the Council if required, be authorized

a) to issue invitations to join the Society to all the persons who have been invited to attend to join the Society and to other persons whom they believe to be in agreement with the aims of the Society and to be able to make contributions to its tasks;

b) to collect membership fees and other contributions to be used for the purposes of the Society;

c) to arrange for conferences either of the Society or of local or specialised groups of members of the Society and to decide, if necessary, for which of the members the expenses of participating in the Conference should be defrayed from the funds of the Society.

d) to arrange for circulation among the members of the Society in duplicated or printed forms of such papers or documents, or translations of such papers and documents, as will assist in the furtherance of the objects of the Society;

e) to arrange, if it should be thought desirable, for the publication of a series of papers, including translations of papers published in other languages, which will assist the study of a free society;

f) to appoint correspondents in the different countries to facilitate contact with members of those countries;

and g) to have power to delegate one or more of these powers to sub-committees or individual members of the Executive Council.

6. that an annual membership fee of U.S. $4.—or its equivalent in other currencies be payable to the Treasurer by each member of the Society.

After some inconclusive discussion on the name of the society the question was referred to a sub-committee to report at the concluding session. Some further discussion took place on the character and size of the desirable membership.

Session 18

Wednesday, April 9th, 1947, 8.30 p.m.

The Present Political Crisis

Dr. Gideonse in the chair.

Professor POLANYI: The crisis is with respect to the position of liberalism, or freedom, in Europe, and arises from a surprising change in the course of history. Assumption that the 1914–1918 war was a war of liberalism. President Wilson said "What we seek is the rule of law, based on the consent of the governed."[1]

Lenin—government by principle that state governs by violence.

Interpretation of history on which this was based was the class war interpretation.

Wilsonian movement had great initial advantages, and spread a wave of democratic reform in several parts of Europe. But the wave of Wilsonian conquest didn't last long. Was thrown back over a large area by class war theory of politics, and was mostly embodied in dictatorships. This

---

1. In his July 4, 1918, address at Washington's tomb at Mount Vernon, Virginia, President Woodrow Wilson declared the goals for which the United States and its allies were fighting, concluding that they might be captured in the single sentence: "What we seek is the reign of law, based upon the consent of the governed and sustained by the organized opinion of mankind."

was interpreted as a <u>failure</u> of liberalism. Spread of theory of "political realism"—not sensible to pursue any moral principles, partly because that only leads to disappointment. Led to a wavering of political action. When the rise of Germany became a threat to the Western democracies as a result: what could the west <u>do</u> about the rise of Germany? <u>Appeasement</u>.

Danger now of communism. Are we going to make the same mistakes over again which were made with regard to Germany, in regard to communism? Are we going to make the same mistakes of appeasement? Or are we going to depart from this attitude, and become firm and resist all claims of communism by force?

There was a conscious desire, in treating Germany, to avoid pitilessness—a mistake. What about policy towards Russia? It has brought America into the field. This is an asset, but, at the same time, a danger, because of the atomic bomb. It has sharpened the internal conflict within Europe, by making the two conflicting parties the liegemen of Russia and America. This phase of appeasement was in a way very tragic. Appeasement was the culmination of that long progress of liberal policy since 17th century which was trying more and more to base human relations on the principles of human confidence and which was suddenly faced, in Europe, with a heresy that denied these principles. We must rely to a considerable extent on these principles, in the present, that fundamentally human beings <u>do</u> obey moral laws. We must learn to combine strength with conquest by persuasion.

Weakening throughout Europe, I think, of the communist internationale. I think it <u>has</u> been shown that strength can be combined with persuasion.

We may be able to make it clear to Russia that we completely trust the U.S.A. But also to tell Russia that she will be fairly treated.

Mr. DAVENPORT: We have to regard present political position. British and American sea and air power keeping the sealanes of the Atlantic open. But reasonable for European countries to grow <u>food</u>.

Some of us don't see how there can be any European unity unless backed by British and American power.

1. American Air Force is at war-preparedness.

2. How to use American credits: I think they should charge <u>no</u> interest.

3. Quality of the power. Is there going to be anything better coming out of America than the skyscrapers? Have the Americans anything better than power to offer to the world? I cannot see how Europe can be in balance, unless with the help of American power.

Professor ANTONI: To conceive of Europe as a mediator, it would need Europe <u>to be</u> something. Europe at the moment is <u>not</u> in that position.

Mr. DE JOUVENEL: 1918: break-up of Austria-Hungary. That was thought to be good. Process of break-up has now reached Germany. It is now not only a matter that Russia <u>could</u> expand, but also that there are countries which would like Russia to expand.

It is to the credit of France that it evacuated the Ruhr, when there was no compulsion. I do not think the same could be said about Russia.[2]

The French people had the opportunity to protest against government policy, but in Russia there is no such opportunity.

Professor KNIGHT: International animosity the one thing capable of preserving unity within the national sphere. Modern man has made a signal failure of discussing those things which are essential if government is to be government by discussion.

Scientism: attempt to apply ideas which work in the natural sciences to the social sciences—it is in that field that the problems lie.

Man is a physical mechanism. Man's success in formulating and dealing with his problems, in order to live together in decent harmony.

---

2. In response to repeated German failures to meet its reparations obligations, in January 1923 the French and Belgian governments undertook a military occupation of the Ruhr. This enraged the German populace and provoked a sustained campaign of passive resistance and civil disobedience. The next year the Dawes Plan proposed a system of reforms and loans that would allow a reinstitution of reparation payments on a sustained basis. Once the plan was implemented and reparations payments resumed, the troops were withdrawn.

No one wants to treat anyone else unfairly. It only depends on what you consider to be fair. Nowadays, it is not the problem of whether people decide to be good or bad, but what they <u>mean</u> by being good or bad.

Dr. POPPER: I'm very impressed with all that's been said to-night. So I don't want to criticise Professor Knight. The present position is one where we nearly despair. But I don't think it quite as desperate as Professor Knight has painted it to be. In a certain sense, one can say that this time in which we live is one of an incredibly high moral standard. Never before in history have so many people had such good intentions as in our time, and particularly is that so with respect to social problems. Even in Germany the Nazis had continually to use moral appeals. What I feel is contributing to the crisis of the moment is the disappointment of so many hopes which were raised during the war of a better world. Russia itself is very weak internally. There has to be a re-affirmation of fundamental principles on our side. If not, external pressure on Russia will be of no real use. I'm quite sure that Russia understands only the language of threats.

Professor KNIGHT: That is, that Russia doesn't believe in discussion?

Dr. POPPER: Yes

Professor BRANDT: We have at least to consider the possibility of a war between America and Russia. This would be the ultimate crisis, in which I see very little hope that Europe would survive.

To what extent can we overcome the demoralisation that has entered the public attitude throughout America, England, and elsewhere in Europe? Power as such has never meant anything in history, unless power is being exercised for moral convictions and moral values. The Atlantic Charter was the only manifesto made during this war which could be compared to the Wilsonian Fourteen Points.[3]

---

3. Like Wilson's Fourteen Points speech, which outlined the principles that the United States would promote at the Versailles Peace Conference following World War I, the Atlantic Charter, a joint statement issued by the United States and Great Britain in August 1941, outlined their goals for the post–World War II world.

Mr. WATTS: Professor Brandt has said most of what I wanted to say. But I think he represents a lot of American public opinion. Growing dissatisfaction in America with American intervention in Europe.

Loss of capital during the war. Capital is not machines, but the human beings behind the growth of machines. Increasing capital is not just a matter of importing machinery. Russian has found this out to her cost, and has found that the machines are just a hollow shell. But Russia is gaining relatively to the other countries, because of the desire for "social gain."

Demand in the U.S.A. to keep the loans at home, instead of letting them go to Europe. But everyone will go communist, unless they're fed.

Solution must be in terms of individuals, rather than with countries.

Professor FRIEDMAN: I don't think Watt's [*sic*] opinions are representative of the U.S.A.

Miss WEDGWOOD: Almost all human beings doubt whether humans do obey moral laws. But we have to act on the assumption that human beings do obey moral laws, and can be won over. I think it is important to keep that tenet of liberalism in mind.

Professor ROBBINS: What moral would all this have had in the appeasement days regarding Hitler, and now regarding Stalin?

I can't see that the march of events would have been affected at all. Is there any reason to believe that concessions would get us any further? You only get further with the Russians if you treat them as though they are not human beings.

Professor POLANYI: Professor Robbins has said what I was going to say, but he's said it very much better. We have one hold on this situation, one hold in the internal life of the countries, where emissaries of Russia are friends. Possibility that, in view of the situation, the Russians might be induced to consider whether there isn't something to be said for accepting the offered guarantees.

Session 19

The Name of the Society

Mr. DE JOUVENEL: The committee suggests "The Mont Pèlerin Society" with the subtitle, "An Academy for the Human Liberties."

Professor ROBBINS: I am inclined to agree with Mr. de Jouvenel. But, for a subtitle, how about "An Academy for the Study of the Philosophy of a Free Society." We don't want to appear as an Academy for <u>action</u>.

Mr. READ: I'd like to support Professor Robbins' suggestion.

Professor EUCKEN: I object to the word philosophy, because of translation difficulties.

Professor FRIEDMAN: Do we <u>have</u> to have a short title?

Various suggestions of Mont Pèlerin Association, Mont Pèlerin Society, and An Academy for the Study of the Principles of Freedom. It was decided to call the society the "Mont Pèlerin Society", with no subtitle to the incorporated name.

Dr. GIDEONSE: We originally expressed gratitude about finance and the administration of the conference.

I should like to express our appreciation of Dr. Hunold, and the amount of work that must have been done before the conference met, and our gratitude to our present chairman, Professor Hayek. Many came largely because of confidence in him as a man and a scholar. Suaviter in modo, fortiter in re.[1] Meeting old friends and new friends.

Professor HAYEK: My reputation may have gone up a little, but it will now be inevitable that you realise my sources of inspiration and information.

I think you should postpone final judgment on this conference until you again mix with other people.

Professor ROBBINS: I should like to suggest a resolution of thanks to the anonymous donors.

Professor RAPPARD: Gratitude for finances and for "absence of strings."

Professor HAYEK: Ought we to issue a statement to the press? Conflicting considerations. I don't want too much publicity. But by trying to keep it secret, we may attract even more publicity.

Professor RAPPARD: I feel some statement is due. Obvious that there will be references to it in the press, so we'd better make the statement ourselves, and we would like Professor Hayek to draft it.

Mr. HAZLITT: Refusal to give a statement would give a very bad impression.

Professor ROBBINS: Preferably a comparatively neutral statement. Preferably no articles writing up the meeting as such, though it would of course be alright to refer to the meetings.

Professor JEWKES: Important job in the next few months of adding to our numbers. So we ought to discuss how big we want the society to be.

---

1. The Latin phrase, describing Hayek, might be rendered "Resolute in action, gentle in manner"—high praise indeed.

Executive committee is free to consult members and council for inviting new members.

Professor ROBBINS: I think it a good idea for members to be given the opportunity to object to the election of any new member, but <u>not</u> to attach any legal status to the objection. But the committee will consider all the support and objections.

Professor RAPPARD: Danger that names become more widely known. Therefore, if the name is circulated, you are more or less <u>forced</u> to elect that person.

Professor ROBBINS: But the advice of the existing members is very desirable.

Mr. MORLEY: I think the executive committee should have a good deal of executive power.

Professor HAYEK: "The executive committee proposes to invite . . . and unless objections are received by such and such a date invitations will be sent out."

Dr. POPPER: "It has been suggested that the executive committee should invite the following people to join. . . ."

Professor RAPPARD: Executive committee should have fair amount of power.

Mr. DE JOUVENEL: Professor Jewkes raised the question of the size of our society. If we're going up to 100 or so, how about breaking into classes, as is the policy of the French Academy?

Professor GRAHAM: Some licence has been given to the members here regarding suggestions of names. Even if the person knew he had been invited, he would <u>not</u> know <u>when</u> he might get an invitation, so he would not worry if were not immediately invited.

Professor HAYEK: This would entail an enormous amount of work for the executive committee.

Professor ROBBINS: I think we should use Professor Rappard's policy.

I hope Mr. de Jouvenel won't insist on carving up the seamless road. No use having an economic section—the meeting would lose its whole point. I'd rather set an upper limit to the number of our members.

Mr. DE JOUVENEL: I agree.

Danger of adding more and more economists rather than of other people.

Professor KNIGHT: I am in favour of an <u>initial</u> limitation of numbers. There ought to be substantial endorsement of a name, before it is passed.

Professor HAYEK: Amount of work for the committee.

Professor GRAHAM: Couldn't we use that method for the <u>initial</u> list only?

Mr. DE JOUVENEL: I would like to suggest Jung, Barth and[2]

Dr. GIDEONSE: No

Professor KNIGHT: Seems to me to be alright to have half of the membership as economists.

---

2. Jouvenel mentions two prominent Swiss thinkers. Carl Jung (1875–1961) was a Swiss psychoanalyst who, breaking with Sigmund Freud over psychoanalytic doctrine, founded analytical psychology. He developed such notions as the "collective unconsciousness," universal unconscious elements that are shared by all humanity, and the "archetypal image," symbols that are found in religious art, mythology, and fairy tales across all cultures. The theologian Karl Barth (1886–1968), renowned for his commentary *The Epistle to the Romans* (revised edition, 1921) and the massive *Church Dogmatics* (1932–67), was the principal author of the 1934 Barmen Declaration of Faith. The latter affirmed that the German Church was not an organ of the Nazi state and became a founding document of the Confessing Church. One presumes that Gideonse's objection was to the suggestion of Jung for membership.

Professor DIRECTOR: Half-way measure: before executive committee acts, it should circulate names to members of the council.

Mr. READ: Prospective members should be good expositors of the liberal philosophy, and be able to make contributions to it.

Professor JEWKES: I hope we <u>won't</u> be desperately restricted. If we include some of the younger members of our own profession, members will increase considerably.

I don't want it to get to 150 or so, and then have a spontaneous explosion from the entire conference "this is too large."

Professor HAYEK: Select among the members for particular meetings.

Professor POLANYI: Limit total numbers by limiting the numbers of economists.

Professor HAYEK: People will be described as sociologists, or by other qualifications.

Professor RAPPARD: "If you've got such and such, aren't I more important than he is" argument might be used.

Professor FRIEDMAN: Select some whose expenses will be paid. Others can either pay their own expenses, or not come. Why limit our numbers?

Professor ROBBINS: I think the executive committee should be given their opportunity to use their own good sense.

Professor RAPPARD: I have been unable to contact Andre Siegfried.

Thursday, April 10th, 1947, 9.30 a.m.

Concluding Session

Professor Hayek in the chair.

After some discussion the proposal of the sub-committee to call the permanent organisation "Mont Pèlerin Society" was generally approved.

Gratitude to the organisers and the anonymous donors was expressed by various speakers and the problem of the information to be communicated to the press, the method of electing future members and the fields to be represented, and the possibility of further conferences were also discussed.

About the Contributors

Bruce Caldwell is a research professor of economics and the director of the Center for the History of Political Economy at Duke University. He is the author of *Beyond Positivism: Economic Methodology in the Twentieth Century* (1982). For the past three decades his research has principally focused on the multifaceted writings of the Nobel Prize–winning economist and social theorist Friedrich A. Hayek. Caldwell is the author of *Hayek's Challenge: An Intellectual Biography of F. A. Hayek* and since 2002 has been the general editor of *The Collected Works of F. A. Hayek*. He is currently working on a full biography of Hayek. Caldwell has held research fellowships at New York University, Cambridge University, and the London School of Economics, and was previously a distinguished visiting fellow at the Hoover Institution. He is a past president of the History of Economics Society and of the Southern Economic Association, a life member of Clare Hall, Cambridge, and a distinguished fellow of the History of Economics Society.

John B. Taylor was president of the Mont Pèlerin Society from 2018 to 2020. Currently he is the George P. Shultz Senior Fellow in Economics at the Hoover Institution and the Mary and Robert Raymond Professor of Economics at Stanford University. Taylor served on the Council of Economic Advisers under three presidents and as under secretary of the Treasury for international affairs. Taylor's fields of expertise are monetary policy, fiscal policy, and international economics. Among his awards are the National Association for Business Economics Adam Smith Award (2007), the Bradley Prize (2010), the Hayek Prize (2012, for his book *First Principles*), and the Truman Medal for Economic Policy (2015).

Image Credits

Photo Section

Hayek's photo album, photos from which appear in the photo section after page 126, may be found in the Friedrich A. von Hayek papers, box 198, Hoover Institution Library & Archives. The brochure for the Hôtel du Parc may be found in the Mont Pèlerin Society records, box 5, folder 1, Hoover Institution Library & Archives.

The photos on the following pages of the photo section may also be found in the Mont Pèlerin Society records, envelope A, Hoover Institution Library & Archives: 1 (*top left and right*); 4 (*bottom*); 5 (*top and bottom*); 7 (*top and bottom*); 8 (*top and bottom*).

Dust Jacket

The photos on the dust jacket, a session during the first meeting of the Mont Pèlerin Society (*top*) and a view of Lake Geneva from the Hôtel du Parc (*bottom*), may be found in Hayek's photo album, as well as in the Mont Pèlerin Society records, envelope A, Hoover Institution Library & Archives. The dust jacket background, the memorandum of association, may be found in the Mont Pèlerin Society records, box 4, folder 1, Hoover Institution Library & Archives.

Index of Names